KU-639-800

Preface

We are proud to present the first edition of ***Electronic Marketing: Integrating Electronic Resources into the Marketing Process*** Instructor's Manual and Test Bank for use by college students, faculty, and professional marketers in the study and teaching of the new fields of electronic marketing and electronic commerce. The Instructor's Manual has been prepared to supplement and expand the course material, whether the course be called electronic marketing, electronic commerce, online selling or online marketing and promotion; this instructive manual is a fresh and up-to-date presentation of interesting, contemporary, and innovative electronic marketing practices. The textbook is developed and written on the realistic premise that electronic marketing tools include more than the World Wide Web. The supposition of marketing on the Internet is too narrow if the marketing actions are limited to online selling by Web site placement. Electronic marketing tools available to the marketer include an array of electronic communications and database adaptations such as online research sites, geo-demographic software, multi-purpose Web site design and sales, online collection for data warehousing and data mining, online commerce, and interactive communications between the customer and the individual, company, or organization. Our premise is that the traditional paradigm of the marketing process, namely situation analysis, marketing planning and marketing implementation, is a model for the present and future marketing management as it has served in the past. Electronic resources can and should be integrated into marketing activities to produce more accurate, analytical, in-depth, and quicker programs for the marketer. These benefits translate into more convenience for the customer.

The textbook and Instructor's Manual as well as the accompanying Test Bank and the World Wide Web site are designed to support in-depth teaching to upper-level undergraduates and graduate students, as well as business professionals studying or working in the sectors of strategic marketing, marketing communications, customer service communications, or marketing management. Its content is appropriate for business or mass communication curriculums based in customer satisfaction. ***Electronic Marketing*** contains nineteen chapters each focusing on an action or decision making stage within the marketing practice continuum. The Instructor's Manual is a balance between marketing strategy content with an equal emphasis on the "what to do" and suggestions on "how to do" electronic marketing. From experience, marketing research and planning are meaningless if the planning and designs are never put in to action.

End of Chapter Questions and Exercises

Electronic Marketing contains end-of-chapter questions and exercises which are posed in "real world" context, asking the student to respond to the question exercise as a business associate might. The student is required to answer in memoranda to superiors, write strategic planning outlines, compose news releases for press or stockholder consumption, or write speech outlines. This tact encourages deliberate organization as well as positioning the information in a varied but persuasive format. The professor can introduce his or her exercises as necessary. The answers to the questions and exercises are suggestions from our business experiences; the instructor may have had different experiences or used different practices.

Teaching Suggestions

As the electronic commerce industry and the electronic marketing discipline are young, dated from 1995 by most observers so pedagogical teaching and learning formats are still being tested and evaluated. However, I [Joel Reedy] have been researching course materials and structure since mid-1996 and launched the first learning session during the spring term, 1997. I have taught Electronic Marketing as a fall and spring course schedule (fifteen weeks, meeting twice weekly in one hour and fifteen-minute class periods and as a summer session (ten weeks, meeting twice weekly in two-hour class periods). The longer terms are preferable since as a comprehensive course, the expedient learning of electronic resources is time-consuming and relies on the building of foundational concepts and applications. In the 10 plus semesters of instruction, I have developed teaching activities and tips that I am pleased to pass along to others. As you develop sound interactive and well-received exercises, please share them with our e-mail link on our Web site. Teaching Suggestions will be called out as separate paragraphs in every chapter.

The course Electronic Marketing is comprehensive in scope and requires the coordination of several marketing and information technology disciplines. For optimum learning, I have called upon the skills and presentation abilities of my university and business colleagues to act as guest professionals presenting the objectives and implementation for their areas of expertise. Before the class begins the Web site creation assignment, I invite a speaker to present the objectives of page design and of HTML conventions such as tags and other elements, creation of colors, using frames and tables, and instruction on survey or order forms. Topics on which technology specialists might speak include general Internet/World Wide Web introduction and history, using listservs as communications tools, online research sites and addresses, HTML instruction, Web site design and implementation, database design and construction, IMC programs integrating online media, customer service response using online forms, and a variety of industry subjects such as e-commerce, e-marketing, information technologists bringing the latest news on information technology and marketing.

Students report that introducing guest speakers enlivens the class and also acquaints them to the personalities, depth of knowledge, and conduct of e-marketing professionals. Socialization of students to the requirements of the marketing industry is a valuable lesson that provides a "window of familiarity" to current content and learning for industry professionals. Educational encounters with working marketers can lead to jobs or internships for marketing graduates or students. If you review the following two syllabi suggestions, you'll see how speaker specialists are integrated into the Electronic Marketing course.

Cases and Commentaries

A selection of online cases and reports represents a broad overview of industries, both consumer and business-to-business, and retail and wholesale commerce situations. These cases date from the late 1990s.

Suggested Online Exercises

The learning objective for this portion of the course is for the student or student groups to spend hands-on time with the computer and online systems, as well as specific communications or database resources. These assignments and exercises are paced to match the electronic marketing project outline; research assignments are placed in the same time frame as the situation analysis step. The marketing planning stage is reinforced by learning HTML conventions, objectives of Web site research and design, prospect selection and database construction, ongoing customer surveys, or prospect questionnaires. Marketing implementation includes Web site production, forms production, and written/oral project development. From experience, an online communications and transactions investigation would follow this process and entail these types of exercises in executing the project. The professor can add or delete these exercises as s/he feels necessary. The completion of these exercises contributes to the point totals in arriving at a semester grade. I use six or seven assignments, counting five for grading. I allow three points per assignment for a maximum total of 15 points for these hands-on exercises.

...Manual and Test Bank to accompany

Electronic Marketing

Integrating Electronic Resources into the Marketing Process

prepared by

Joel Reedy
University of South Florida

Shauna Schullo
University of South Florida

with assistance from

G. Bernard Yevin
Fontbonne College

THE DRYDEN PRESS
A Division of Harcourt College Publishers
Fort Worth Philadelphia San Diego New York Orlando Austin San Antonio
Toronto Montreal London Sydney Tokyo

Cover Image by Lamberto Alvarez

ISBN: 0-03-031099-7

Copyright © 2000 by Harcourt, Inc.

All rights reserved. No part of this publication may be reproduced or transmitted in any form or by any means, electronic or mechanical, including photocopy, recording, or any information storage and retrieval system, without permission in writing from the publisher.

Requests for permission to make copies of any part of the work should be mailed to: Permissions Department, Harcourt, Inc., 6277 Sea Harbor Drive, Orlando, Florida 32887-6777.

Address for Domestic Orders
The Dryden Press, 6277 Sea Harbor Drive, Orlando, FL 32887-6777
800-782-4479

Address for International Orders
International Customer Service
The Dryden Press, 6277 Sea Harbor Drive, Orlando, FL 32887-6777
407-345-3800
(fax) 407-345-4060
(e-mail) hbintl@harcourtbrace.com

Address for Editorial Correspondence
The Dryden Press, 301 Commerce Street, Suite 3700, Fort Worth, TX 76102

Web Site Address
http://www.harcourtcollege.com

THE DRYDEN PRESS, DRYDEN, and the DP LOGO are registered trademarks of Harcourt, Inc..

Printed in the United States of America

9 0 1 2 3 4 5 6 7 8 023 9 8 7 6 5 4 3 2 1

The Dryden Press
Harcourt College Publishers

UNIVERSITY OF HERTFORDSHIRE
HERTFORD CAMPUS LRC
HERTFORD
BIB 0339071
CLASS 658.84 REE
LOCATION OWL
BARCODE 4405333555

L182693

A sample syllabus

Electronic Marketing Syllabus
(MAR 4933-001)
Marketing/Promotional Strategies Using Electronic Resources

Instructor: Joel Reedy, MBA
Office: BSN 3222 (Marketing Department)
Office Hours: Tuesday & Thursday, 11:30 a.m.-12:30 p.m., 2:30-3:30 or by appointment
Phone: 974-6184, voice mail (recorder in office) or 974-4201 (USF Marketing Department messages)
E-mail reedy@coba.usf.edu

Course Description

This course is designed to introduce and expand students' knowledge and usage of electronic marketing resources for application in the process of marketing planning and promotional strategy. The accomplishment of these objectives requires that student groups investigate and write a marketing strategy for a proposed business entity, either product or service based. Students will obtain familiarity with online and hard copy marketing research resources and will develop a marketing plan employing electronic communications tools; the course offers hands-on experience using reference data which delineate product-prospect-place-promotion-performance decisions.

Course components include usage of the Internet, usage of online marketing intelligence sources and geo-demographic software, usage of the World Wide Web as a communications medium, database software for customer tracking, and online communications for ongoing customer relations. All of these tools will be incorporated in preparing a marketing strategy (situation analysis, marketing planning, and marketing implementation).

Course Objectives

The course objectives are to familiarize students with electronic marketing and research tools that enable students to formulate and write precise, effective, and efficient marketing planning documents. Specifically, objectives are:

1. To expose students to the electronic marketing and communications environments that are available in today's fast-paced business world (the emergence of online information, the need for speed in introducing new products, the availability of new media, the ability to profile new buyer prospects).
2. To familiarize students with online marketing tools and electronic communication vehicles.
3. To demonstrate the marketing planning process through the step-by-step formulation of a highly targeted marketing document.
4. To introduce students to the sources of extensive information available for consumer or business-to-business marketing.
5. To encourage students to improve team-working skills and task delegation.

Skill Building Objectives

You should expect to develop the following marketing skills when you complete this course: foundational knowledge, critical thinking skills, using marketing tools, communications skills, computer usage skills, team-building skills, and hands-on experience.

Course Requirements

1. My first requirement is that students have a basic familiarity with e-mail and the Internet, or at a minimum, have a fierce desire to learn these skills quickly. We shall develop advanced research and World Wide Web competencies together.

2. Two texts are required: **Electronic Marketing** by Reedy, Schullo, and Zimmerman (ISBN 0-03-021107-7) and **The Online Student** by Reddick and King (ISBN 0-15-503189-9). Reference books on the Internet or World Wide Web are available in the USF library or at bookstores.

3. In the first days of class, if you do not have one, you will open a student e-mail account to gain access to various class exercises. This account is free to USF students and is administered by the Academic Computing office (LIB 608) on the sixth floor of the library. You will have to go there in person; the first days of class, you'll find a table in the lobby to assist you. The telephone number is 974-1222. If you need additional assistance, you might contact the Business Computing Help Lab. That office is BSN 2400; telephone is 974-4208.

4. Online exercises and team reports: There will be several online exercises which you will retrieve from my USF Home Page (http://coba.usf.edu/Reedy) which is accessed through the Marketing Department Web site. My e-mail address is (reedy@coba.usf.edu). It will be your responsibility to maintain access to the USF computer network or similar access. The group you form will execute the exercises and project throughout the semester. Several of these exercises will be posted to my Home Page; these assignments can be e-mailed to me or handed in as a hard copy.

5. In the first week of class, I expect you to form a team of three students who will then develop assignments throughout the term. There should be approximately 5 to 10 teams available within the class. Be sure to select group members on the basis of skills, home locations, time availability for meetings, and flexibility of work schedules. It will be your responsibility to prepare group assignments, the research project, visuals, and presentation details among team members.

6. Group marketing project: The group project is the most important element of the learning process in this course. The project will be divided into three parts:
   - A. A situation assessment of your selected product or service.
   - B. A marketing plan containing assumptions, prospect, product, price, distribution and promotion elements for your venture. An outline for the project's content has to be retrieved from my Home Page.
   - C. An implementation plan is the third step; this portion will detail the execution and specifications to put your marketing plan into action.

   This marketing project will be prepared by independent teams. Each group will develop a product or service concept that is to be researched and marketing via electronic information, communications, and transaction tools. In general, most projects support either an online selling or exposure of a consumer or business product or an informational site such as a service site for a health-related organization. At the end of the term, teams will be responsible for developing a 30-minute class presentation that summarizes and demonstrates the major points of their research/marketing/promotional program. A written marketing/promotional plan will be submitted at that time. All team members will present a portion of the oral presentation. I must be provided with an agenda, executive summary, and detailed outline on or before July 6.

7. Two exams are scheduled, a mid-term and a final exam. Materials to be covered will be discussed in class prior to each exam.

8. Class attendance and participation: attendance will be taken at each class. Since a portion of your grade is derived from your verbal participation in class, you will improve your "batting average" if you attend class faithfully and comment intelligently. Should any student incur an excessive number of absences, I reserve the right to lower that student's score by one full letter grade. Encouraging class participation, you should feel free to ask pertinent questions and to make comments or observations at any time. Students who anticipate the necessity of being absent from class due to the observation of a major religious observance must provide notice of the date(s) to me, in writing, by our second class meeting.

9. Written work and class participation will be graded on the basis of quality and quantity, with more attention given to quality. Late assignments will be penalized.

10. Grades: Final grades will be determined by the student's point total at the end of the semester. Total points (100) for assigned activities are:

    35 - design and implementation of team project
    15 - online exercises (total of 5 assignments)
    20 - mid-term exam
    20 - final exam

10 - class participation and attendance
100 points (100%)

****

Example class schedule for a summer term

Date	Subject
May 16	Orientation and expectations; each student to confirm that his or her account is open through the Academic Computing office on the sixth floor of the library (974-1222) or in the lobby table. Read *Electronic Marketing,* Chapters 1 and 2; Begin reading *The Online Student*, complete reading by date of midterm.
May 18	History of the Internet and World Wide Web, and its role in an AMC program; guest speaker - begin first work session (sign on to MAR 4933 listserv) Discuss group project requirements; attention to proper Netiquette.
May 23	Introduction to the practice of e-marketing and the e-marketing process. Retrieve marketing process outline and electronic exercises from my home page. Read *Electronic Marketing*, Chapters 3 and 4.
May 25	Introduction to the world of Electronic Commerce; discussion of virtual commerce and appropriate products and services. Hand in group names of three persons and define product or service concept to be developed next class.
May 27	Concept of the virtual store for marketing products and services. Read *EM*, Chapter 6.
May 30	Discussion of e-marketing resources' roles, advantages and disadvantages and of integrating electronic marketing tools into the traditional marketing process. Start second exercise work session, monitoring listserv for three weeks with written report, due day of midterm (June 10). Read *EM*, Chapter 7.
June 1	Analyzing and segmenting the target market; introduction to geo-demographic software for prospect identification and selection. Third exercise, the geo-demographic analysis is a take home exercise, due next class. Read *EM*, Chapter 8.
June 3	Integrating the promotional mix lecture; introduction to the WWW as a promotional vehicle; objectives and synergy. Demonstration of creativity and interactivity; added value activities and online services. Read *EM*, Chapter 9.
June 8	Guest speaker-World Wide Web communications in action. Fourth exercise assigned, Web site reviews, three reviews per person. This is not a group exercise, due July 6. Read *EM*, Chapter 10.
June 10	Mid-term exam.
June 17	Guest speaker – Web page content objectives; design and use of HTML conventions. Work session to explore HTML page design. Read *EM*, Chapter 11.
June 22	Finish HTML work session; group status report on marketing plan development; each group to report to me the progress of your project.
June 24	Guest speaker-Discussion of customer database tracking, using Access software. Work session to explore information retrieval objectives and capture. Customer database assignment due, a written rationale and listing of customer characteristics that you plan to capture in your customer database, next class - one to two pages per group.

June 29	Guest speaker – strategy for customer communications on purchase satisfaction and opinion surveys. Fourth exercise (Web site reviews) and sixth exercise due, write a customer survey to solicit opinions and improvements to service, product, or new product ideas for customer completion online. Can be order form also. One to two page report per group. Read *EM*, Chapter 13.
July 1	Establishing and promoting the virtual storefront. Demonstration of cybershopping sites and resources. Introduction to security on the commerce site. Read *EM*, Chapters 14, 15.
July 6	Special opportunities for business-to-business commerce and the future of electronic marketing resources lecture. Hand in agenda for presentation. Read EM, Chapters 16, 19.**
	**NOTE TO INSTRUCTORS: Instructor assignment of Chapters 17 and 18 is suggested as optional depending on time constraints and learning objectives.
July 8	Group presentations with oral report on marketing strategy.
July 13	Finish group presentations with oral report on marketing strategy.
July 15	Final Exam

If changes to this schedule are required, you will be notified in class.

****

Example class schedule for a spring semester

Date	Subject
Jan 11	Orientation and expectations. Each student to confirm that his or her account is open through the Academic Computing office on the sixth floor of the library (974-1222) or in the lobby table. Read Chapters 1 and 2, *Electronic Marketing*. Begin reading *The Online Student* which is to be completed by the day of the midterm.
Jan 13	History of the Internet and World Wide Web and its role in an IMC program. Introduction to online browsers and data searches; attention to proper Netiquette. Read Chapter 3, *Electronic Marketing*.
Jan 18	Guest speaker - first work session (sign on to MAR 4933 class listserv). Discuss marketing process/project outline and assignments from my Home Page. Read Chapter 4, *EM.*
Jan 20	Discussion of virtual reality commerce; appropriate products and services. Review product and service suggestions from Chapter 3. Choose group of three persons and define product or service concept to be developed.
Jan 25	Introduction to the Internet lecture; Read Chapter 5, *EM*. Start first exercise work session, sign-on to marketing or special interest listserv.
Jan 27	Discussion of marketing resources for online prospect profiles and behavior/usage. Second exercise due, one to two page report per group on proposed product or service to be developed. Read Appendix C, *EM*.
Feb 1	Concept of the virtual store for marketing products and services lecture. Read Chapter 6, *EM*.
Feb 3	Work session, explore research/information sites in your group. Brief me on your group's progress on your project.

Feb 8	The tools of electronic marketing resources lecture and demonstration. Read Chapter 7, *EM.*
Feb 10	Analyzing and segmenting the target market lecture; introduction of geo-demographic software for prospect identification and selection. Third exercise, a take-home geo-demographic worksheet due next class. Note that this is not an online exercise. Read Chapter 8, *EM.*
Feb 15	Integrating the promotional mix lecture; introduction of the World Wide Web as a promotional vehicle; objectives and synergy. Read Chapter 9, *EM.*
Feb 17	Using the Internet lecture; Discussion of creativity and interactivity; added value activities and online services. Read Chapter 10, *EM.*
Feb 22	Guest speaker-World Wide Web communications in action. Fourth exercise assigned, reviews of Web sites. Nine critiques per group (three reports per individual) using supplied form.
Feb 24	Mid-term exam
Feb 29	Web site/page design. Guest speaker-Web page objectives and design using HTML source code lecture. Read Chapter 11, *EM.*
Mar 2	Guest speaker-Tables and colors, practice home page construction. Work session, explore HTML tags/page design.
Mar 7	Guest speaker-Explanation of customer database tracking, using Access software. Read Chapter 12, *EM.*
Mar 9	Work session, explore information retrieval objectives and form design by constructing practice database and conducting simple queries in Access. Fifth exercise due, one to two page report per group, written rationale and list of characteristics to captured in customer tracking effort.
Mar 13-17	Spring Break
Mar 21	Group status report on marketing plan development; each group reports to me the progress on your project. Group work sessions in class while other groups report to me.
Mar 23	Guest speaker - Strategy for customer communication for purchase satisfaction and opinion surveys. Sixth exercise assigned, one to two page report per group, written rationale and list of questions to be asked of project target. Either prospect or customer questionnaire, pre- or post-analysis. Read Chapter 13, *EM.*
Mar 28	Establishing and promoting the virtual storefront lecture. Demonstrate examples of cybershopping sites and resources. Read Chapter 14, *EM.*
Mar 30	Security on the E-commerce site lecture. Read Chapter 15, *EM.*
Apr 4	Seventh exercise due, oral reports on local businesses using e-marketing.
Apr 6	Finish seventh exercise.
Apr 11	Special opportunities for business-to-business commerce. Read Chapter 16, *EM.*
Apr 13	International e-marketing implications lecture. Read Chapter 17, *EM.*

Apr 18	Guest speaker: E-commerce wrap-up (or career panel of e-marketing graduates). Assigned readings: Chapter 18, 19 of *EM*.
Apr 20	First two group presentations/oral report on marketing strategy and Web tools.
Apr 25	Group presentations.
Apr 27	Group presentations.
May 2	Final exam

****

A memorandum structure regarding online assignments for a fall semester

January 5, XXXX

MEMORANDUM

TO: Electronic Marketing students
FROM: Joel Reedy
SUBJECT: Retrieval and assignment dates for online exercises

As indicated on the Electronic Marketing Syllabus, there are a number of online exercises and reports due throughout the semester. This memo contains the assignment topic and due dates. You are responsible for bringing your team together and thoroughly preparing each assignment on time.

Each assignment (unless noted) is to be typed and posted to my e-mail account at USF. My e-mail address is reedy@coba.usf.edu. I will make note of the date and time received.

Due date	**Assignment**
Wk of Jan 6	Open e-mail account, retrieve assignment memo and marketing project outline (not a graded exercise). Assignment 1: sign on to a marketing listserv and monitor content of list for three weeks. Write two or three paragraphs per week; submit as an individual report. Due on day of mid-term, February 12.
Jan 23	Assignment 2: A one to two-page report on the product or service your team has chosen to research and market is due. Refer to our class lecture on appropriate products or services for online marketing. Team members will be identified (not a graded exercise).
Jan 30	Assignment 3: analyze and complete the geo-demographic worksheet to answer the corresponding questions. Note that this is not an online assignment. Turn the take-home worksheet in for our next class.
Feb 11	Assignment 4: starting this date, I want your team to report on nine Web sites (three critiques per person), with written critiques of each site. Comment on purpose of the site, graphics, level of interactivity, types of "hot buttons," and any other notable features. Report is due March 25.
Mar 4	Assignment 5: due this date, design a one to two-page report/format for customer profile input. Use your product/service project as the criteria for designing your customer selects retrieval. In your report, tell me why you chose the profile terms in relation to your project. Use the format of the database program, Microsoft Access. Turn this group report in at our class meeting.

Mar 18 Assignment 6: due this date is a one to two-page report/format for online customer service survey and tabulation strategy. Use your product/service project as the criteria for designing your survey. In your report, tell me why you chose the lines of questions in relation to your project. Turn this group report in at our class meeting.

Mar 25 Assignment 7: start this date, each group will make a short oral report giving two examples of local individuals or companies engaging in Internet/Web marketing. Interview these people to share a ten-minute report per group.

If you or your team have questions, please contact me by posting your message to my e-mail account.

****

Table of Contents

Preface iii

Instructor's Manual

Chapter 1	Introduction to the Resources of Electronic Marketing	1
Chapter 2	Concept of Electronic Commerce and the Traditional Marketing Process	9
Chapter 3	Marketing Planning Stage for Online Activities	17
Chapter 4	The Actions of Marketing Implementation	27
Chapter 5	An Introduction to the Internet	33
Chapter 6	Concept of the Virtual Store for Marketing Products and Services	41
Chapter 7	The Tools of Electronic Marketing Resources	49
Chapter 8	Segmenting and Analyzing the Target Market	57
Chapter 9	Integrating the Promotional Mix	65
Chapter 10	Using the Internet	75
Chapter 11	Web Page Design	81
Chapter 12	Capturing Customer Profiles and Data Management	91
Chapter 13	Considerations for Ongoing Customer Communications	101
Chapter 14	Establishing and Promoting the Virtual Store	109
Chapter 15	Security on the E-commerce site	117
Chapter 16	Special Opportunities for Business-to-Business Situations	123
Chapter 17	Implications to the International Marketing Program	131
Chapter 18	The Ethics of Electronic Marketing	137
Chapter 19	The Future of Electronic Marketing Resources	145

Test Bank

Chapter 1	Introduction to the Resources of Electronic Marketing	157
Chapter 2	Concept of Electronic Commerce and the Traditional Marketing Process	162
Chapter 3	Marketing Planning Stage for Online Activities	167
Chapter 4	The Actions of Marketing Implementation	172
Chapter 5	An Introduction to the Internet	177
Chapter 6	Concept of the Virtual Store for Marketing Products and Services	182
Chapter 7	The Tools of Electronic Marketing Resources	187
Chapter 8	Segmenting and Analyzing the Target Market	192
Chapter 9	Integrating the Promotional Mix	197
Chapter 10	Using the Internet	202
Chapter 11	Web Page Design	207
Chapter 12	Capturing Customer Profiles and Data Management	212
Chapter 13	Considerations for Ongoing Customer Communications	217
Chapter 14	Establishing and Promoting the Virtual Store	222
Chapter 15	Security on the E-Commerce site	227
Chapter 16	Special Opportunities for Business-to-Business Situations	232
Chapter 17	Implications to the International Marketing Program	237
Chapter 18	The Ethics of Electronic Marketing	242
Chapter 19	The Future of Electronic Marketing Resources	247

Instructor's Manual

Chapter 1
Introduction to the Resources of Electronic Marketing

Chapter Summary

Electronic marketing resources such as electronic mail (e-mail), the World Wide Web, database management, and online ordering and payment systems are revolutionizing the efficiency and effectiveness of the traditional marketing process. Using these electronic tools delivers speed, accuracy, access, and interactivity, all customer conveniences over and above the traditional marketing elements. The purpose and function of the various electronic resources is the focus of this chapter.

The chapter also focuses on the appropriateness of employing electronic resources by either large or small companies with a conclusion that size is unrelated to electronic marketing activities. The question of the planning strategic or tactical actions afforded by the capabilities of the Web with other electronic resources such as e-mail or database management is addressed in the chapter, and both planning practices can be executed equally well. Strategically, entire targets of technology users can be exposed to Web advertising as well as engaging the Web for online sales campaigns targeted to existing customers. Tactical efforts are particularly well served because of the speed and accuracy of electronic resources. Transactions are quickly consummated and recorded because of the interactivity between the purchaser and the merchant; intuitive databases can be "mined" for purchasing habits and cycles. The student should recognize that the strength of the World Wide Web is its capability to create a "real time" dialogue due to the interactive nature of online communications.

The chapter closes with observations how electronic commerce is reflective of the speed in which business is conducted and how electronic marketing is the process by which contemporary business can evaluate, plan, and produce goods and services acceptable to the ever changing public demand. The attributes of speed, accuracy, accessibility, and interactivity of employing electronic marketing resources make possible a higher level of customer convenience and satisfaction.

Core Concepts

- To introduce and explain various electronic marketing resources that can be integrated into the traditional marketing process to cultivate the ultimate goal of successful electronic commerce systems
- To demonstrate how electronic marketing resources increase "value added" uses and perceptions to the products and services of e-commerce
- To differentiate the strategic and tactical uses of electronic marketing resources

Chapter Outline

I. The Marketer Enters the Online Age
   A. Technology has entered just about every business
   B. Technological advances are now enabling the marketer to identify specific prospects to deliver specific products for consumption
      1. Narrowcasting
      2. Listservs
      3. Discussion groups
      4. Hotspot advertising
      5. Online press releases
      6. Online conferences
   C. Electronic commerce is the conducting of business communications and transmissions over networks and through computers, specifically the buying and selling of goods and services, and the transfer of funds, through digital communications
   D. Electronic commerce can also include all inter-company and intra-company functions
      1. Electronic mail

2. EDI (Electronic Data Interchange)
3. File transfer
4. Fax
5. Video conferencing
6. Workflow
7. Interaction with a remote computer

E. Electronic commerce can include: buying and selling over the World Wide Web and the Internet
1. Electronic fund transfer
2. Smart cards
3. Digital cash

F. Electronic marketing is all the online or electronic-based activities that facilitate manufacturing goods and services by the producer to satisfy the wants and needs of the consumer

G. Electronic marketing resources are those technological or electronic marketing tools that are used to complete the marketing directives
1. World Wide Web
2. Interactive Web sites
3. Shopping agents
4. Avatars representing people objects in virtual reality environments
5. Cyber shopping malls
6. Fax-on-demand information
7. CD-ROM presentations

II. Listening to the Consumer Speak

A. Commodities that a consumer values in today's marketplace? The recurring answers are saving money, saving time, and enhancing convenience

B. Marketers can improve or streamline these traditional marketing processes

C. The logic and consistency of the marketing process, namely situation analysis, marketing planning, and marketing implementation

III. The Importance of Electronic Marketing Resources in Business Today

A. The better you know your customers, the better you can serve, and hopefully anticipate their needs

B. Consumers demand "instant gratification" which means that speed of delivery and accuracy in fulfilling the order are crucial

C. Introducing the premise of "added value" services to each and every one of your clients or customers

D. Adding value to your product or service, you can achieve a higher, perhaps more predictable brand equity and reputation that none of your competitors can match

E. Business situations for which online marketing resources are very appropriate
1. Company communications
2. E-mail address
3. Marketing research
4. Marketing planning
5. Productivity innovations
6. Business-to-business exchanges

F. The value of e-commerce to the consumer
1. Time and access to commercial sites
2. Audiotext

G. Electronic Marketing Resources
1. Customer loyalty
2. Affinity marketing
3. Globalized reach
4. Competitive intelligence
5. Cost management

6. Partnering and logistics become easier to maintain through online marketing
7. Telecommuting
8. Corporate recruitment's

H. Additional benefits which ease the cost of technology
1. Intranets-a company can share resources
2. Extranets-communications networks maintained for outside suppliers or other external groups, also efficiently disseminate privileged

IV. Commerce for Large or Small Companies
A. There are no parameters yet for fitting e-commerce into traditional marketing and sales programs, only the commitment to thorough and appropriate use of marketing strategy
B. "Online retailing has left the experimental phase and is accelerating into the mainstream"

V. What Electronic Marketing Tools Are Shaping the Future
A. Speed, accessibility, accuracy of information, and competitive advantages are four of the major forces
Driving business
B. The ability to personalize the message with the product or service order, the payment system, the delivery date, and even the hour of the day, and the marketer, the retailer, and the wholesaler can offer the consumer an unheard-of package of convenience
C. Systems are designed to distribute information to solve specific organizational problems
D. Categories of electronic marketing resources include:
1. Online information and research
2. Computer and software based resources that include:
a. Web-based advertising and sales promotions
b. Proprietary inventory management networks and software
c. Geo-demographic
d. Proprietary database management
e. Online customer service and fulfillment
f. Customer and prospect surveys
g. Videoconferencing
h. "Smart cards"
i. Virtual reality environments
3. Telephony resources that include:
a. Fax and fax-back systems,
b. Pagers
c. Beepers
d. Telemarketing
4. Network-based resources include:
a. The Internet
b. World Wide Web sites
c. Intranets
d. Extranets
e. News release networks
f. Electronic Data Interchanges
g. Transactions
h. Authentication networks
5. In-store resources such as:
a. Optical scanners
b. Electronic coupon dispensers
c. Electronic kiosks
d. Low frequency radio "broadcasting"
e. Electronic price shelf tags

f. Video shopping carts

6. As their places in the marketing process are reached in the book:
   a. Fax-back systems
   b. Customer tracking methods
   c. Customer surveys and order forms using HTML (Hypertext Markup Language) editors
   d. Smart cards
   e. Optical readers
   f. Cybermalls
   g. Efficient communications systems

VI. Electronic Marketing Resources, Strategic or Tactical?
   A. Yes, electronic marketing tools can be utilized in strategic planning and in tactical execution
   B. A model for integrating Internet applications, which places interactions with the customer at the center of a networked information management system, provides a framework for redesigning traditional business functions for maximum advantage
   C. The tactical application, those shorter term activities, that make the marketing implementation come alive by putting the strategic ideas into action

VII. Navigating through a World of Change
   A. Marketing is being tested to handle continual and momentous change

Teaching Suggestions

The student should understand the difference between electronic commerce and electronic marketing, electronic commerce being defined as the practice of satisfying customer and business' wants and needs through online procurement. Electronic marketing is defined as any activity that facilitates the electronic commerce exchange process. The student should think of electronic marketing as the means to the end of transacting electronic commerce. A distinction should be made between the concepts of closed networks, in the past called "online" systems, as opposed to open networks, originally designated as an "internet". In the early 1990s, an example of a closed, online network would be CompuServe or America Online. As the open network of the Internet grew rapidly, the line between online fee-for-service access and the open access of the Internet blurred. In our text, online and Internet networks are used interchangeably.

The efficiency and effectiveness of performing online market research, delivering messages and expediting consumer or business' transactions through electronic marketing should be stressed in following the model of Integrated Marketing Communications (IMC). IMC practices coordinate the objectives and strategies of the promotional mix of advertising, sales promotion, public relations, direct marketing, and personal selling; online activities enhance each of these elements through speed, accuracy, and interactivity, benefits to the user.

At every practical instance, the Instructor should demonstrate the use of electronic marketing resources, from initiating ISP access to opening the browser and explaining the tool bars to using search engines and printing Web pages. These skills are learned by hands-on experience, first demonstrated and then executed by the student. Many students are afraid of information technology delivered by PCs; assure them that they will not break the machine or the software. Building the student's confidence is an important component of this Electronic Marketing course.

Answers to Questions and Exercises

1. Within the framework of the traditional marketing process of situation analysis and marketing planning, in which step do you think electronic marketing resources are most valuable and best suited?

An argument can be made to the value of electronic resources in all three stages of the marketing process. However, given the benefits of electronic marketing—the speed, accuracy, accessibility, and interactivity—most marketers can envision the customer convenience delivered by the marketing implementation stage. Marketing implementation actions could include faster order placement, more accurate inputting of merchandise specifications, product or credit card numbers, or delivery instructions and addresses. The implementation and delivery of advertising offers and sales promotions could also be accelerated using online means. Database management of customer references and habits are generally conducted in the marketing implementation stage as well as ongoing customer communications.

While electronic resources can expand marketing research to national or international sources and speed up research retrieval, many e-marketers unfortunately do not engage in market research or customer communications. The situation analysis stage is left to opinions and reenacting previous years' programs without consideration to market changes. Electronic resources have less value in the marketing planning stage compared to the implementation stage; creativity and experience, the human touch, determine the valuable characteristics in managing the marketing mix of Ps. Product, pricing, promotion, and distribution strategies emerge from the marketing planning stage but with little assistance from electronic resources.

2. Every technological advancement has its advantages and disadvantages over the previous system in place. What are the advantages and disadvantages of using electronic marketing resources in the marketing process? Be prepared to discuss these points in the next class.

Some advantages include: marketing services can be delivered much quicker than traditional methods. Examples are downloading brochure and specification materials, as well as company information such as annual reports or press releases. Market research can encompass larger areas of smaller or bigger geographies. Also, primary research studies can be conducted more quickly with more accuracy than traditional means and secondary research sources can be retrieved from numerous sources, nationally and internationally, quickly and cost effectively. Marketing communications can be targeted to segmented groups thus increasing effectiveness and efficiency of message delivery. Electronic marketing resources can be used for consumer and business-to-business marketing efforts and delivery of certain services such as software and information can be downloaded instantly.

Some common disadvantages include: enhanced technology comes with a cost, either in the initial system installation, potential user fees, or expensive ongoing maintenance. Hardware and software technology can become obsolete in a very short time. Plus, customers or prospects must have the proper equipment and access to the World Wide Web. Also, substantial amounts of time and resources may be required to instruct employees on proper usage of the technology and support must be secured at the highest levels of the company to spread the technology approval to lower tiers of staff and line workers.

3. Interview a businessman who is involved with electronic marketing or electronic commerce. What has been his or her experience in integrating electronic tools into the present company systems? Has this integration met with success or failure compared to traditional marketing efforts? Is it too early in this businessperson coffeehouse opinion to make a judgment? What are the performance criteria used to judge success or failure?

In Appendix D, there is a set of questions that the student can use to conduct an interview or supplement questions the student might develop him/herself. Encourage the student to consider service or product firms, large or small companies, high tech or basic manufacturing concerns. If the results reported by the businessperson are negative, have the student relate the facts. Not all companies or industries can execute electronic marketing properly. The results of this interview are to be written as a news release for dissemination to the local business press.

4. Discuss why a company would choose *not* to employ electronic marketing resources throughout the enterprise. Should certain departments always be equipped with electronic tools, or should certain departments always be excluded it from using them? Prepare an outline of your thoughts.

Because of fear and uncertainty in changing business practices, some businesspeople may reject different forms of information technology. Also, because of budgetary constraints, some officials believe that enhanced technology is too expensive for the company's finances. These mangers can be unaware of the technologies' availability. As far as information technologies' appropriateness for all departments, all levels of work processes can benefit. E-mail is ubiquitous in most contemporary companies, from the home office to branch offices. The shop floor maintains work-in-progress records or schedules for inventory purposes. Accounting has financial records to maintain. Any work unit that has to communicate either internally or externally with other parties or has to keep records of various kinds via database management is a candidate for electronic resources.

5. Many marketing situations are tradeoffs between the optimal and actual choices. If you were required to make an either/or choice, which would you, the marketer, select: a good product with bad online promotions or a bad product with good online promotion? Write your stockholders a short memo justifying your position.

While no marketing manager should condone or be forced to work with inferior products or insufficient marketing resources, most astute managers would work only with good products while trying to improve the quality of online promotional results. Good promotion promises benefits from products and services featured; good promotion brings awareness to the inferior products hastening their demise

6. Go to your college library or access the library online to investigate the stories of five companies that have recently announced the establishment of its first Web site. Print out the news story and write a one-page report summarizing the purpose of the new company Web site.

Good resources for technology items can be daily news featured on home pages of search engines, weekly newsletters published by Iconocast, Digital Digest, Forrester Research, or various marketing newsletters prepared by e-marketing companies. Many e-marketing companies' addresses can be located through search engines. Also, stories can obtained using the PR Newswire (www.prnewswire.com) or Business Wire (www.businesswire.com) as well as business news services such as Point Cast (www.pointcast.com), a program that can be downloaded from the Web.

7. Online communications cover a broad marketing spectrum of customer contact from customer characteristics databases to interactive Web activities to online customer service after purchase. In which category of the promotional mix (advertising, sales promotion, public relations, direct marketing, or personal selling) to you feel the World Wide Web is best classified? What would be the second best fit of promotional element? The third best? Write a one-page memo to your boss explaining your thoughts on the promotional mix and the World Wide Web.

It is generally accepted that e-marketing on the Web has greatly enabled the capabilities of direct marketing thus impacting this promotional element more than the others. Traditional direct marketing has been the tool of choice in reaching select groups because of its segmentation, personalization, and interactivity. The Web offers these provisions plus speedier transactions and low-cost customer communications.

The Web probably serves public relations/publicity efforts or sales promotion programs, tying for second or third place. Publicity can be widely disseminated to many constituencies, from editors in the press, to customers and the general public, to stakeholders and stockholders. Sales promotions can be instantly acted upon once the viewer reaches the page. Interactivity and convenience of response are important factors for customers to move on impulse.

Web advertising is still a fledgling effort, with few "rules" to follow for capturing consumer awareness and purchase intention. Measurement standards produce uncertain or ambiguous results sometimes delivering understated or inflated response statistics. In many cases, the Web is used to supplant personal selling programs and staff. However, e-marketers are learning that some products and services (high priced, complicated, extensive information purchases such as life insurance, home buying, or complex technology products still require one-on-one presentations to conduct the sales process). Perhaps in the future, the advertising process will become more structured in approach highlighted by interactivity, producing more dependable results. Likewise perhaps the Web will become a more substitutive communications and transaction medium to allow field salespeople to cover more territory and service customers with more extensive product or service data.

8. Web sites can be used for various purposes. Access sites with the following purposes: print out the home page or supporting page. Write a paragraph explaining the purpose (new product announcement, general image awareness, specific product sales, publicity support, product or service relationship, employment, and customer survey page) of each site or page.

Most any large corporation, Oracle or IBM for example, will contain several pages of the previously listed content. Follow the hyperlinks to the page or site of interest.

9. What is relationship marketing? How can electronic marketing resources assist in developing or supporting ongoing relationships with customers? E-mail your answers to your professor.

Relationship marketing is the combined promotional efforts used to create and sustain a long-term exchange association with a customer. This relationship is mutually beneficial to both parties, and many times a trust is built between the two. This trust is called customer or brand loyalty. Many electronic tools can add convenience (keeping a record of customer purchases that can be accessed by the customer), provide information (creating e-mail newsletters or online announcements of special sales), produce savings (shopping bots to search for merchandise not carried by the merchant), and shaping customer service (creating discussion groups centered on learning more about customer needs and wants of the manufacturer's products).

10. Access the Internet from either your college's computing lab or from your online service at home to research the five largest business-to-business vendors' sales volume over the last three years. Use a resource such as Deja.com or Fortune 500 listings to check the various manufacturing or service companies' sales figures. Record the performance of these five companies and hand your findings in at the next class.

Using a data archive such as the Pathfinder Web site for Fortune, Time and Money magazines (www.pathfinder.com) or the Wall Street Journal industry reports (www.wsj.com), a student can access this information easily.

Chapter 2
Concept of Electronic Commerce and the Traditional Marketing Process

Chapter Summary

Chapter 2 explains the similarities of electronic marketing and traditional marketing, noting that each performs the identical process steps of situation analysis, marketing planning and marketing implementation. The difference between the two processes is that of speed in online retrieval of research, expanded reach of online research to global resources, and accuracy of online survey analysis for the situation investigation. Once facts and opinions are established, the marketing planning stage can manipulate the marketing Ps in untold iterations. Web communications and persuasion materials are designed and innovative distribution system can be developed. Lastly in the implementation stage, the marketing designs are put into action, consummating the Web site design, ISP connections, transactions systems, database and customer service forms construction. The steps are identical, only the methods differ.

The chapter continues by establishing estimates of demographic, psychographic, behavioral, and e-commerce potentials, and explains why companies should consider using e-marketing. In considering why a company should develop Web presence, management should discuss having a strategic plan for employing Web capabilities, goals for communications integration among employees, customers, and suppliers and responsibilities for the Web site operation. Does the company have the patience to "grow and nurture" the online resource? Does senior management support and use electronic tools? If not, electronic marketing efforts will be viewed as unimportant and pilot programs will probably be unsuccessful.

The chapter ends with discussion of the culminating concept of the situation analysis investigation, a statement of the niche opportunity. The niche opportunity is a balance of the marketer's product or service, manufactured and serviced profitably to meet and satisfy a prospect or customer group's needs or wants. Usually the niche opportunity is smaller rather larger in numbers in an effort to provide quality products and experiences.

Core Concepts

- To examine the audiences and potentials of electronic commerce
- To describe how the e-marketing process affects electronic commerce
- To explain how electronic marketing resources can monitor the situation analysis

Chapter Outline

I. Is Anybody Out There?
   A. Matrix Information and Directory Services (MIDS, www.mids.org) estimates that presently 57 million consumers are using the Web, and by the year 2000, more then 700 million people will have Web access
   B. The research company further states that 7.5 million persons use the World Wide Web, and 7.3 million use the Internet at home
   C. Company estimates that 700,000 of 1.1 million children use the Internet at their schools
   D. Reports that 62 million U.S. adults ages 18 years plus now have access to the Internet
   E. (GVU Ninth User Survey 1998) In this April 1998, survey more than 10,000 Web users, 38.7% of Web users are female
   F. Forrester Research (www.forrester.com) a highly regarded online consultant, estimated the female population on the Web accounted for 43% of the Web traffic during 1998, with 45% projected for 1999

II. Why Should Companies Consider Using Electronic Marketing?
   A. Requires efforts for more situations than one "standard" approach

- B. The Internet can be made by long-established companies looking for fresh approaches
- C. Entrepreneurs might use the Internet to "jump-start" a startup business or one that has some history but no money
- D. Ongoing domestic company sees a product or service fit to a selected market within a selected country or region
- E. Review the reasons why electronic commerce is right for the firm
- F. How is business using the Internet?
  1. Approximately 47% of businesses use the Internet-for gathering information
  2. 14% of business Web users purchasing products or services in 1996
  3. A proposed 46% of business are using the Internet for communications purposes
  4. 20% use the Internet to download software
  5. 16% of the firms are selling products
  6. 30% are purchasing products and services

III. The Virtual Retailer

- A. The front door, roof, and back door of a virtual store are the flat surface of your monitor
- B. One of the main driving forces includes the fact that each retailer serves customers with different demographic, psychographic, and behavioral characteristics
- C. Marketers hire communications specialists such as:
  1. In-house designers or Web masters to create and maintain the company's Web stance
  2. Companies might be a one-person operation or a national interactive advertising agency
  3. Third participant is the Internet provider (IP) or Internet service provider (ISP)

IV. Comparing the Traditional Marketing Process Model

- A. Marketers must understand the current dynamics of the marketplace
- B. The first step in your marketing overview is to initiate a situation analysis

V. Evaluating the Online Marketing Situation

- A. Knowing at what point to start is always the key to successful marketing efforts; the stalwart queries of "who, what, when, where, and why" are the conventional, tried embarkation concepts for the investigation
- B. Initiate an online awareness as an extension of the product's or service's promotional program
- C. An advantage of Web messages is the ability of encouraging interactive response
- D. The capability to improve the dialog and react quickly to customer service inquiries
- E. Considered set of Frequently Asked Questions (FAQ's) can oftentimes substitute as an "answer key
- F. Technical support can be enhanced by e-mail communications
- G. Benefits is that technical information can be dispensed with a greater quality of consistency if fewer people are dealing with customers
- H. The Web is conducive for testing new product or service concepts
- I. Customer tracking has become much easier and more accurate as companies have instituted database development programs
- J. Online marketers are discovering that employee recruitment

VI. Defining the Information Search

- A. Relevant market research and input to help set direction for the future marketing plan
  1. Primary research
  2. Secondary research
- B. Steps in the Research Process
  1. Step one is to define the required relevant research
  2. Second step in the research process is to ascertain if and where the information can be obtained

VII. Proposed Market Description
  A. The environmental factors are defined
  B. Market should be described, perhaps two or three market segments could be appropriate for communications and consumption targets
  C. Setting expansive prospect parameters allows the marketer to being construction of the marketing strategy, as the marketing planning evolves, more narrow and clearer profiles will start to emerge

VIII. New Product or Service Definition
  A. Concisely describe the concept of the new product or service, if the marketer cannot, it is unrealistic to expect the audience to work to understand
  B. The product or service must satisfy some need or desire of the target market
  C. A marketer must think in terms of expected benefits that are attractive to the intended audience
  D. Framing the product or service concept, there are several facets to consider: general utility of the good, convenience of procuring the good, timely delivery of the good, and the sales environment where the good is purchased
  E. Many new products are developed as marketers keep tabs on market trends within their industry
    1. Customer recommendations
    2. Industry publications
    3. Online industry resources
  F. Service are more difficult to establish than products

IX. Environmental Factors and Market Trends
  A. There are four major categories of environmental factors that the marketer must monitor
    1. Economic environment
    2. Cultural environment
    3. Legal environment
    4. Political environment
  B. Each of these four environments is equally important since an imbalance in area can create unexpected
  tremors in others

X. Demographic and Other Characteristics
  A. This is the area of change that applies to the people portion of the marketing equation
  B. Demographic information comes from the ten year census initiated in 1790
  C. Psychographics are attitudinally constructed, and many attitudes are difficult
  D. Segmenting populations into similar groups, a marketer can analyze many factors as supplied by the Census data
  E. Other interesting information to consider:
    1. Households can be described in several ways as total number by county, zip code, Census tract,
    or radius in miles or by heads of households
    2. Age profiles
    3. Income clusters
    4. Educational level
    5. Occupational status
    6. Psychographic or lifestyle analysis can uncover lifestyle characteristics for which the marketer is searching

XI. Company History and Competencies
  A. Behind every successful business lies skills or competencies that sets the enterprise apart
  B. The marketing manager can perform an internal audit (or external audit among supplies, current customers, or past customers) to evaluate perceived and real strengths and weaknesses; these competencies should be reflected as benefits

C. Their contention was that every competitor, either company, brand or service, vies among like rivals in product categories, and each is ranked by the consumer

XII. Competitive Analysis and Evaluation

A. Conducting research on competitors' products or services has been facilitated by Web usage because so many Web sites contain so much information

B. Surfing for competitive information is a good idea, particularly if the marketer is entering new fields or new territories

XIII. Assessment of the Niche Opportunity

A. Analysis of the marketing factors and forces, the marketer will be able to establish the product or service niche, a narrower rather than broader market segment

B. Probably the best balance in a marketing relationship is derived as a market segment's needs are met satisfactorily while the company's operation is profitable and efficient

C. The market opportunities can come from existing customer bases, such as extending current offerings into new products

Teaching Suggestions

The student should be aware that there are many forecasts and estimates of e-commerce and Web growth which should be tempered in planning and executing marketing programs. Conservative plans are best received early in electronic marketing efforts as promising some results is better than promising great results. Research from various sources support business use of the Web. The most frequent activities that businesses engage Web usage are: gathering product information, researching competitors, collaborating, vendor support, and internal communications

I ask students to examples of their experiences in the business world and ask whether or not the companies they observed used electronic resources. If not, would work processes be improved if the companies embraced these electronic tools? I also demonstrate the online research sites by accessing the Web addresses to show what the Census Bureau, iVALS, Internet World, Iconocast and other information sites contain. The Census Bureau site has an interesting innovation, the "Population Clock" estimating the American population at that precise minute while National Decision Systems has another imaginative feature, the MicroVision Lifestyle Game (http://laguna.natdecsys.com/lifequiz.html) that provides psychographic information for the zip code you input. These resources are full of information and present data in interesting ways.

Structuring student groups should be discussed early in the term, preferably on the first day. I have found that the online marketing plan is best produced by a group of three students. It can be an overwhelming and intimidating assignment should one student try to execute the research, planning, and implementation alone. Within the group of three, one student may possess strong research skills, another might have interests in constructing the marketing mix while the last student might have been exposed to HTML editing in another class or in a personal project. Checking group dynamics early is also wise since conflicting work schedules, where students live, and other limiting conditions can plague group work. I ask for the students to form a group by the third class meeting (the names written on paper or as an e-mail to me) and the project's product or service concept after the lecture on appropriate e-commerce items. I have found that many groups need coaching to focus their concept into a researchable, marketable, executable project. I have scheduled class periods solely to meet with each group to discuss progress and to make suggestions on the project direction and development.

Answers to Questions and Exercises

1. Your boss says in a meeting, "Always keep sights on our customers. They continue to be moving targets." What did she mean by this statement? Translate this remark into an e-mail message to the staff reporting to you.

The points to be communicated could include:

- Continued research of the market to know what the current needs or wants might be.
- Knowledge that customers are fickle and always ready to buy the newest fashion, lowest price, or some other more attractive product or benefit even if you don't stock the product or offer the service.
- That customers are subject to added-value conveniences that you may not think of or supply.
- Awareness that competitors are always snipping at your customers through promotional efforts, either online or traditional activities.
- That environmental trends such as demographic movements could render your markets, selling techniques, store locations, and products or services obsolete through the passage of time.

2. Evaluate and expand upon the statement, "Electronic marketing resources are the means to the end of electronic commerce." Write a one-page memo, with examples illustrating your points. Explain this concept to a Basic Marketing class.

Points to explain this concept statement might include:

- The concept of "a means to an end," that processes are designed to enable an objective, a finished product or activity
- An explanation of the marketing process as a series of steps or decisions
- A comparison of the steps involved in the workload of traditional marketing versus electronic marketing
- That the situation analysis, the planning of the marketing mix of Ps, and the marketing implementation stage can be translated by electronic resources.
- That electronic resources such as electronic data analysis, databases, communications networks, customer interactivity, and robot shoppers are merely marketing functions or activities enhanced by information technology. A Web page can be considered a traditional print advertisement that allows instant interactivity between the buyer and the seller.
- Strategically e-commerce is the "what" enabled by the "how," the activities of e-marketing.

3. How does the traditional marketing process differ from the electronic marketing process? Which elements are the same and which are different? Write a one-page memo to your boss explaining the concept.

The stages of the traditional marketing process differ little from the stages followed in the electronic marketing process. The information to be investigated, the strategic and creative formulations of the marketing planning stage are similar, and the actions of marketing implementation are alike. The difference between processes becomes noticeable in the speed of retrieval of information or the speed of delivery of communications, hallmarks of electronic resources.

4. In the text discussion, the recommended starting point for a marketing review is the situation analysis. Many marketers deal with their products and companies for years and years. Given this long experience, is it even necessary for the seasoned marketer to pursue the situation analysis, often reaffirming what he already knows, or should he skip this stage to begin with the marketing planning? Be prepared to discuss your thoughts in class.

Because of the speed of change in almost every facet of an individual's life or business environments, it would be foolish for the marketer to ignore the situation analysis process. An analogy might be to compare the marketing process to preparing a roast or Thanksgiving turkey. The food must be cooked, sliced, and served. To save effort, the cook could skip the first step, probably the most time-consuming activity. The marketer could do likewise and a similar disaster would occur. The environmental influences in shifting attitudes, economics, politics, regulations and laws as well as consumer demographics are unwise to ignore, and consumer tastes and expectations can change overnight with examples of gun control or violence in schools. Entertainment such as motion pictures and television can produce powerful desires among all age groups, therefore, generating demand for products or services that were nonexistent in previous years, such as Beanie Babies, Giga Pets, or Furbys.

5. Of the three stages of the marketing process that are discussed in the text, which step (the situation analysis, the marketing planning, or the marketing implementation effort) is most important? Write your response as an e-mail to a colleague who is starting her first marketing management assignment.

In concept and practice, the marketing management process is a continuous effort with no one stage or activity taking precedence over another. In marketing as in other professions and labors, a manager should realize that "there is no finish line" and that the marketing process is circular, with the findings of the situation analysis providing a foundation for the marketing planning designs that are then brought into action in the marketing implementation and measurement stage. The results of marketing measurement become input into the next situation investigation and the process begins again. The marketing manager must be careful to balance her efforts and enthusiasm for the three stages.

6. You are the head strategic analyst for a newly established division of a one-hundred-year-old candy company. Many of your brands lead in the categories important to the consumer. For the last six months, you have been gathering market intelligence that will be crucial in launching a new brand targeted towards upscale department stores' candy counters. Much of the information, however, is contradictory, such as the target market's interest in quality chocolate while at the same time eschewing purchasing luxury goods. Which data source should you may most attention to—industry statistics, company statistics, consumer opinions, or customer survey opinions? Prepare your response as a speech outline that you will be giving to a stockholder meeting.

Points that might shed direction on your new luxury confectionery and could be shared with the stockholders (and the students) include:

- Your company has a hundred-year history and experience in serving and satisfying candy-buying customers.
- Over this period, the company established a reputation and image for producing quality sweets.
- The company has a close connection with its customers and listens to their opinions, both supportive and critical.
- Department store clientele are discriminating and expect quality merchandise.
- The company advertises sparingly, explaining that it puts the promotional money into better quality ingredients and relies on word-of-mouth referrals.

The strategic analyst would be best served by conducting customer opinion surveys since the company has a constituency of loyal customers. If these relationship customers indicate the product is needed, their opinions should be heeded over industry statistics or general audience attitudes.

7. You are the customer satisfaction manager, and you are reviewing customer comments sent to you by e-mail. You know that one in ten prospects purchase your product, which means that nine potential customers leave your store without purchasing. Prepare a proposal that would survey by e-mail those non-buyers leaving your stores, and project what you would expect to learn from this electronic study.

The first decision in this information search is defining what information is needed such as "what factors are keeping non-buyers from buying?" After the information needs are established, deciding what method of survey is appropriate for the most complete and reliable results is the next step. This decision may or may not include an e-mail survey depending on your customer base and product category. If the product is competing in an economy class, the penetration of online access may be low; thus, many non-buyers would be missed. Supposing the product is mid-priced to luxury priced and a discretionary purchase, a method of collecting e-mail addresses must be devised. What the marketer should expect to learn will be only as good or complete as the survey instrument. A well-crafted questionnaire might uncover prospect resistance to some obvious objection such as a perceived high price or an overlooked obstacle, such as poor nighttime lighting in the parking lot.

8. The various influences that shape the competitive environment in which businesses must operate are discussed in the chapter. In your opinion, rank from most important to least important those environmental factors—economic, cultural, legal, political, and demographic trends. Write a memo to your boss explaining why these influences are important and in what order they should be studied.

This is a difficult question to answer because there is no one influence that can be singled out as "most important." Marketers in the early 1970s were caught off guard when the Arab oil embargo was imposed on the U.S. Few marketing programs could succeed if consumers were unable to drive to stores or shopping malls. A logical approach to responding to the influences of these environmental factors is:

1. *Legal and regulatory trends.* Government and legislative opinions must be monitored because laws prohibiting the sale of the product category will close any business.
2. *Economic trends.* Since marketing impacts the economy and the economic health of a region or a nation impacts marketing, economic indicators such as interest rates, new home sales, rates of inflation, and monetary exchange rates can drastically speed up or slow down consumer or business-to-business purchasing.
3. *Demographic trends.* The marketer must have a sufficient customer base to which to sell, though demographic changes may be slow to recognize. Many previously successful companies such as Montgomery Ward or W.T.Grant have struggled or folded because of changing demographics and customer tastes. Some management personnel refuse to change strategies and policies to the result that longtime customers abandon the retailer's establishments.
4. *Political Trends.* Political trends can swing from conservative to literal to moderate all within a six-year period according to the two-year elections for the House of Representatives. While marketers strive to be "politically correct," these swift swings in opinion may swing back before any negative marketing influence can be detected. Conscious marketers will keep in touch with the political pulse as part of the standard "environmental watch". Also, the U.S. hosts so many cultures and ethnic groups that marketers are almost always offending some constituency. As segmentation and target marketing spread among companies' strategies, more focus will be given to homogeneous groups of consumers. Marketing messages and programs should mesh better with the culture of the group. Cultural sensitivity is important, but marketers are already attempting to learn the mores and taboos before a marketing program is launched.

9. Using the tactic of positioning, many brands have created unique images for themselves. Either watch television commercials, read a popular consumer magazine, or walk through a department store or supermarket to pick out ten examples of successful products or services and their positioning lines. Are they used on the product's Web site? Write a brief paragraph identifying the positioning and explain the benefit(s) being offered by the brands.

This is a field exercise and the brands will vary depending on students' tastes or interests.

10. As a brand becomes more and more successful, marketing managers often begin to reduce marketing efforts and expenditures. This seems to be sensible to save valuable monetary resources in the near-term. Considering electronic marketing activities, do you support or reject this line of thinking? Compose an e-mail to the chief financial officer stating your position on the proper strategy and level of marketing expenditures.

Support of saving money in the near-term:

- Perhaps the product is fashion or fad-oriented in which demand might disappear overnight.
- Establishing costly electronic systems might be wasted if the product becomes obsolete.

Rejection of saving money in the near-term:

- A more realistic thought process would be to consult sales representatives, distributors, and to watch competitive products' sales before any arbitrary alteration of the marketing after or budget is considered.
- With electronic marketing resources, changes in direction can be made quickly because of the nature of the electronic media.
- Distributors or retailers may drop the line if promotional efforts are reduced.
- Reducing the electronic presence might signal some danger sign to the customer base.

Chapter 3
Marketing Planning Stage for Online Activities

Chapter Summary

This chapter draws parallels between traditional marketing planning concepts and illustrates how they are integrated in to the electronic environment. Marketing planning in an electronic environment is stressed. The application of the traditional marketing techniques of the Marketing Mix (marketing Ps), product/service image development, market segmentation, benefits analysis, positioning strategy, pricing, promotion, distribution, and budgeting are reviewed and then the ways in which they can be utilized in an electronic environment are highlighted.

The premise that the electronic environment will create more knowledgeable consumers is stressed and attention is given to strategic and tactical marketing planning and marketing plan development in light of a more informed and savvy customer base. The real-time access to information by the consumer and their increasing demand for instant response from marketers to their inquiries will provoke e-marketers to re-think their traditional use of marketing techniques while developing innovative applications of new technology to meet the demands of consumers in the newly competitive electronic marketplace.

The chapter also shows that marketers must think and strategically plan in tandem between traditional and electronic marketing environments, and each must compliment the other to be totally competitive.

Core Concepts

- To define the e-marketing mix elements of product, price, promotion, distribution, and measuring performance
- To introduce the methods of market segmentation
- To explain how electronic marketing resources can enhance the traditional marketing activities of effective and efficient marketing planning strategy

Chapter Outline

I. Planning with Electronic Ps
   A. Marketing planning and marketing implementation are last steps in the marketing process
      1. Marketing plan based unfortunately on their own misinterpreted data
      2. Marketers lack the knowledge and skills necessary to initiate a marketing program because they are overwhelmed with marketing data and become confused as to the next step to take
      3. In marketing planning, the marketer draws upon the findings of the situations analysis and constructs future activities according to structuring the marketing Ps
   B. Marketing on the Web parallels traditional marketing
      1. Tools change-from traditional to electronic resources
      2. Findings of the situation analysis beget the market niche to be filled
      3. Which begets a product need and definition
      4. Manufacturing a brand by fashioning image parameters
      5. A new product offering is formed
         a. identify desired image benefits
         b. create the product identity
         c. coordinate image and identity so all marketing materials speak with "one voice"

II. Crafting a Unique Online Image and Identity
   A. Essence the marketer's product or service does for his clientele

1. With an attractive concept and solid product execution, hopefully the offering cannot be easily duplicated by a competitor
2. Given a perceived or real uniqueness, the marketer can build a niche strategy online
3. Establishing a singular benefit sets some companies in an exclusive position

B. Electronic marketing considerations start with the product name

1. Attention should be given to the URL address name so that it is distinctive and readily reminds the user of the product name
2. What will be your server name, that of your ISP or your own server?
3. What is the proper domain designation?
4. Will you use the prefixes in your address?
5. Will you choose to hyperlink to other sites, and wi8ll you reciprocate?
6. What types of hyperlinks will you allow on you pages
7. With what types of search engines will you register you Web site address?
8. Will you print-block your Web pages so that the viewer cannot print your page?

C. If the marketer's strategy is to introduce an existing product to the Web, she can prepare an audit of the advantages and disadvantages of Web exposure

1. What has made your brand what it is today, and for what reasons do you have a product following?
2. What attributes does you audience value and why?
3. Which of these benefits do your customers value?
    a. Quality as in durability or reliability?
    b. Faster and friendlier service?
    c. Technicians with high levels of expertise?
    d. On –time service?
    e. Twenty-four hour convenience?
    f. Money-back guarantees?
    g. Twenty-hour tracking service?
    h. Perhaps well-trained and caring store personnel?

D. Competencies can you leverage into your online marketing efforts

1. Accurate product prices on your Web site
2. Quick replies to e-mail inquiries
3. Correct policies
4. Frequently Asked Questions
5. Responsive modem connections
6. Up-to-date product offerings

III. Building the Marketing Plan

A. The objectives of the online marketing effort-No different from traditional marketing

1. Objectives are usually set as numeric goals
    a. Percent of market share
    b. A dollar sales volume
    c. A dollar sales quota per sales representative
    d. A percentage or dollar return on investment or asset
    e. A dollar sales volume per territory

B. Marketing Direction

1. Additional sets of objectives can be established
    a. Market target descriptions
    b. Communications objectives
    c. Sales
    d. Media
    e. Public relations objectives

C. Having established numeric objectives, the marketer will be able to compare the program's performance at year's end

- D. Input into the next year's planning
- E. Establish goals?
    1. Consult current literature
    2. Interview fellow staff members
    3. Check with industry associations
- F. Marketing programs will differ depending on:
    1. Stage of the product life
    2. Level of competition
    3. Size of the sales territory
    4. Type of product entry
    5. Whether the product is a seasonal good or services

IV. Selection of Prospect Groups
- A. Investigation of prospect clusters begins now
- B. Segmenting the market:
    1. Geography
    2. Demographics
    3. Psychographics
    4. Behavioral characteristics
- C. Benefits analysis
- D. Develop the product or service positioning strategy
    1. Positioning line

V. Framing the Ps of the E-Marketing Plan

VI. Defining the Product or Service
- A. What are some of the categories that are being sold on the Web?
    1. Better
    2. Faster
    3. More convenient
    4. More unique
    5. Last longer
    6. Feature a better warranty
- B. Specific categories can include:
    1. New or existing products or services
    2. Harder-to-find products
- C. The Web as a delivery vehicle
    1. Information services
    2. Tangible products
        - a. Compact packaging
        - b. Overnight or two-day delivery
        - c. Installation as simple as possible
    3. Research
- D. Benefits of the Web
    1. Interactive capability of dialog between the viewer and the marketer
    2. Electronic in nature and therefore will be attractive to the technological crowd
- E. Availing an existing product or service to an online presence

VII. Pricing Knowledge Will Become Universal
- A. Consumer
- B. will have "perfect knowledge" of the marketer's price structure
- C. Strategy for protecting quality and profit margins against cutthroat
    1. Quality-related information about the product or service

2. Differentiating brands within a category

D. More intense price competition with the infusion of interactive home shopping (HIS)

VIII. Distribution Decisions

A. Logistics activities include:

1. Strategic planning
2. Transportation
3. Purchasing
4. Warehousing
5. Materials handling
6. Inventory control
7. Forecasting

B. Distribution function as an input and an output system in which customer communications is the initial input (or order) that leads to an output (product or service delivery) with continual customer contact to start the process over again

C. Online tools improve the distribution cycle

1. Thread of speed
2. Accuracy
3. Efficiency runs through the logistics strategy

IX. A Targeted Promotional Strategy

A. Promotion mix

1. Advertising
2. Sales promotion
3. Public relations
4. Direct marketing
5. Personal selling

B. Online media fits best into the direct marketing category, direct marketing may be renamed "interactive marketing"

X. Formulating the Marketing Budget

A. Objective and task method

B. Zero-based budgeting

Teaching Suggestions

First, it is helpful to define the traditional promotional mix of the five persuasion elements: advertising, sales promotion, public relations, direct marketing (under which we have categorized Web marketing), and personal selling to describe each effort's advantages and disadvantages, and then to demonstrate various Web sites and their online counterparts. Easiest to find are banner ads that populate search engine home pages. Sales promotions are always found on CD, book, video club sites such as Blockbuster (www.blockbuster.com) or Columbia House (www.columbiahouse.com) pushing incentives such as eleven CDs for one penny. Most corporate sites such as Visa (www.visa.com) or Merrill Lynch (www.ml.com) have information for the press and a repository of past news articles about the company, its financial performance, its products, and many other newsworthy items.

As we discussed, any consumer or commercial sales offering on a Web page should be considered a form of direct marketing (other forms include direct response advertising on television or in newspapers), and Web direct response activities are improvements over the traditional form because of the interactivity capability. Speed in placing the order, accuracy in merchandise and customer databases while still maintaining the ability to personalize through e-mail or on invoices provide convenience for the e-shopper. Personal selling programs also benefit from electronic resources as field sales representatives can fax inquiries, probe customer databases, and e-mail instructions to the home office while sitting in her home office or the client's. Electronic marketing resources enhance these practices, not replace them. Within the traditional marketing paradigm, the Web becomes another information medium, and electronic marketing programs rely on traditional media such as newspapers and magazines, trusted and tested, to extend awareness of the existence of the Web site, expand penetration to offline audiences, and spread retention of the Web address.

The text continues to explain the strategy of product branding which can be confusing to the student. Branding is the concentrated effort to create a unique and desirable "personality" for a product (Campbell Soups), service (Metropolitan Life Insurance) or idea (Disney Imagineering). The tools marketers and advertisers use for crafting a unique online brand (and extending the concepts to offline usage) are image and identity-building processes. Brand image is the "what awareness" the marketer wants to conjure in the prospect or customer's mind. A nostalgic example is Campbell's branding of a long line of soups, all made with tasteful ingredients represented by the "Campbell Kids" characters, testifying that the soups were "Um-umm, good." The identity materials include the positioning line, "Um-umm, good," the illustrations of the Campbell Kids are a de facto logo when the Campbell name is not used, and the continuity of the red and white label design is highly memorable. The late artist Andy Warhol used the label and can as the subject matter to represent Campbell's as an American icon. Building a successful and desirable brand name and image is a popular method for introducing new products under the accepted brand.

In discussing the logic and framework for building the marketing plan, students should have a clear understanding of planning terminology by way of an understanding about the difference between objectives and strategies (what versus how), strategic versus tactical (long-term versus short-term) and so forth. Other definitions to cover should include the alternate method of segmentation: geographical, demographic, psychographic, behavioral, and benefits derived. The differences and situations for use were described in Chapter 2. For executing this online marketing plan, the best segmentation strategies for the student to research are demographic and psychographic characteristics.

The chapter presents a discussion of appropriate products for e-commerce. I encourage student groups to create "fantasy" products or services that do not exist to give them reign over the marketing mix. They should make assumptions on product characteristics and manufacturing, the features of previously nonexistent services, accommodating pricing, full or select distribution as well as achievement of product placement in the outlets students choose. I believe that their creation of nonexistent but desirable products and services provides freedom in thinking and implementation. Some students choose to execute a project for developing an online presence for existing companies that are not marketing on the Web. Many students attempt to produce an online marketing plan for companies owned by friends or family; this type of project tends to be grounded in reality (the limitations of real budgets, product manufacturing specifications, and distribution restrictions). These "real" projects have a tendency to be less dynamic and imaginative particularly if the student acts as a consultant to the family operation and tries to create a marketing plan that is to be implemented online.

The student groups should also understand that their projects are planning prototypes NOT to be published online. Students will not have to worry about filling orders, maintaining stock, or processing transactions because the project is an e-commerce simulation.

In this planning stage, students have difficulty in constructing a marketing budget. I begin with an explanation and example of a reasonable sales revenue projection and ask them to estimate the number of total hits and what a reasonable conversion to sales might be (my research has a conversion to sales between .0025 percent for high traffic sites to 2 percent although these figures vary according to industry, viewer interest, and the effects of more persuasive marketing programs). Then I ask what retail unit price they expect to sell the product for; for simplicity sake, the quantity sold times the unit price because the project sales revenue for the period the students choose. Some groups figure outlandish revenue estimates that I ask them to explain and revise. I present the rationale of "percentage of sales," not the best budgeting method for real companies but a simpler, more arbitrary method that students seem to understand. I discuss the components of the marketing and promotional elements and suggest they budget for each one. This leads to a presentation of objective and task (also called zero-based) budgeting in which the marketer outlines all materials and programs, estimates the cost of each to arrive at a master budget total. This taste of the budgeting process, albeit simplistic, helps the student recognize how the marketing budget is derived from the gross sales revenue.

Answers to Questions and Exercises

1. Bill Gates has said, "Everyone will have access to most of the world's information." From a marketer's point of view, is this a positive or negative occurrence? Or does it depend on the situation. Justify your answer in a three-paragraph statement to your company's CEO.

To an ethical marketer this is a positive happening because the more information s/he has, the better a decision s/he will make when purchasing goods. The information must be quality, meaning accurate and usable. With quality information the buyer can better satisfy her needs, take advantage of beneficial pricing, compare offerings from several vendors, and be apprised of product availability and delivery schedules. This situation could almost be termed "perfect knowledge" in that the buyer and seller are privy to equal information. The seller also benefits because the buyer should return fewer products, associate positive purchase experiences, and enjoy positive referrals from satisfied customers while sellers could manage inventory and cash flow better. The seller could also monitor the prices of the competition more fully.

Only the unethical marketer would object to this free flow of full information. By withholding true prices, this marketer could manipulate pricing that held exorbitant, inflated profits unfair to the consumer. Perhaps the only exceptions to this statement could deal in areas of general population health care such as managing epidemics or in matters of national security.

2. What is the difference among branding, image, identity, and positioning as a marketer creates a perception for a new business-to-business product or service? Which tactic is the most important in setting a public perception forth the new product? Write a one-page strategy statement your division's new product plans for your company's manual report.

This exercise might take some imagination on the part of the student to fabricate new product plans. You might give them a scenario of a light truck manufacturing division venturing into a sports utility vehicle line (SUV). These are popular vehicles today and manufacturers currently use branding, image advertising, identity packaging, and positioning to create memorable messages for their products.

In general, positioning would be most important in setting a public perception because evaluations of the brand, the image, and the identity are filtered into the shaping of the market positioning. Further positioning takes into account the perceptions, messages, and identities of competitive products to create this unique new position. The establishment of a positioning perception would evolve only after substantial product, prospect, and competitive offerings research is analyzed.

3. The coordination between image and identity is critical since all marketing materials should speak with "one voice." Marketers generally accept this statement as true. Can you think of special circumstances in which a vehicle might take a different voice? Write a one-page memo advising your public relations director of your deviation in the marketing plan and why this change makes sense.

Some companies follow strict identity guidelines set forth in "identity manuals" which prescribe how corporate image is to followed, from the size of the logo in half-page magazine advertisements to the placement of a logo on product packaging or company vehicles. Continuity and reinforcement of identity elements are supported by contemporary marketing thought.

The reverse of a quality producer producing mid-line goods usually calls for divergence from the "one voice" strategy. This frequently occurs in the practice of "private branding," when a manufacturer has excess capacity and produces goods under independent store's name brand.

4. Much of the promotional strength of online communications comes from "word of mouth" endorsements through Usenets or discussion groups. Consumers using Usenets can post their dissatisfaction about products. Select a product you either strongly like or dislike and log onto a discussion site such as Deja.com or eGroups to monitor what other people are saying about your product. Write and e-mail to your professor summarizing public opinion about your selected product.

The students can explore eGroups, www.egroups.com or Deja.com, www.deja.com, to investigate public opinion concerning the favored or disliked product. They can also follow the thread of the conversation to report on the development of the positive or negative product opinions.

5. Perhaps a disgruntled ex-employee fired from your company for stealing supplies stated in a newspaper interview that your spring water company was actually selling tap water drawn from the city water supply. This allocation was false but to combat rumors, you commissioned a product testing study that confirmed the purity of your water from a natural source. To reach your well educated, techno-savvy consumers, what would be the best tactic to state your case and findings: posting the study on the company Web site, placing online ads, sponsoring an online conference, or employing Usenets? Write an action strategy to submit to your marketing director.

Realistically a rebuttal should include both traditional marketing efforts such as a public relations and publicity campaign and targeted online communications such as the creation of a specific discussion group for the purpose of presenting research study findings and answering questions concerning the issue. Placing traditional and online ads might not be wise because bringing attention to the issue through advertising could rekindle general public debate or make those customers who are unaware of the allegation become suspicious. Sponsoring an online conference for general public users will also rekindle the issue or bring unwanted awareness to those unfamiliar with the original publicity as would postings to a Usenet group. A moderated discussion group would probably circulate the correct information to interested users.

6. We discussed a second method of differentiated marketing, product differentiation, which focuses on offering products or services with different features but within the same category. Think of General Motors' array of differentiated brands such as Chevrolet, Pontiac, Oldsmobile, Buick, and Cadillac, with economy to luxury features that have made the brand famous. In your opinion, which strategy, market segmentation or product differentiation, is more customer-oriented and, therefore, more attentive to delivering customer benefits? Prepare your thoughts as a five-minute talk with basic marketing students.

Contemporary marketers generally agree that market segmentation centers on prospect or customer needs or wants; this focus is directed to satisfying rational or emotional demands. Market segmentation allows the marketer to concentrate the needs and wants of smaller, more homogeneous groups rather than a "one size fits all" product mindset. Marketing resources can be expended more wisely to achieve market segment satisfaction rather than producing a line of products that the consumer may not want, a financial gamble of the product differentiation strategy.

7. Market identification strategies of demographic, psychographic, geographic, and behavioristic segmentation are each very different ways to profile your market segments. Define the bases of differentiation for each such as numeric, and state the advantages of each strategy. Be prepared to support or defend each method in a class discussion.

Demographic segmentation - numeric quantification, sums and percentages

- Advantages: Updated by the government every ten years; specific characteristics measured such as age, income, gender, household size
- Disadvantages: Movement of changing markets between the ten-year Census; many attitudes and behaviors are not demographically driven; using smaller and smaller niche markets

Geographic segmentation - measurement by specific geographical units, such as zip codes, counties, states, etc.

- Advantages: Boundaries are specific such as roads, zip codes, county lines; regions can be numerically compared against one another; targeted marketing plans can be prepared for specific geographical areas such as Florida, and another program prepared for California
- Disadvantages: Movement of changing markets between the ten-year Census; imprecise mix of segment characteristics causes uncertainty of profile and benefit; choosing too small a geographical area to which to market may be uneconomical or inefficient

Psychographic segmentation -measurement by lifestyle clusters such as "outdoor" or "workaholic"

- Advantages: Provides a richer portrait of consumer than simple demographic information; identifies market segment by patterns in an individual's pursuit of life goals
- Disadvantages: Psychographic variables are more difficult to deal with because of qualitative Descriptions and requires considerable resources; Some researchers question the validity of this segmentation approach

Behavioral segmentation - measurement by product knowledge, habits or consumption

- Advantages: Consumers will self-identify as to product knowledge, links about products and brands, and reason for purchase; consumers are promotionally sensitive and will react to incentives
- Disadvantages: Consumers vary in consumption habits between categories of products or services; behavioral research requires considerable resources

Benefits segmentation - measurement by consumer value systems and perceptions of brands in a product class

- Advantages: Seeks to identify customer needs and wants with products and services with desired benefits; considered very consistent with the approach to marketing suggested by the groups
- Disadvantages: Benefits segments change over time; benefits research requires considerable resources and must be performed periodically

Geo-demographic segmentation - measurement by grouping demographic variables such as age and income, as identified by a geo-demographic variable such as a zip code

- Advantages: Method identifies clusters of like-minded prospects, assumes that "birds of a feather flock together"; considered more accurate in targeting promotional efforts
- Disadvantages: Geo-demographic research relies on Census data which is recorded every ten years and requires modeling toward the decade; geo-demographic research requires considerable resources

8. Distribution/logistics has long been overlooked as a promotional element to create competitive advantage. Name electronic marketing resources that have produced tactical advantages in the marketing plan, and how these attained cost or time efficiencies. Write a memo to your chief financial officer.

- *E-mail networks, domestic and international* - Messaging between offices faster and more economical, saving postage and stationery
- *Intranet and extranet* - Efficient communications among internal offices and selected suppliers or clients partnering and collaboration over distances
- *EDI* - Efficient and rapid exchange of data between clients, commercial vendors, and internal record keeping
- *Electronic data warehouse and data mining* - Selection of preferred customers for promotional targeting, recording sales movement, and lean inventory management
- *Internet order processing and downloading/delivery of electronic services* - For more efficient and accurate order transactions and delivery of selected information technology items

9. In the *Journal of Marketing* article about interactive home shopping, the authors stated a considerable amount of distribution costs is borne by the customer when unsatisfactory merchandise is returned. Within the distribution scheme, how can electronic marketing resources prevent these costs to the consumer? Assuming no one buys a

product merely to return it, formulate five distribution policies that could be used in junction with electronic ordering and transactions systems.

1. To improve accuracy of order filling, adopt a product numbering and bar code system.
2. Implement an optical mark/character reader scanning system that would read bar codes.
3. Schedule training sessions for all warehouse and order entry staff on operation of the bar code system.
4. Conduct a quality review of all promotional materials including Web offerings and product catalogues as to reflecting correct product numbers.
5. Create an automated e-mail system to confirm online orders to purchasers before the product is shipped.
6. Establish a call center to periodically check on order fulfillment and satisfaction.
7. Transmits an e-mail customer satisfaction survey or mail a hard-copy survey asking customer satisfaction questions and ideas for service improvement.

10. Given that company operating policies are usually driven by either budgetary efficiencies such as an being "low cost producers" or "benefits bundling" to enhance effectiveness for products of less price sensitivity. In which scenario, cost efficiencies or marketing effectiveness, do you think electronic marketing resources performed better? Are your thoughts an either/or answer, or must other factors the considered? Why are these factors? Be prepared to present your thoughts in a class discussion.

Because most companies producing products of less price sensitivity are producing discretionarily, those products that fulfill wants rather than needs, products, cost to the consumer is of minor consequence. Thus, marketing strategies such as "benefits bundling," for convenience or ego satisfaction, must perform well and provide the promised product or service satisfaction. In a marketing-oriented company, this question would not have an either/or answer. Customer satisfaction would reign, and marketing programs' costs would be built into the product or service's price.

Chapter 4
The Actions of Marketing Implementation

Chapter Summary

This chapter addresses the techniques of marketing implementation, or "putting the plan into action." Marketing realities, both traditional and electronic, are created by continually reassessing and answering the questions of "who, what, when where, and why?" Since marketing actions and their implementation must be logical and orderly to attain efficiency and effectiveness, the answers to these questions will define the strategic and tactical direction the marketer must take to attain business goals.

The electronic environment provides faster access to larger quantities of customer data, which must be consistently monitored to quickly respond to changes in the competitive market. In an electronic environment, customer tracking will take on new meaning and broader roles in responding to the needs of the consumer. Electronically communicating with customers and responding to their needs will dictate a twenty-four hour a day, seven day a week effort as consumers will demand this increased level of attention.

Not only will these concepts apply to customers, they will apply to suppliers in the business-to-business sector, in which marketers also deal. Confidentiality and security issues are taking on more importance in e-commerce due to the quick accessibility to vast quantities of personal and commercial information.

Performance assessment of electronic marketing is introduced in this chapter.

Core Concepts

- To describe the tactical issues that face hands-on execution of the electronic marketing mix strategies
- To explore the tasks, advantages, and disadvantages of engaging outside suppliers
- To establish performance objectives to determine whether marketing progress achieved corporate objectives

Chapter Outline

I. Minding the Details
   A. Good marketers prepare workable and realistic implementation plans
   B. Marketing planning is future oriented
   C. Marketing plans are put into action

II. Consumer Tracking Strategies
   A. Customer tracking system
      1. Record individual purchasing habit or special interests
      2. Inventory tracking devices in medium to large companies
      3. Purchase dates
      4. Length of warranty
      5. Categories of merchandise
      6. Gift or personal use
      7. Payment preference
      8. Different characteristics are important to different industries
   B. Reporting formats
      1. Mailing lists of customers, dealers, wholesalers, or prospects
      2. Customer service or maintenance records
      3. Sales movements in planning future advertising expenditures
      4. "Coupon keys"

- C. Tracking software also will organize the information into easy-to-read and understand reports with color graphs or charts

III. Keeping in Touch with the Customer
- A. E-mail notices
- B. Global positioning satellite system (GPS) is a valuable differentiation factor in transportation
- C. Sample of customer inquiries is electronically forwarded to the marketing department every day. Follow-up questions or replies can be issued within a time standard, such as twenty-four hour promise of response

IV. Setting Priorities for Action
- A. Marketing implementation can be simple or complex
- B. Can require national, regional, or local efforts
- C. It may bring together manufacturers, wholesalers, and retailers
- D. Importance of organization and delegation
  1. Outlining the tasks
  2. Determining who will implement these tasks
  3. Breaking down the big program into bite-sized portions
  4. Coordinate internal personnel and tasks as well as external resources for e-commerce
- E. Online implementation can be complex since longer lead times are required by telecommunications or hardware suppliers
- F. Suppliers can be of great help, many marketers will outsource some crucial activities
- G. Suppliers, key people or organizations working outside the company
  1. Delineate what final outcomes are expected
  2. How the work or systems are to be designed
  3. How progress is to be measured
  4. Who the people that comprise the supplier's staff are and what qualifications the staff has
  5. What the length of the engagement is expected to be
  6. How ongoing maintenance of the Web site is to be performed
  7. How or when the supplier is to be paid
     - a. prepayments
     - b. installments payments
     - c. milestone payments
- H. There are mixed opinions on the value or flexibility in using outside suppliers
  1. Supporters position on hiring an outside firm
     - a. Supporters pose that engaging outside software developers adds fresh thinking and objectivity
     - b. Introduces experience gained from other assignments
     - c. Pushes overhead costs to the consulting firm
  2. Opponents position on hiring outside the firm
     - a. Consultants charge up-front retainers
     - b. Lack necessary proof or promise of successful completion
     - c. Many people have trouble visualizing the end product or service
     - d. Worry outside suppliers is that the supplier staff is incompetent
- I. Checking Suppliers
  1. The supplier firm's credentials are easily checked by calling current and past clients
  2. Speaking with suppliers that have done business with the company
  3. Financial inquiry report such as Dunn and Bradstreet financial profiles
  4. Marketer learns about the supplier's business practices
- J. To assure that equal attention is paid to the client
  1. Write into the business contract who will be the company contact
  2. Identify the software design team

3. Identify who in each firm will be the arbitrators should problems or misunderstandings arise

K. Concern with confidentiality and security issues

1. Careful screening of the software firm and its associates
2. Nondisclosure agreements should be signed by all parties, including supplier and client interests
3. Fortifying buildings
4. Security personnel for building visitors from check-in to checkout
5. Verification of authenticity with credible companies that supply services to the building
6. Should be suspicious of liaisons such as hiring the brother-in-law's software company or employing an old college chum of the CEO

V. Assigning Program Responsibilities

A. Efficiency

1. Cost per thousand
2. CPM (cost per thousand)
3. GRP's (gross rating points)
4. TRP's (target rating points)
5. Page hits
6. Clickthroughs
7. "Unique visitors"

B. Effectiveness

VI. The Disadvantages of Implementation

A. Do not have a thorough understanding of what they have created

B. How to maintain

C. How to evolve

VII. Planning for the Entire Year

A. Effective manner of bringing the marketing process of life is through planning

1. Sets out specific tasks
2. Setting objectives for various exposure vehicles such as Web page design or newspaper or allied traditional media
3. Developing the copy and graphic approach for the media
4. Selecting and budgeting for media support
5. Planning the distribution
6. Training the retailer and salespeople
7. Identifying many other potential objective

B. Object and Task Method

1. Concurrent activities
2. Linear activities

VIII. Measuring Performance

A. Any marketing plan that does not estimate acceptable goals and the time and budget allocated to reach the goals is an incomplete marketing plan

Teaching Suggestions

The material in this chapter is pedestrian because it pertains to detailed-oriented activities in executing the marketing plan. Yet, this could be the most important chapter in the entire textbook because if actions do not put the plan into motion, no marketing effort happens; or if the execution is shoddy or delayed, efficiencies and effectiveness of the synergy of an IMC program slide. We have discussed the two optimal qualities of the marketer personality, that of organization and persuasion; this chapter describes the tasks and responsibilities of marketing implementation and its needed foundation for organizational abilities.

In an earlier end of chapter question, the strength and appropriateness of electronic marketing resources relative to the stages of the marketing process, i.e. which stage benefits most from the use of electronic resources, and it was suggested that this stage, marketing implementation, gained the most advantage. Electronic resources help to mind the details provided by automation.

There is a discussion on using outside suppliers or in-house staff for the implementation of certain marketing projects. These decisions depend on company policy, expertise needed, cost considerations, or deadlines set for project completion. Students are cautioned to check suppliers' credentials carefully to ascertain if the supplier is qualified to execute the project. Many companies use outside suppliers to gain top-notch talent on a project without incurring full-time staff expenses.

The text continues by explaining the setting of priorities, strongly stating that "the marketer must know where to start to know where and when to finish the project or program plan. Students become confused with all the data, deadlines, and promotional strategies they wish to execute. They should remember the simple critical thinking model of "who, what, why, when, and where" word questions that lead to how the program plan will be prioritized. Most students I've taught are linear thinkers, completing one full element before going on to the next step. Most excellent marketers are "random abstract" thinkers, able to handle several assignments at once without confusing one with the other or making mistakes. I've found also that the two patterns cannot be taught, a student comes equipped with one or the other. So, conscious effort in setting marketing implementation priorities must be stressed. Examples for implementation planning are included in the chapter.

After the implementation planning discussion, the chapter closes by presenting the rationale for a carefully recorded and scrutinized measurement system. There are marketing performance software packages available for analysis of efficient marketing and advertising costs and there also are statistics packages which can be adapted to Web site measurement counting hits, clickthroughs, amount of time the viewer remains on the site, most popular pages accessed, and more profiling information. Electronic marketing is like any other operational expenditure; it must be measured for results or lack of results. Without measurement criteria, how can a marketer judge if objectives and goals are being met?

Answers to Questions and Exercises

1. You are hiring an assistant marketing director to help you run a two-person marketing department. What are the 5 most important personality characteristics you will be looking for in your view hire, and why are these characteristics important? Make a written list to refer to as you interview.

From the chapter discussion, two personality traits are important for the marketing professional. One is the ability to organize, to maintain order amid chaos as well as to direct a marketing effort from beginning to and. A second trait is the ability to persuade, to develop marketing programs and be able to able to communicate the logic and value as to why the company and its customers will benefit from these actions. Other good characteristics include: the ability to listen carefully and empathize with your markets to understand their points of view, having a strong sense of persistence in problem solving, being creative in abstract planning, having a balance between self-confidence and flexibility in working as a team is necessary, and the ability for clear and concise communications among the marketer's superior, her market, her associates, and her suppliers is uppermost.

2. You are a production manager working on producing a new Web site for your company. You have the designs for various Web pages but you have no further input about the assignment. The marketing director of your company is on vacation for two weeks, and she expects the site to "go live" the week after she returns. What questions would you e-mail her if you needed more information in implementing this assignment?

This question concerns the level of initiative possessed by the production manager. If s/he has been through the introduction process of launching a Web site, s/he may proceed with the project based on past experience. If the production manager is new or inexperienced, s/he should refer to the written marketing plan to see what the implementation schedule requires. If a marketing plan and/or implementation plan has not been developed, the production manager should contact the marketing manager to ask for the preparation of the document.

3. In implementing an e-mail order system confirmation, you recognize that the primary purpose of the system is to acknowledge order receipts to customers. What are other benefits, some psychological, that comes with this type of customer contact? Prepare a one-page memo on system benefits that will be used in training customer service representatives.

The most obvious confirmation is that of the product price, quantity, shipping details as well as delivery date. Customer contact of this sort can help build positive relationships to let the customer know that the company appreciates the business and is working to fulfill its commerce duties to the highest expectation. Customer appreciation, recognition, satisfaction, and the reliance on a trusted retail resource might be feelings a customer could harbor as proactive customer service is rendered. In the event of errors, customer replies through the e-mail system could stop orders before they are shipped. This action could make a potentially unsatisfied customer happy with the company, save shipping or delivery charges, and save the customer the aggravation of having to return the merchandise. With a fast and accurate e-mail confirmation system, credit card accounts might not be charged because mistakes could be caught before shipping. Lastly, the customer could be contacted by e-mail to announce special sales not publicized to the general public, which would make the customer feel like part of a "select group." E-mail systems can enhance customer service by complimenting the merchant's efforts towards special treatment of the clientele.

4. You are in charge of implementing a large proprietary database system that will contain all company financial, client project and employee records. Your publicly-traded construction company has sales of over $3 billion. You report to the Chief Operating Officer, and he is extremely nervous and paranoid about losing control of this data. For certain phases of the transition, from integrating three databases from the old system to your new consolidated information network, you will need to use an outside firm that specializes in data proprietary software and that could make the whole system operate 25 percent cheaper in processing costs, run 35 percent faster, and produce construction estimates in half the time with15 percent better accuracy.

Most arguments should be considered from both objective and subjective standpoints. The most obvious answer is numeric, to save 25 percent in processing cost, and to increase productivity by faster execution and estimating in half the time with better accuracy. Most CFOs would support these monetary gains of the new system. No financial data or proprietary information will be disclosed because of the legal non-disclosure agreements that the database supplier has agreed, too. Your company has control of the language of the non-disclosure agreement and can structure the document to protect company interests and with the consolidated system, you will be able to create "competitive advantage" over other construction firms because of the faster, more accurate cost estimating system. With this proven software, your firm will benefit from previous work on other companies' systems development and you will be able to take advantage of state-of-the-art information technology without having to hire permanent staff to create or maintain the system.

Fewer rational counter-arguments can be offered, but some are that you have never worked with this data warehouse supplier so you don't have first-hand experience with its performance, and while every system's consolidation is different, the assignment may be too complex or inappropriate for the database company's proprietary software solution. Besides, the three legacy systems may prove to be incompatible after all work is done. It would be wise to learn why your boss is so paranoid about hiring outside suppliers and frame your arguments to allay his fears.

5. Implementation planning requires an organized, logical mindset to be able to think in linear and concurrent time frames. You keep notes from meetings, double-check your figures, and write progress reports highlighting weekly developments. Over coffee one morning, you describe your activities to a marketing assistant in another division, and he laughs at your diligence. "Can't you keep this in your head?" he taunts. What is your answer to him?

Prepare six scenarios that might occur to you as you organize your work on paper and in spreadsheets and what might occur to him if he keeps everything in his head.

We have discussed the multitude of details and deadlines required in producing a marketing program. Few professionals rely on their memories to include the execution of every point in the implementation plan. Some possible outcomes of keeping notes, writing down your thoughts, or planning with an electronic spreadsheet could be:

- Certainly due dates are important, and by careful tracking, you can discover which assignments are on schedule or behind schedule. Rarely do marketers enjoy working ahead of schedule.
- Keeping track of each assignment and who is to be charged with its completion is an important management activity. Those jobs assigned to no one are never started or completed.
- Many competent production professionals keep "tickler files" that contain entries on their electronic calendars reminding them to check on the assignment status two or three days before its completion is scheduled. Checking up beforehand helps to smooth out any interruption.
- Written reminders assist in avoiding overlooking any critical bottleneck that could delay other linear production assignments particularly important, high cost jobs such as television or film shoots.
- Looking into little details such as checking tomorrow's weather forecast may save thousands of dollars in special events' staging, photography sessions, or commercials, production.
- Preplanning sessions aid in the staff's understanding of the project and what is to be done by each individual. At these planning meetings, rough budgets are discussed. The wise marketer makes note of these figures to follow expenditures because over-budget items are never recovered. Catch them early.

6. The text spoke of completing implementation projects "on spec, on budget, and on time." As a marketing manager, which objective do you feel is most important to the benefit of your job? What is most important to the benefit of your division? To the benefit of your company? Are there conflicts? Write a one-page outline summarizing your wants on achieving goals at these various level of personal and company interests.

A well managed marketing program will be delivered on spec (according to the program design and elements), on budget (the expenditures are estimated in advance for approval and the work is completed according to the cost agreement), and on time (marketing programs are usually time-sensitive and must be completed on schedule). To the marketer, the driving force is delivering a quality, response-producing program as his mark of successful, therefore, delivering on spec or specification is fulfilling the quality and effectiveness promise by his creative thinking. In the eyes of the division, the greatest benefit would come from delivering marketing programs on cost and that marketing successes could be delivered within the budgets set by the marketing management while the company is concerned with delivering on budget which keeps the financial pro-forma balance according to projections.

Many times there are conflicts in the goals and benefits among company interests. Some marketers focus on winning awards for their marketing efforts; some divisions cut corners to achieve their sales projections, therefore earning their bonuses. Some companies look to the bottomline within every company function. Recognize that different factors influence management decision making, and that your goals may not match other parties' interests.

Chapter 5
An Introduction to the Internet

Chapter Summary

The Internet has evolved considerably in the three decades since it came into existence. It was created in the era of time-sharing, but has survived into the era of personal computers, client-server, peer-to-peer computing, and the network computer. It was designed before local area networks came into existence, but has accommodated that new network technology. It was envisioned as supporting a range of functions from file sharing and remote login to resource sharing and collaboration, yet has also spawned electronic mail and more recently the World Wide Web. Most importantly, it started as the creation of a small band of dedicated researchers, and has grown to be a commercial success with billions of dollars of annual investment.

This chapter discusses the Internet, revisits the history of how it got started, what made it so popular, and where it is today. Details of who, what, where and when are provided to give the student some background information and allow them to get their bearings in the scheme of the Internet as a whole. This includes all aspects of the Internet, not just the World Wide Web.

Since the Internet became a graphical, easy to use tool, the Web has been all the rage. The later portions of this chapter discuss concepts that are in line with this trend. They examine topics such as consumers buying online, current Internet usage and trends and how marketers can use the Internet to their advantage. This chapter provides an overall review and general knowledge acquisition for the technology we call the "Internet."

Core Concepts

- To offer insight into how and why the Internet was developed
- To introduce and clarify the operation and technology of the Internet
- To discuss the Internet resources that will be most vital for use in the process of electronic marketing and e-commerce

Chapter Outline

I. The Internet as a Whole
   A. The Internet began as a federal government project and is still growing-because of the support of the government
   B. More recently, the Internet has evolved to satisfy the demands of commercial interests
   C. What is the Internet exactly?
      1. The Internet is a worldwide computer network accessed via modem, special communication lines or even satellite
      2. The Internet connects universities, government laboratories, businesses, and individuals around the world
      3. It can be thought of as a virtual community of cooperation, which covers the entire globe, spanning political, economical, and cultural spectrums
      4. The Internet is "virtual" in that it has no physical "home" or dimension, weight, or texture
   D. There is a significant difference between the Internet and commercial online services
      1. The online services are centrally controlled and programmed to serve the like of the subscribers
      2. The Internet is decentralized with little control by any party

II. History of the Internet
   A. In the Beginning

1. The first recorded description of interactions through networking was in a series of memos written by J.C.R. Licklider of MIT in August 1962
2. In 1969, an experimental computer network called ARPANET was created to provide a test-bed for emerging network technologies
3. In 1973, Bob Kahn of DARPA posed an Internet problem that initiated the "Internetting" research program to develop communication protocols or agreed upon standards, allowing networked computer to communicate transparently across multiple, linked packet networks
    a. "Packets" information would be broken into many smaller units that would be easier to route through the network
    b. In "packet switching" the information, be it a text message, a photograph or illustration, notion, or sound would be disassembled at the origin of the message into smaller packets
    c. The system of protocols, which was developed over the course of this research effort, became known as the TCP/IP Protocol Suite
    d. In 1971, Ray Tomlinson of Bolt Beranek Newman (BBN, www.bbn.com) invented the first e-mail program that could send messages across a distributed network
    e. In 1972, the first e-mail utility to list, selectively read, file, forward, and respond to messages
    f. The evolution of Telnet was developed by the National Center for Supercomputing Applications (NCSA) and File Transfer Protocol (FTP)

III. An Online Community Begins
- A. During 1980 through 1981, two other networking projects, BITNET and CSNET, were initiated
- B. Computer Science NETwork (CSNET) was initially funded by the National Science Foundation to provide networking services for university, industry, government, and computer science research groups with no access to ARPANET
- C. At its peak, CSNET had approximately two hundred participating sites and international connections to approximately fifteen countries

IV. The Revolution Starts with the Explosion of Personal Computers (PCs)
- A. In 1982 and 1983, the first desktop PC began to appear
- B. During 1985 through 1986, the U.S. National Science Foundation connected the nation's six supercomputing centers together. This network was called the NSFNET, or NSFNET backbone, and today, provides a major backbone communication service for the Internet
- C. In 1986, the Internet Engineering Task Force and Internet Research Task Force (IRTF) came into existence under the IAB to assist in the organization and standardization of the Internet
- D. One of the first hard times (and resulting negative publicity) for the Internet came in 1988 when an Internet worm burrowed through the Net, affecting approximately 6000 of the 60,000 host computers
    1. Soon after the worm incident, DARPA formed the Computer Emergency Response Team (CERT)
- E. In 1989, in order to keep up with the demand for information, the NSFNET backbone was upgraded to "T1", meaning it was able to transmit data at speeds of 1.5 million bits of data per second, or about fifty pages of text per second
- F. In 1991, the University of Minnesota developed Gopher
- G. The European Laboratory for Particle Physics in Switzerland (CERN, www.cern.ch/) released the World Wide Web (WWW, www.w3.org/)
- H. To ensure privacy on the newly formed Web, Pretty Good Privacy (PGP), a security program was released
- I. In 1992, the Internet Society (ISOC) was chartered; this organization is a voluntary membership whose purpose is to promote global information exchange through Internet technology

J. The first audio multicast (March 1992) and video multicast (November 1992) were seen and heard on the Internet

K. In 1993, the NSFNET backbone network was upgraded to "T3" meaning it is able to transmit data at speeds of 45 million bits of data per second, or about 1400 pages of text per second

V. The World Goes Graphical

A. During the period of 1993 through 1994, the graphical Web browsers Mosaic and Netscape Navigator were introduced and spread through the Internet community

B. WWW Worms are joined by Spiders, Wanderers, Crawlers, and Snakes are programs which make it easier to find information on the Internet

C. Communities began to be wired up directly to the Internet

D. The Web has edged out Telnet to become the second most popular service on the Internet, behind e-mail

E. In 1995, RealAudio (www.realaudio.com), an audio streaming technology, let the user of the Internet hear in real time, as near to the actual event as possible

F. The Web surpassed FTP in March 1995 based on byte count

G. Registration of domain names was no longer free; beginning September 14, 1995, a $50 annual fee was imposed

H. The year, 1996, the Internet allowed phone companies to sign up users allowing the user access to the Internet; and various ISPs suffered extended service outages, bringing into question whether they would be able to handle the growing number of users

I. In 1997, the American Registry for Internet Numbers (ARIN) was established to handle administration and registration of IP numbers to the geographical areas currently handled by Network Solutions

VI. Current Internet Usage Trends

A. A good place to start looking at the statistical data on Internet trends and usage is at Yahoo (www.yahoo.com/Computers_ and_ Internet/Internet/Statistics_and_Demographics/), where many useful sites are listed under the topic Computers and Internet/Internet/Statistics

B. Stat Market (www.statmarket.com), a global site that keeps statistics on most used browsers, operating systems, busiest times of the day, and other useful Internet usage research

C. Through a Web address additional information on Web travelers can be obtained

D. You can glean some information about the person or organization that created a Web page by the address or Uniform Resource Locator (URL) of the page you are viewing

VII. Current Internet Operation and Tools

A. The architecture of the Internet is simple. Based on the concept of a client-server relationship between computer and a line of transmission

B. E-mail stands for electronic mail. It was designed for personal and business communications through the Internet

1. To use e-mail, a user must have an electronic post office or e-mail address. This address is comprised of:

a. A user name

b. A machine or host name

c. A domain

2. Along with e-mail come List Servers or listserv

C. Telnet

1. Host have gateways to other hosts

2. Access remote Multi-User Dimensions (MUDs)

3. Multi-User Simulation Environments (MUSEs)

D. File Transfer Protocol

E. The World Wide Web

F. Search Tools

Teaching Suggestions

The content of this chapter introduces the history and capabilities of the Internet in its academic and research context to its commercial subset, the World Wide Web of today. Most of the learning will from the text information and demonstration of the sites mentioned such as CERN, the laboratory in which Tim Berners-Lee developed the conventions for hypertext markup language (HTML) in Switzerland in 1989. Other sites of significance are the National Science Foundation, the computer Emergency Response Team (they react to security problems such hacker terrorism, virus infections and rumors, or network outages among other issues), the domain naming site, and interNIC, operated by Network Solutions. Background information on the creation and development of the Internet should be reviewed in order to develop the pedagogical parameters for this chapter.

Answers to Questions and Exercises

1. The Internet has become one of the buzzwords of the marketing world. Write a two-page paper describing what the Internet is and what impact it is expected to have on marketing in the future. Will the Web expand its presence beyond the direct marketing element? Why?

Each student, depending on the grasp that they currently have of the Internet and technology will answer this question differently. However, below is a definition of the Internet from the chapter and some guidelines on how a student may attempt to answer this question.

There are many definitions for the Internet, from the ambiguous technical description to one that can be readily understood by everyone. The Internet is a worldwide computer network accessed via modem, special communication lines, or even satellite. It connects universities, government laboratories, businesses and individuals around the world. In 1998, this global system connected an estimated 100 million users, and more than a hundred countries were interlinked to share information. It is a vast mechanism for information dissemination and a medium of collaboration between individuals without regard for geographic location. It can be thought of as a “virtual community” of cooperation, which covers the entire globe, spanning political, economical, and cultural spectrums. The Internet is "virtual" in that it has no physical "home" or dimension, weight, or texture. Users of the Internet can communicate with each other, sending electronic mail, transferring files, and accessing information at speeds that, a few years ago, were not even imagined.

However, the Internet has not finished changing. It will continue to change, evolving at the speed of the computer industry in order to stay in the game. The availability of the Internet along with powerful affordable computing and communications in portable form (i.e., laptop computers, two-way pagers, PDAs, cellular phones), is making possible a new paradigm of mobile computing and communications. This development will bring us new applications such as Internet telephones and, slightly further out, Internet television. New methods of access and new forms of service will breed new applications, which in turn will continue to drive the Internet revolution.

2. From what you have learned in this and previous chapters, list five business activities that you can accomplish by putting your company on the Internet. Give specific examples of electronic research, communications, or transactions and their purposes. Be prepared to discuss examples of how this is currently being done by others, or explain original ideas as appropriate in your next class.

The student may choose many different activities and sites as examples for this exercise. It is important that the activities contain some of the following communication tools and that they seem to understand how and why they would be used. Although it will be hard to give appropriate examples, valid original ideas should be given ample credit as well.

- *Competitive intelligence*. Taking a look at competition and consumer preferences via demographic research sites, viewing your competition and conducting consumer surveys. Example may consist of a good survey being conducted by a company via the Web to stay in touch with your consumer or business market.
- *Extending reach and building image.* Increasing communications accessibility by using e-mail, list servs, and forums. Increasing advertising power via online ads, search engines and other Web-based methods. An example could be any of the large online bookstores or computer companies.
- *Increasing sales.* Adding online commerce options to provide ready access to products and services via e-commerce and online transactions. There are many examples of e-commerce available. The student should present some aspect of e-commerce or online transactions in his/her answer.
- *Enhancing customer support.* Strengthen customer feedback and response mechanisms via Web-based forms and e-mail. This is an important topic and examples can readily be found on the Internet.
- *Adding value*. Providing value-added incentives to increase repeat customer visits. A good example of this is the Nabisco site. At Nabisco, consumers can get many added value items such as coupons and free recipes sent to them via e-mail or through the Web.

3. The Internet has not always been as widely known or popular as it is today. Certain events in the history of the Internet have increased this phenomenon. Which major invention stimulated popularity for the Internet and why did it take this piece of the Internet for the business world to determine it was beneficial for their organization?

During the period of 1993-1994, the graphical Web browsers Mosaic and Netscape Navigator were introduced and spread throughout the Internet community. Due to their intuitive nature and graphical interface, these browsers made the Web and the Internet more appealing to the general public and more appealing to the business world. Now, businesses and media have really begun to take notice of the Internet and Mosaic took the Internet by storm. The Web propagated at a 341,634% annual growth rate of service traffic. Communities began to be wired directly to the Internet. This ensured that consumers were not far behind, giving businesses a new medium to reach consumers. So, commercial shopping malls, cyberstations (RT-FM), the ability to order pizza from the Pizza Hut, and the first cyberbank, First Virtual (http://www.firstvirtual.com/), opened for business on the Internet. This was the beginning of the Internet we now use for Internet commerce and marketing.

4. Listservs are useful for communicating with a large number of people with like interests. How would you as a marketer use this to your advantage? Find at least two lists (preferably active ones) that are of interest to you and subscribe to them. After three weeks of observing the list traffic and participating in the discussions, write a short paper on the content and tone of the discussions and the positives and negatives of e-mail lists for marketing intelligence gathering.

The content of the papers received here will depend on the lists chosen by the student and will vary by their interests. A few key elements should be present in their discussions to assure that they actually participated in the list discussions. A good place for students to start looking for a list to join is www.listz.com, which is mentioned in this chapter. Some students may have difficulty signing on to a list or may have signed on to a low traffic or inactive list (particularly during summer sessions). The Instructor should ask weekly how the activity is for the students' listservs. I have had to extend the assignment because of problem sign ons or low volume postings.

1. Students should have a general understanding of the list concept and be able to explain the content of the discussion list they choose. They should be able to describe the tone of the list and offer an opinion on whether or not the list was interesting and useful to them personally and in a business sense. He or she should know how to follow the discussion thread to understand what opinions were expressed to develop the positive or negative comments. They should discuss the pros and cons of listservs for marketing purposes.

5. In a very short time, the Web has been transformed from a plain-looking black-and-white visual text to a full color, sound and motion communications vehicle. Using your imagination, describe three visions of how you see the Web's marketing or commerce capabilities in the year 2020. Remember that marketing serves customer interests and satisfaction; how will your visions support these objectives? Write a one-page outline describing the marketing opportunities, the technology needed, and company benefits and consumer benefits of each of your three

ideas; address your comments to the director of Strategic Planning in your company.

This is a personal and open-ended question. It will be best answered with the creativity and insight of the student. In the year 2020, who knows where technology may have taken us?

6. Search tools are very important to the marketer for many reasons. List some examples of advertising or promoting on a search engine home page and how they would be useful for providing exposure for your company. These examples might be advertising banners available with the click of a mouse, listings high on the search hierarchy, or sponsorships of news such as headlines or weather. Conduct these searches on the Internet and print samples of five promotional elements. Be prepared to share your examples and explain how different promotions might reach different targets contained within your marketing program.

Here is a brief summary of the concepts on search engines from the chapter and additional ideas that students may present. This is, of course, not an inclusive list; there are many possibilities.

An example of being listed high on a search hierarchy can be accomplished by using proper metatags and using them wisely. Searches such as these count the number of matches that incur between the search terms and the keywords found in the metatags. This is a very important step.

Registering your company with a major directory service such as Yahoo would provide you with the benefit of being listed in certain categories and easily found when consumers are searching for topics that your products or services fit. It is important to choose the proper categories and understand how the directory works.

Other search engines provide advertising possibilities via banners that are run at the top of the pages when consumers are searching or additional advertisements that can be added to pages when a consumer searches. These are clickable ads that can be randomly generated or generated by the search the consumer has entered. They are not free, but are often quite effective.

Similar to the clickable ads is a link that is included at the top of a search referring the consumer to additional information on a topic. A good example of this is the ability to look for a book on the same topic as a consumer searches for via Amazon.com or barnesandnoble.com. Many search engines have added this feature to their portals for consumer convenience and a marketers benefit.

As with the regular yellow pages, it is useful to add your business to the online yellow pages. This will allow any consumer who is looking for you to find you quickly. The yellow pages are usually a part of the search engine portals and are easily accessible by most consumers.

Search engine home pages are popular locations for advertising. The student can select and print a Web page that features promotion on a search engine on a home page such as AltaVista or Yahoo! Advertising on other search mechanisms could include a shopping robot such as Jango (www.jango.com) or an internal search engine such as those on the Blockbuster or Reel.com. Any of the search features on Excite search engine such as "People Finder", or telephone or business directories are locator tools, therefore popular sites for promotion. Banner advertising is common on "public" sites as well as insert ads on news reporting sites. As the student surfs for different sites, he will see that advertising or sales promotion adorns almost every other site.

7. The proper domain name and URL can be important in a marketing strategy. Does your company need its own "unique" domain name? How do you decide? Explain why this is important, then find two examples of companies that have a perceived image advantage due to their domain name and two who missed out because someone else got there first.

A domain name is important for customers to find a company on the Internet. If the proper and descriptive domain name is available, those customers trying to find you by guessing the URL have a better chance. For example, say you were looking to buy hockey equipment. You might try typing www.hockey.com to see if some smart company had registered this domain to bring in the Internet business it would generate. Large companies need to have a sensible domain name for the same purpose. One would easily determine how to find companies with domain names like, nabisco.com, pillsbury.com, ford.com, saturn.com, etc. As an assumption, the URLs of American Express (www.americanexpress.com) or BMG Music (www.bmgmusicservice.com) indicate that these two companies missed their opportunities for a simpler URL such as amex or bmg.

8. Marketers use demographics and trend studies to determine the best way to approach their target market. In this context, why is it important to know who uses the Web? Discuss in five paragraphs how you would go about determining the information you need to know about Web users. Be sure to cite any Web sites that you would use to find your information.

A wise marketer should investigate and ascertain which computers consumers are using for processor and modem speed, version of software, color versus B/W monitors, or the type and version of browser. She needs to know what her market's wants or needs are to fill the voids. She needs to understand where the marketing efforts should be directed to reach the greatest online audience. It should be clear where the target markets are "hanging out" on the Web.

To do this, there are many resources available on the Web. A good place to start looking at the comprehensive statistical data on Internet trends and usage is at the Yahoo! site (http://www.yahoo.com/Computers_and_Internet/Internet/Statistics_and_Demographics/), where many useful sites are listed under the topic "Computers and Internet/Internet/Statistics". These sites cover statistics relating to the Internet, derived from published estimates or supported by public surveys. It is not always the most current statistical collection, but it contains pertinent information for marketing program usage. From this site, there is a link to the GVU's WWW Users Survey. So far, it is one of the best places to investigate each of the concerns listed above. Students should be able to print graphs of information to cover many of these concepts and then explain how they effect the marketing strategy.

9. It is always important to know where consumer trends are going, and the good marketer knows that he can learn from the past. Take a look at the Web sites containing Internet usage trends discussed in this and previous chapters. What are the most important trends? Is Web access and computer usage growth of concern to the marketer? Write an e-mail to the European manager of your company listing ten trends to watch for on research from your internet marketing experience in the U. S.

The student should make a visit to the usage sites discussed in this chapter. A starting point is (http://www.yahoo.com/Computers_and_Internet/Internet/Statistics_and_Demographics). From this data, an example of current trends should be printed and supporting verbiage should be included. The student might also be asked to access the GVU studies to compare ten trends or features longitudinal from the last three studies, the tenth, the ninth, and the eighth. The Instructor can choose the features or allow the student to do so. The GVU Web address is included in the previous question.

10. Now that you have a general understanding of how the Internet was developed and what tools are available, you should be aware of how you might use it to support your marketing efforts. Besides supporting sales or creating a corporate presence, what are some other ways within the promotional mix that the Internet can support marketing efforts? E-mail a short response to your professor.

Few tactics of the traditional promotional mix cannot be replicated by online promotional tactics. Advertising can be made memorable with sound and motion exceeding the capabilities of traditional print advertising. Traditional television and radio awareness is eclipsed by Web advertising through interactivity with customers. Global reach can be achieved with electronic marketing and advertising resources. Even monstrous outdoor billboards have an equivalent with electronic interactive ad banners residing on Web pages. Sales promotions to gain customer e-mail address lists, incentives complementary to the products and services being featured, electronic coupons, and electronic newsletters and catalogs are possible and offer the same, if not better, accountability of traditional sales promotion. Public relations programs such as community service and humanitarian campaigns populate corporate Web pages, and online press releases are archived on pages of news about the company

We have discussed that electronic marketing and advertising efforts are considered outgrowths and extensions of traditional direct marketing. Web advertising and transactions target contact with select markets in faster time of delivery. The messages of Web advertising to customer lists can change daily depending on customer interests, inventory, or special offers. Personal selling activities now benefit from faster answers on products such as life insurance, home sales, or other transactions dealing with mounds of information or approvals.

The shortcomings of electronic promotions are those activities that dispense tangible items such as sampling programs in that consumption of food or use of personal care items is the objective. Marketing programs that distribute perishable products also fall into this same category. Innovation and creative alternatives to physical distribution (an alternative could be electronic vouchers or coupons) may provide suitable substitutes for e-marketers' programs.

Chapter 6
Concept of the Virtual Store for Marketing Products and Services

Chapter Summary

This chapter presents retailing in the context of the electronic environment. The question, "What is a store?" is an under-riding issue that is continually present in this chapter. The nature of retailing is changing with the development of the virtual marketplace. As traditional retailers start to market their products and services through their web sites on the Internet, the concept of retail establishments requiring a storefront in a mall has dramatically changed.

Concepts and practices of retail marketing in the electronic environment are discussed and the advantages and disadvantages of the virtual store are presented in detail. As customers adapt to electronic shopping, their demands and expectations of customer service change dramatically. Servicing the customer electronically is not the same as it is in a mall, and the e-marketer needs to clearly understand the differences, which are presented in this chapter.

The logical evolution of the cybermall from the virtual store is presented, as well as is its marketing implications. Security again becomes an issue as the volume of electronic purchasing increases. Strategies for identifying online marketing objectives are discussed, as are techniques for product and service differentiation.

Core Concepts

- To differentiate between the practices of virtual retailing and traditional retailing and relate each to e-commerce
- To present the advantages and disadvantages of opening the virtual store
- To discuss the strategies in building awareness for the virtual store

Chapter Outline

I. Retailing Approaches: Virtual versus Tangible
   A. Virtual stores are novel, electronic retailing and wholesaling still follow these principles but do so in a "back office" manner, hidden from physical contact to the public
      1. Compromised of invisible electronic data (Web site merchandise or offerings)
      2. Housed and promoted on an electronic medium (Web sites, e-mail, listservs, discussions groups)
      3. Delivered by an electronic distribution system (often the World Wide Web)
   B. The JCPenney monster Web site presents a most ambitious home page
      1. Directed to shoppers
      2. The community in general
      3. Stockholders or investors
      4. Home page produces a three-page printout that appears to have something for everyone

II. Virtual Store
   A. The advantages of a virtual store:
      1. To expand her distribution to a wider geography
      2. Company to choose what is to be the purpose of the Web site:
         a. Online sales
         b. Online advertising
         c. Online customer service
         d. Sales or communications activities
      3. Capital expenditure is much less in starting consumer or business to business directed marketing programs

4. Flexibility is such that an entrepreneur could maintain sales and service from any location
5. Web sites operate twenty-four hours every day, and this capability is valuable for those firms that market overseas
6. Firm's credentials and qualifications, the retail Web site can dispense marketing or sales materials automatically on request
7. Electronic systems to update prices, specifications, or other product or service data hourly if necessary
8. Company-sponsored promotions that are translated into the company's Web site
9. Customers inquiries can be investigated more quickly
10. The Web allows the company to render fast and responsive customer services
11. Order status can be ascertained immediately
12. The opportunity to test new products or services may be one of biggest advantages of the Web
13. Experimentation with new technology is also possible using Web-based testing
14. Discussion/listserv environment is on in which an effective marketing program could tap selected test markets

B. The disadvantage of virtual store
   1. Not every product or service is appropriate to Web sales exposure. Goods like perishable or dated good are not being sold on the Web as of yet
   2. Site offerings, communications, and maintenance require many hours, days, or weeks of a Web Master's attention. It might even require the work of multiple Web masters.
   3. Web marketing is a time intensive activity
      a. Good Web master should be surfing the competition at least an afternoon during the week
      b. Double checking the position of her Web page ranking on all the major search engines
   4. The twenty-four hour service pledge is a double-edged sword
   5. The marketer's organization is dependent on its equipment, communications software, and its ISP connections
      a. Redundant system
   6. Another double-edged sword is the anonymity of identity inherent to the Web
   7. Today is that of limited penetration and exposure to the general public at present
   8. Virtual storefront continues to present merchandise or services as long as the server is running or the Internet provider is being paid

III. The Value of the Virtual Storefront and the Cybermall

A. Strategic plan by playing from your strengths
   1. Reliability
   2. Consistency
   3. Privacy
   4. Accessibility
   5. Accuracy
   6. Responsiveness

B. Retailing power builds on the fundamentals usage nature of the Internet
   1. Demographics of connectivity
   2. Content
   3. Customer motivation

C. Several cyberstores band together, thus giving the merchandise in one location or address, this gathering of Web sites is considered to be a cybermall

D. Alternative to banding with a cybermall is to be a "linked storefront" in which the storefront address is hyperlinked within a popular general interest site

E. The security concerns the following reasons for not purchasing online:
   1. Providing credit information online is "just plain foolish"

2. Providing credit/purchase information online
3. Toll-free call/fax is tied with secure transmission. There seems to be some residual reservations about electronic transactions
4. Clear preferences for the involvement of a third party in the transaction preference for involvement by a credit card company or a bank

F. What are online information seekers seeking?
1. Men are more frequent purchasers than women, and men make purchases exceeding $50
2. Common items of interest are software, hardware, and electronics
3. Purchase is consummated, it represents price shopping for less expensive products

IV. Building the Cyberstore's Awareness
A. Empathy for the customer's wants and desires is one of the key ingredients for storefront success
B. Minding the corporate or division objectives should be stated in the corporate marketing plan

V. Deciding the Online Marketing Objective
A. What are the appropriate goals for online marketing
B. "Competitive difference" of this online vehicle compared to the traditional media is the online opportunity for interactivity
C. Sampling might include free inducements, such as an online demonstration of a free e-quotation for auto

VI. Commerce Image and Identity Development
A. Identify qualities would your target market value in online awareness and delivery of a product or service
B. Building image is the part of the "impression" of the good to consumers
C. A big part of a brand name is to differentiate similar products

VII. Searching for the Product or Service Differentiation
A. As part of the initial marketing plan, the marketer should consider the trait or traits perceived or real, for differentiation that no other product or service can easily match
B. Strategy of selecting different features valued by different people is called a niche marketing strategy
C. Customization and particularly personalization are critical factors in creating and sustaining competitive advantage on the Internet
D. Personalization of services and the development of new services such as online help facilities based on the experience of multiple users
E. Capture more of the "value chain" for their product-for example, by eliminating distributors or suppliers
F. Other differentiation strategies have been developed from:
1. From countries of origin
2. From ethnic groups
3. From geographic locations
4. Usage patterns
5. Special occasions
6. Celebrations or time

Teaching Suggestions

At this point, we have laid the foundation for establishing the electronic marketing process, introduced the communications capabilities of the World Wide Web, and explained how electronic marketing resources fit into the e-marketing process. We have reviewed the strengths of electronic resources as producing new levels of speed, accuracy, accessibility, and organization for transaction services with customers. We have also discussed the unique ability of the Web—two-way interactivity—which sets the medium apart from traditional marketing mix vehicles. An instant capability to respond to e-merchants is a powerful tool that more customers and prospects are exercising each day.

In this chapter we explore the introduction and role of the "virtual retailer," the online merchant that has no physical establishment, no merchandise to touch and feel, and no eager sales people to affect your shopping experience. Retailer approaches are discussed with the differences between the retail strategies of virtual selling versus tangible selling environments. Several successful consumer and business-to-business sellers' online efforts are reviewed: JCPenney, Wal-Mart, and Oracle. The home pages of typical e-commerce firms are demonstrated as to design, content, and elements added for customer convenience.

The chapter continues by presenting the advantages and disadvantages of a virtual stores. Some advantages include: expanding a store's distribution channels, easier communications with customers via e-mail, reduced capital expenditures for retail outlets, flexibility in work locations (a cyberspace location can be operated from almost any Internet access point), the capability of 24-hour, seven-day "store" hours, a vehicle to react to volatile market conditions by inventory suppliers, a 24-hour marketing information repository which can be downloaded on demand, an enhancement to corporate image with an ability to tell its goodwill programs or store its press articles, a customer-friendly system for tracking orders, a vehicle for launching test products and services, and an opportunity to sell globally if so desired.

The disadvantages of operating a virtual store include: not every product is appropriate for selling on the Web, operating a commercial Web site is time intensive and staff intensive and may require hiring staff such as a Web master, twenty-four hour selling is difficult to staff, order entry and inventory/shipping personnel must work around the clock, the Web merchant is dependent on equipment or information technology that can be down or under construction, commerce on the Web is operating in the blind; the merchant or the customer knows little about the honesty of the other party and the quality of goods being transacted, at present Internet access is low estimated at less than 25 percent of American households, probably a lower number is realistic for households worldwide.

The value of the virtual storefront and the cybermall is discussed to compare conventional shopping habits at shopping malls and emerging habits of consumers shopping online. Retailing power builds on the fundamental usage nature of the Internet: the demographics of connectivity, content, and customer motivation. User demographics are stated and it is stressed that the typical Web user is an attractive customer potential.

The chapter closes with two important decisions: the marketer deciding the appropriate online marketing objectives and the marketer's searching for her product or service's differentiation

In achieving the marketing missions, the marketer must decide what objectives will be appropriate for the new (or existing) Web marketing activities. These marketing decisions require a full knowledge of product or service history, retailer or distributor relations, customer expectations, in other words, a full familiarity of the offering's strengths, weaknesses, opportunities, and threats. As a promotional element, the Web presence and its mechanisms cannot "sell" as many clients or corporate officers might expect. The Web presence, likewise for print or broadcast advertising, can only inform and create interest or curiosity; with this interest established, the job of selling is transferred to a "real" salesperson, the staff of a call center, or to the ordering apparatus on the Web site. It is wise to keep the abilities of various promotional elements in mind to have realistic expectations for marketing programs. What are the appropriate goals for online marketing? As in traditional marketing, new products can be launched from a unique site or from a company offering. Perhaps the objective is to extend the brand franchise awareness such as Colgate Total toothpaste, toothbrushes, and floss (www.colgate.com/products) for being blessed by the trusted Colgate name. As we have discussed, the online objective might constitute

- Improving response time on customer inquiries
- Extending brand awareness
- Launching new products or services, or brand extensions
- Developing a new channel of distribution
- Launching public relations efforts to stockholders

- Establishing a press center with a news article repository
- Testing new products or new "direct marketing" promotional programs with incentives

The chapter ends with a discussion of awareness building using strategies of brand image and identity development. Students can become confused in differentiating image (the "what" the marketer wants the consumer to think of when a brand is seen or spoken of) and identity. The identity efforts (the "how" the visual or auditory messages are presented) integrate the image onto the marketing elements such as consistent use of the image, logotype, positioning statement, colors, or other graphic identity items.

Answers to Questions and Exercises

1. What are the factors that could encourage a traditional retailer to invest time and mining in developing a Web presence and site? Write your answer as a memo to the merchandising executive of your company, either supporting or rejecting an online sales tool for your company.

These factors are discussed extensively in the chapter. Supporting points could include:

- expanding a store's distribution channels
- easier communications with customers via e-mail
- reduced capital expenditures for retail outlets, flexibility in work locations (a cyberspace location can be operated from almost any Internet access point)
- the capability of 24-hour, seven-day "store" hours
- an vehicle to react to volatile market conditions by automatically adjustment ices or inventory suppliers
- a 24-hour marketing information repository which can be downloaded on demand
- an enhancement to corporate image with a ability to tell its goodwill programs or store its press articles
- a customer-friendly system for tracking orders
- a vehicle for launching test products and services
- an opportunity to sell globally if so desired

Factors to reject online marketing:

- Not every product is appropriate for selling on the Web
- Operating a commercial Web site is time intensive and staff intensive; may require hiring staff such as a Web master
- Twenty-four hour selling is difficult to staff; order entry and inventory/shipping personnel must work around the clock
- The Web merchant is dependent on equipment or information technology that can be down or under construction
- Commerce on the Web is operating in the blind; the merchant or the customer knows little about the honesty of the other party and the quality of goods being transacted.
- At present Internet access is low estimated at less than 25 percent of American households; probably a lower number is realistic for households worldwide.

2. Create an outline of the steps you would take in adopting a virtual store strategy and prepare a proposal to present to your management on the benefits of the operations, finance, and marketing functions. Write the proposal as a pros and cons view of the effort, telling management what results to expect after the virtual store goes online.

This question reinforces the understanding of the three stage marketing process and the understanding of the benefits of electronic marketing resources to the business functions of operations, finance, and marketing. After the pros and cons are listed, the student should promise conservative results that might take two or three years to realize. The student must grasp that e-marketing is rarely an overnight success but rather takes persistence and flexible planning to establish a viable commercial resource.

3. If you were charged with opening a Web site directed to the consumers on mainland China offering current music videos with choices of either Szechwan or Cantonese-dialect subtitles, create a list of steps you would perform in establishing a Chinese language Web site. Write a memo to the director of Asian operations for your music reselling chain. Detail your thoughts on payment, shipping, and distribution systems for the selling operation.

This question also asks for a restatement of understanding of the marketing process. Music video customers' habits and preferences should be researched and this input should be weighed in decisions concerning the Web site content. Concerning the implementation stage, research should be performed on preferred and realistic pavement systems, shipping methods and restrictions, and traditional distribution systems in the formally closed but now opening economic landscape of China. Reforms are surfacing quickly, then taking a few steps backward, and then resurfacing with newer and different methods for doing business. Environmental scans might be done monthly to check conditions and anticipate the paths that business and government regulations might pursue.

4. From the text discussion, investigate a successful story of a traditional retailer moving to the Web as alternative sales channel. Isolate four reasons why the opening of this sales and/or communications function was successful and present your views as substantiation. Pick an industry you are familiar with and treat this exercise as a competitive intelligence report prepared for the president of your company.

This is a field research assignment of which the student can select the company success story of her choosing.

5. As in the exercise above, report on an unsuccessful Web experience by a traditional retailer that closed its online sales operation or converted it to another purpose such as technical support or customer service. Isolate four reasons why the opening of the Web function was unsuccessful and present your views as substantiation. You may have difficulty a terminated Web activity, so you might ask your friends for leads or check a local Web address directory for retailers. Input the addresses and see if they are still in operation. Treat this exercise as a competitive intelligence report prepared for opening a company of your own.

This is a field research assignment of which the student can select the company failure story of his choosing.

6. Prepare a three-minute speech on how a disadvantage of using the Web or commerce can also be an advantage of the medium. An example might be that stringent security protocols may add time in processing each order; the advantage is that the merchant is more likely to be paid for each transaction. Select your topic, discuss it with your Instructor, and support your topic with two to three examples of the advantage/disadvantage proposition.

Possible advantages/disadvantages combinations:

- Dissemination of information on the Web travels quickly; in certain cases, this advantage can be a disadvantage because the information might be inaccurate or libelous.
- Information technology systems such as powerful database management can be of great assistance to be marketing effort; these technology systems can be inefficient if the technical staff is ill trained or the transaction volume is low.
- Information technology systems can be complex and difficult to implement; once implemented, the same company system can be replicated worldwide.
- Inventory maintenance to match Web stock descriptions is tedious work; as maintenance is performed, the accuracy of specifications, prices, availability is improved.
- Buying on the Web requires access to the Internet; the cost of Internet access is a factor in the Web's producing qualified buyers.

7. In your opinion, what would be the top two attributes of competitive advantage for the following businesses that are "establishing a Web presence?"

- A chain of flower shops: Regional or national reach in order delivery, convenience of ordering and seeing selection displayed on the Web site
- A manufacturer of sticky labels: Displaying the variety of products and the ability to sell directly to businesses or consumers
- A hospital bill reviewing/consultant service: Exposure to upscale viewers, some of which might have had recent hospitalizations and are using search engines, and Web site content on hospital fraud as a goodwill service
- A nationwide chain of shoes for infants: Web site advertising targeting to women, national reach of ordering, display of shoe selection
- A regional group of insurance agencies: Web site exposure via search engine, ability to dispense marketing materials and applications from printing from the Web, Web advertising targeted to young males

8. How should a company decide on a differentiation strategy for execution on the Web? What steps should it consider in establishing a "unique" differentiation from others in its category? Assume the company is in the technical/trade educational business. Write a strategy selecting points of differentiation on its Web site. Also assume the company has a twenty-five year track record in graduating successful technical people from its eighteen-month programs.

This question tests comprehension of initiating the Integrated Marketing Communications program strategy. Adopting a Web differentiation strategy should, in most cases, follow the "uniqueness," positioning, or the Unique Selling Proposition strategy chosen, not deviate from it. The IMC coordination suggests that all programs and media should be structured to reinforce the message, in a synergistic manner. Please note that this question does not contain enough information for concepting a differentiation strategy. The twenty-five year history alone is insufficient around which to build a consumer benefit strategy. More research and information is needed to make conclusions from the situation analysis and marketing plan decisions.

9. Your company is a manufacturer of asphalt roofing shingles and has long employed a premier position in the home building business because of the unusually long twenty-year warranty of your shingles. In the last two years, a boom of new home construction has brought new competitors into the marketplace, and you recently learned that a newcomer to the shingle business is now offering a thirty-year warranty. The differentiation of your shingles being known as the "Two-Score Shingle, the Nation's Longest Warranty," is no longer true. What Web message strategy should you adopt? Do you change your differentiation/message strategy, ignore the competitor, or take other actions? This message will be used beyond Web messages to be incorporated into an integrated marketing communications program. The prepared to form a three to four-person marketing committee to present your strategy to the class.

As in the previous question, positioning strategy is larger than merely for usage on the Web. This situation could be used as a mini-project if you so choose. Regardless of the purpose of the assignment, the students/groups should do research on the building industry, specifically the roofing industry, to evaluate factors and influences in the use or purchase (as in reroofing an existing home) that drives purchase decision. Building products are one of the many business-to-business products that are purchased over the Web, and are experiencing new levels of competition because of the "shopping comparisons" that the Web affords. A twenty-year guarantee may be sufficient for certain segments of the market so perhaps a new segmentation plan should be considered. The positioning line probably should be changed since the twenty-year promise is no longer the longest.

The important points to consider are:

a) Prospect/customer expectations
b) Product alterations if any, e.g. should you make changes to the product to match or better the thirty-year warranty?
c) Promotional considerations. If you change the product to match the thirty-year, what will be your new positioning rationale and positioning line?
d) Will you use a different differentiation strategy for online communications?
e) Distribution considerations. If you choose to market to a different market segment such as to do-it-yourself, would your channels of distribution change? If you have specified product alterations, what would be the rubber distribution strategy?
f) What would you anticipate your competitors' reactions to your marketing strategy?
g) Are there better marketing alternatives or strategies to consider for selling asphalt shingles to builders or consumers?

10. Of the possible competitive advantage online action attributes of speed, accuracy, accessibility, or convenience, which one do you as an e-merchant consider most important? Write an e-mail justifying your selection to your college professor when she asks about the marketing direction that you set for your photo finishing company.

In general, the value of the attribute depends on the business category; it would be difficult to make a blanket statement that one characteristic is greater than all the others. In this example, a photo finishing company, possibly a marketing differentiation could be an e-mail alert that the photos and negatives are ready to be picked up. Or perhaps you are offering an archive service to keep the negatives at your shop. The customer could call in for more reprints from a proof sheet that is accessed from your account. You could then pick the negatives you want printed, the size, and the quantity. Here convenience might be more valued by the customer. So depending on the business operation, the segment of customer that you are trying to satisfy the type of merchandising (economy to luxury), the Web offers different benefits to different business models.

Chapter 7
The Tools of Electronic Marketing Resources

Chapter Summary

This chapter serves well as a directory of hardware and software, which are important electronic marketing tools. They are presented in detail and discussed in an integrated manner to show the reader how they work with each other to provide enhanced efficiency and control to the e-marketer. In addition to showing how they provide advantage to the e-marketer, their advantage to the e-consumer is also presented. Not only are the advantages of these e-tools given, their limitations are also discussed.

Core Concepts

- To introduce the tools and software applications of electronic marketing
- To anticipate the problems associated with maintaining a marketing Web site

Chapter Outline

I. The "Electronic" of Commerce
   A. Electronic marketing resources have proliferated over the last ten years, and most notably, the reach for most marketers has been inward from communications to mass markets to markets of one, as in individual purchasers or prospects
      1. The focus on electronic marketing resources will broaden to include other essential electronic tools marketers can use for communications, segmentation, or memory enhancements of customer preferences
         a. Videography
         b. CD-ROM
         c. Interactive kiosks
         d. Pagers
         e. Optical scanners
         f. "Smart cards"
   B. Power of the e-communications is the capability that provides the strongest link between the vendor and its customer because of the gratification factor of speed, accuracy, or convenience

II. The Data Warehouse and Enterprise Reporting
   A. Most of you probably see a transient medium of communication
   B. The Web was viewed as the next paradigm for distribution of marketing communications
   C. The Web is a truly interactive way of captivating the audience
   D. The Web introduced a new component of the otherwise familiar frame of data processing: instantaneous, massive volumes of incoming and outgoing data
      1. Including e-mail addresses
      2. Your machine or computer
      3. Length of time on the site
      4. Mouse clicks
      5. Your most recent session is then paired up to other information already from other visits on the Web

III. E-mail, a Hardworking Messenger
   A. E-mail has become the most prevalent communications tool for exchanging messages at the local, national, or international scope
   B. Low-to- no cost e-mail providers

C. Companies have embraced e-mail systems because e-mail is a low-cost messaging system that is very flexible for reaching internal individuals, groups, or company wide audiences
D. External communications such as links to customers, business partners, and prospects
   1. The lists can be private
   2. Messages are posted to the site without supervision
   3. E-mail can be anonymous
   4. E-mail is a quick response
E. Where does e-mail "work"?
   1. One e-mail account that they access from home (25%)
   2. 42% of interviewees report having one e-mail account
   3. 56% report having more than one
   4. 30% Europe versus 20% U.S.
   5. Europeans are also more likely to access their accounts only from work
   6. Older respondents are more likely to access accounts from home (65%)
   7. Single account (74%)

IV. The Internet's Interconnections
A. Internet's origins
   1. Historically the Internet began as a government defense project in the late sixties
   2. Government's goal was to prevent interruption of telephone or satellite communications' links in case of nuclear war or natural disasters
   3. Eventually was turned over to the National Science Foundation (NSF) for use by the research and education constituencies
B. The Mosaic browser developed at the University of Illinois, and now represented by the various versions of Netscape Navigator and Internet Explorer

V. The Wonders of the World Wide Web
A. Relatively new marketing and communications resource that was introduced to the public in 1991
B. Coming of color monitors, faster modems, sound cards with speakers, along with the sharpened expertise of Web designers
C. Several years, commercial Web sites have come alive with addition of motion and sound as well as the manipulation or colors and graphics
D. "Killer application" among marketing circles because of the visual, sound, and interaction capabilities
E. Improved information retrieval is integrating a site research engine
F. The advantages and disadvantages of a Web presence
   1. Flexibility
   2. Updated as often as the marketer wishes
   3. Flexibility in how the customer or prospect can interact with the Web vehicle
G. Transfer technology is the method of employing touch-tone, or voice-recognition, menus to route calls to the appropriate department
H. Hold statistics technology allows the customer to know fairly precisely how much patience she will be required to exhibit in order to get the attentions she is requesting
I. The global commerce potential is most attractive particularly with the emergence of free market economies throughout the world

VI. Growing of Internet
A. Internet culture blossoms
B. The spread of interface culture brings together technology and culture elements to demonstrate how these pervasive interfaces have earned a rightful place in homes and workplaces.

VII. Robot Shopping Agents
A. Comparing prices from site to site could ensure the lowest expenditure for the consumer

- B. These automatic shoppers are becoming a great convenience to the consumer, possibly an inconvenience or a sale-robbing threat to the e-merchant
- C. Beware that not all sites will participate with shopping robots

VIII. The Extended Memory of CD-ROMS
- A. Marketers are finding more applications for these plastic, aluminum-coated disks than just for playing music
- B. While speed is important to the marketer, the multimedia capabilities offer even greater benefits
- C. CD-ROMs have also become a transfer medium for software

IX. The Benefits of Database and Other Software Marketing Tools
- A. Improving corporate memory has been the goal of database management applications for many years
    1. Small firms might use Microsoft Access as their database application customer roster to keep minimal inventory records
    2. Large companies have the opportunity to use several powerful database packages, such as Oracle Developer 2000 or Oracle Data Warehouse
- B. There is a database management tool to fit the situation
- C. Sources:
    1. Hire an in-house software developer
    2. Engage an outside software development company

X. Front-End or Back-End Application Devices arrange multiple software applications used together to build data systems.
- A. Front-end of a system, one that provides the client software and the client inputs data, probably in marketing or IT/IS/MIS departments
- B. Back-end might be composed of an Oracle system database located wherever the server is located
- C. Front-end—back-end combinations act as the back-end to send the message or retrieve the information

XI. Communications Networks
- A. Communications are gravitating to service specialized audiences, no longer addressing mass audiences
- B. Intranet, a private access communications network designed most frequently for the employees within an organization
    1. Addresses issues of interest to the company's constituencies
    2. Repository for work-in-progress where project files can be accessed in meetings on-site and other distant offices or by employees working at home
    3. Intranet can contain a plethora of information including company notices, work schedules, or even classified ads offerings
    4. Intranet can be a source of pride for the staff
- C. Network is a company extranet, a private access communications network that includes selected external suppliers and clients
    1. This outside-the-company networks helps to coordinate projects or participants that are distant in geography or those who infrequently are involved in the project

XII. Software Working Hand in Hand
- A. So rapid communications are vital to the response and success of the management
- B. Provides a competitive advantage that can be derived from more powerful and reliable tools
- C. Communications systems might wed server software to an on-demand, automated fax-back system, heavy volume of fax requests and responses create records in Lotus Notes database

XIII. Reporting and Planning Systems

A. Business requires clear and concise decision-making and frequent reporting project status to management and to peers
B. Reports have become more visual in the last five years
C. Software systems must be able to access, analyze, and develop accurate assessments for making strategic decisions
D. Resulting data must be easy to read and understand
E. In particular, large projects with horizons of many years benefit from planning applications to set direction and timelines, milestone points, and overlap, and down times

XIV. Optical Scanners
A. Incorporated into new and varied services manufacturing, in the medical industry, in the aircraft industry, in lumbering, in measurements
B. Electronic tool saves many hours in pricing and counting inventory, coupons, or contest entries
C. Optical scanners often dispense coupons
D. Scanners assist marketers increasing performance tracking results of sales promotions, by counting units sold, by checking prices, by verifying identities, or by hundreds of other marketing and operations considerations

XV. Fax-Back Systems
A. The Facsimile, has been reborn to serve the distribute information systems, more so than on a one-on-one transmission

XVI. Web Portal Sites
A. Web super site; the portal is the entry point that offers a broad array of resources and services, such as e-mail from the Web site, forums, a variety of search engines, news broadcast, personal Web pages, and online shopping malls
B. American Online (AOL) is still the largest and most successful portal in history as a one-stop service to access the best on the Web.
C. Marketer might look at advertising exposure on several portal sites as he would analyze programming on a television network
D. AOL is creating a two-tier portal
1. One with fewer features
2. One more heavily laden perhaps with resources such as personalized news, choices of e-mail options, free Web pages to users, and smarter search engines

XVII. The Limitations of Electronic Marketing Resources
A. With every improved business practice or convenience, there is a tradeoff, usually price
1. Cost benefit analyses are usually conducted as a starting point determining the cost of the proposed new marketing system can save money over the current system involved
B. Investigating her options in scalable software and hardwired or other high tech equipment for future growth
C. Systems are becoming more and more complex
D. Resourceful companies spend handsomely on training to retain their best employees.
E. The low penetration of the World Wide Web into American households
F. General lack of faith in financial transactions over the Web
G. Acceptance of electronic commerce is proving varied according to industry
H. For international marketers, stumbling blocks could be the limitations on language, laws, and currency, possible cultural differences in the exchange process
I. In understanding and balancing your electronic marketing requirements is communicating your real needs to your suppliers so that the proper trilogy-software system, hardware, and budget is attained

XVIII. The Problems with the Web Site

A. The most commonly experience Web access problem is that of taking too long to download pages
B. The growing problem of broken links or dead Web pages
C. The content on the Web
D. What equipment does the user own to access various Web sites
E. World Wide Web has also caused an impact in the customer service capabilities

Teaching Suggestions

This is a chapter of further explanation and demonstration of the electronic tools that the student groups will use in their e-marketing project. By this time, the student should be familiar with information transfer and operation of the World Wide Web and Web browsers. Browsers are integral in opening the consumer and business-to-business worlds for the e-marketers. The Instructor should demonstrate and explain the electronic resources as they are listed in the text.

Answers to Questions and Exercises

1. As a written exercise, define the following terms:

Software - consists of programmed computer instructions or data. It includes anything that can be stored electronically. The term software is often used as both a noun and an adjective.

Hardware - analogous to the pages and the ink of the book; the storage devices and display devices of a computer. Hardware refers to objects that you can actually touch such as disks, disk drives, display screens, keyboards, printers, boards, and chips.

Intranet -Any network that provides similar services within an organization to those provided by the Internet outside it, but which is not necessarily connected to the Internet.

Extranet - the extension of a company'sintranet out onto the Internet to allow selected customers, suppliers, and mobile workers to access the company's private data and applications via the World Wide Web.

Data warehouse - a generic term for a system of storing, retrieving and managing large amounts of data.

Data mining - analysis of data in a database using tools which look for trends or anomalies without knowledge of the meaning of the data.

Frontend/Backend Application - For software applications, the term "front end" refers to the user interface. In client/server applications, the client part of the program is often called the "front end" and the server part is called the "backend". Compilers, the programs that translate source code into object code, are often composed of two parts: a front end and a back end. The front end is responsible for checking syntax and detecting errors, whereas the back end performs the actual translation into object code.

Enterprise reporting - the process of gathering information throughout the organization in order to use it in comprehensive reports, rather than working among scattered, unconnected business reporting.

Program for Internet News and Mail (PINE)a-tool for reading, sending, and managing text-based electronic messages.

2. As an inventory manager of a medium-sized hospital supply company, you are approaching an important date: the annual inventory of merchandise. In the past, you have used an outside supplier to perform this task, but the supplier's charges have grown rapidly over the last four years. You wish to investigate buying or leasing your own database resources. Outline the steps you would take in developing a cost/benefit analysis to compare the costs of

using a supplier, leasing equipment, and buying your own hardware and developing software systems. Input your projections into an Excel spreadsheet for the financial officer to review.

The Instructor should provide some direction on preparing a cost/benefit analysis for this exercise. The students should realize the complexity of inventory management particularly in this hospital supply example. Hospitals, clinics, and medical offices use "pieces of inventory" frequently. In inventory control, the manager must consider "hard" and "soft" costs that are often subjective or intangible. The hard costs are easier to quantify such as computer equipment and accessories, optical scanners and accessories, bar coding equipment and supplies such as labels, and software systems. All of these would constitute an inventory management system. There are "soft" costs, probably more subjective, such as employee "reengineering," sensitivity to employee morale because of the change in operations from a familiar to an unknown system, or recruitment costs should present employees leave. Soft costs are difficult to estimate and some arise unexpectedly. Thus, the "make versus rent" decision involves more than purchasing equipment and software.

The first decision is setting the objective for the operation. Is it to improve continual inventory replacement? Is it to track the largest users of inventory and what those inventory items are? Is it to trace "shrinkage," mysteriously missing inventory usually stolen, or sometimes not delivered by the supplier? Knowing what the objective is usually defines what resources will be required in making the "make or rent" decision. Since particular costs will be difficult for the student to obtain, you might direct them to set up only the planning spreadsheet format.

3. After reading this chapter, what would be the three and only three electronic marketing resources you would choose for operating your bicycle manufacturing company? Assume that you are in a startup situation and the company can afford only three resources. Justify each resource in a one-page memo to your stockholders.

****

<u>Memorandum</u>

To:	Stock holders
From:	Marketing Director
Subject:	Electronic Marketing Resources
Date:	June 19, XXXX

In order to have a presence in this new technological age it is imperative that we begin our company with the proper online presence. Although our startup funds are limited, there is one important resource that would facilitate the image that we desire. This resource is a well-designed Web site, which could be utilized to reach our target audience and solicit new customers. After the initial startup cost, a Web site is an inexpensive way to advertise and communicate with customers. Besides the maintenance and updates required, this resource should require little additional monetary input.

Coupled with the Web site, the use of electronic mail or lists would promote communicate with consumers providing an effective and timely solution to some of the customer service that is necessary for us to get off in the right direction. E-mail would also be fairly inexpensive and give us a broad reach especially in tandem with current phone and postal mail approaches.

A third resource that would be beneficial to our startup endeavors is a database system that would keep track of important data such as products, customers and services. This could eventually be coupled with the Web site to provide online catalogs, e-commerce and searchable customer service information. The addition of the database would allow us to service customers in a more efficient manner.

In our opinion, a startup company would benefit most from the electronic marketing tools of a content-filled, image-oriented Web site, a well planned e-mail system, and a marketing-oriented database.

****

4. You are planning to open a virtual storefront selling wildlife and scenic photography calendars and prints of various sizes. Will you allow robot shopping agents to enter your site? Consider your products to be medium priced. Write an e-mail explaining to your brother-in-law and partner what the advantages and disadvantages of your decision may be. Would you change any of the marketing mix elements (raise or lower your prices or cut or increase promotional elements for instance) depending on your decision? Fully justify your marketing decision.

The decision to participate with shopping bots is generally a marketing decision, though it can be affected by your financial position. The marketing considerations are derived from your marketing strategy. Is your site offering premium priced merchandise or economy merchandise? Many upscale products do not compete on a price basis (as in offering the lowest price or matching the lower price of a competitor) but rather on features such as quality workmanship, selection, or accessibility to justify their higher prices. Cooperating with a shopping bot would be futile if you produced hand-carved chess sets if the bot was searching for "chess sets." An alternative marketing strategy for retaining a medium price would be to adopt a differentiation feature popular to your market. This differentiation should be a feature that shoppers are looking for. Your prints could be sold with mounting and matting at no extra charge. Prospects would qualify themselves by searching with terms such as "dry mounted posters," "matted prints." Perhaps your company makes wooden lawn furniture or beach chairs. Shoppers might input search terms such as "wooden," "beach," or "chair," but no reference to price. Your product might be selected because price was not a search criterion.

You may choose to participate with the shopping bot service if you do pursue a low pricing strategy. The advantage here is the sales traffic that many shopping bots might bring to your site. This plan would match a volume selling operation, probably at narrower margins.

5. You are thinking about opening a virtual storefront to sell pop culture T-shirts internationally. These T-shirts will be colorful to be displayed on a Web site and will feature timely slogans or headlines in English. This will be a part-time venture, so the site must operate almost autonomously. What topics should you be investigating to provide excellent customer services to your purchasers? List and explain these topics as to how you will operate the twenty-four hour site.

That the company will be a part-time venture and operate twenty-four hours a day, seven days a week makes using the Internet an excellent decision. One of the advantages of using the Internet is the ability to provide better customer service and ordering opportunities without the need for a person to sit at the other end of the line. This allows for the possibility of a part-time, twenty-four/seven day a week operation.

First, Customer Feedback and Automated customer service via e-mail can be facilitated with an auto-responder and then daily return of messages at the convenience of the company. However, it is important that mail is responded to in the time that the auto-responder says that it will. Next, you should provide the capability for browsing your online product catalog. This will allow consumers to shop not only at your convenience, but also at theirs. The catalog can be likened to online purchasing or orders can be taken by e-mail or phone. Be sure to provide proper responses and feed back to customers who look through your site. Decide in which language the Web site is to be published. Over 90 percent of the sites are in English, but you may have a country-specific product (such as World Cup merchandise) that is inappropriate for English language messages or for which English-speaking populations might have little interest.

Online purchasing or electronic commerce can then be implemented to automate the process even more. With the addition of a product order form, a customer can via a secure transmission and the sales can almost run themselves. *Almost*. There is the need to follow up and add a human touch that only you can do. Be sure to include ways for customers to contact your company when they have questions or problems, and be sure to provide a privacy policy to alleviate customer fears.

6. In the Bayer Pharmaceuticals case, what other means of communications could the field sales staff have considered in gathering accurate information to supply to physicians? Make a list of alternative communications channels and technology to accomplish this same goal. For each alternative, list the advantages and disadvantages to either the physician, the salesperson, or the Bayer corporation. Submit this list to your instructor acting as your sales manager.

The Bayer Pharmaceuticals marketing manager decided on building an information gateway based on an intranet knowledge management system. Alternative knowledge systems might have included:

- A manual retrieval of individual information requests. The volume of inquiries would overwhelm manual retrieval, thus taking too much time to return the information.
- An open Internet-based system. Proprietary Bayer information would have become public.
- A paper-based "library" system. This solution was already in place, was too awkward because of all the resources to be consulted, and was performing too slowly.

7. In the Introduction to this chapter, a statement was made that "interactivity produces gratification for the user." Interpret this statement from the marketer's and consumer's viewpoint. Cite examples as you write a one-page explanation of the concepts for the sales staff.

The customer is always right, right? Then it is important that we, as marketers, make their stay on our Web site the best experience that we can. To do this we need to investigate what kind of interaction initiates customer gratification. Do the customers want to get in and get out in a hurry? Is this really happening? If so, the navigation scheme may need to be examined. You may also need to look at the size and number of our graphics files. Are they loading quickly or are people who visit the site having to wait? Do our customers like to stay and browse to be sure they are getting all they can? Is there enough content for them to browse? Does the content provided have kick? Feedback from customers falls partly on the shoulders of sales staff and each sales person needs to look at the site from both the perspective of a marketer and a customer.

From the marketing perspective, we want the customer to stay and become comfortable with our site so they will have a favorable opinion of our company and products. We want them to come back often. We would really like for them to purchase our goods and services, but most importantly, we need them to find satisfaction by returning the next time they need something that we have.

The site should also be viewed from the customer's point of view. Is it easy to get around? Can you find what you want? Do you feel as a customer that the company is providing you with the satisfaction and gratification that you deserve? If this is not the case, changes and adjustments will need to be made.

8. One of the problems of Web operations is maintenance of the existing site. The Web site should be continually evolving, updated frequently with fresh content and product services offerings, and consistently accessible by the server. The tasks and skills of a Web master are discussed in detail in the text. Should this Web master be a staff employee (subject to using his singular style and subject to stagnation of new ideas and promotions) or should the Web master be an outside supplier? Consider the advantages and disadvantages of both situations and be prepared to discuss the Web master scenario in a class discussion.

Having an in-house Web master can have its ups and down. It is very convenient and more cost effective. A Web master that knows the company mission and goals can keep your Web site on track. On the other hand, they can also be too close to see new ideas and a fresh set of eyes can be a good thing. For this reason, I think a combination of in-house and external resources should be utilized in the creation of the appropriate marketing Web site. By having an experienced and skilled outside supplier involved in the creation of the original site or major programming projects, you alleviate the need to hire strong programmers or graphic artists for this rather large endeavor. However, this outside supplier should work closely with the in-house staff, creating a working relationship that can be called upon again if needed. In-house staff can perform the maintenance and updates, allowing for changes to be made well within the time frame required. When major revamping is required, the design team should be called in again to work with the in house Web master on the new content and design. This process of brainstorming and teamwork should provide better Web based design ideas for a stronger Web presence.

Chapter 8
Segmenting and Analyzing the Target Market

Chapter Summary

In contemporary strategic marketing planning, the value of the tools of mapping, household cluster analysis, geo-demographic analysis, psychographic segmentation, and database marketing is widely accepted without question as fundamental to segmenting, analyzing, and identifying prospective target market segments. This chapter starts with a detailed review of these tools, their use, application, and the data they provide in traditional marketing settings and then concludes with an introduction of their application in the electronic marketplace.

Core Concepts

- To understand the concepts involved in using geographic, demographic, and psychographic research
- To understand the value of electronic resources in identifying demographic and psychographic prospects in the marketing segmentation process
- To be able to analyze geographic, demographic, and psychographic data in making informed marketing decisions

Chapter Outline

I. Basics of Geo-Demographic Analysis
  A. Searching through 130 million households
  B. The services of these database-enabled, geo-demographic companies are broad and thorough
    1. Many reporting, many are mapping
    2. Demographic characteristics of households
    3. Psychographic reported in clusters
  C. The value of marketing databases is the classification of like items into smaller groups whereby the marketer finds communication and service easier tasks
    1. Demographics, socioeconomics, housing characteristics, lifestyles, and consumer purchasing behavior
    2. SIC code (Standard Industrial Classification)
  D. Why are the concept and practice of segmentation so important?
    1. Demographers have found that people of similar demographic, economic, and social characteristics tend to live among other similar persons, and for marketing purposes, these clusters of people with similar means, aspirations, and motivations can be matched to products and services related to their life circumstances.
    2. Discovery important of whom the intended prospect is
3. These two profiling situations give the marketer considerable direction in the promotional program
  E. Investigating the typical demographic report
    1. Demographics
    2. Demographic updates and projections
    3. Age by income
    4. Business

II. Psychographics, the Clustering of Households with Similar Lifestyles
  A. Psychographics is about lifestyles
  B. With psychographic data, marketers can segment, locate, quantify, and target their best prospects within any defined demographic area

- C. Each market segment represents consumers with a unique pattern of purchasing, consumption, media usage, and financial behavior
- D. Psychographics measurement identifies the number and percent of households and population in each market segment to give the marketer an index of measurement
- E. Researching the habits and the lifestyles of your chosen markets can improve your effectiveness in all of the promotional tools including media vehicle selections, appeals, advertising scheduling, and sales promotions
- F. There are many lifestyle niches in which an individual can occupy, hence the study and application of group psychographics becomes an important key to marketing
- G. The marketer must define his best profiles, one or more that will be most receptive to purchasing his product or service
    1. Selection process should be ranked by number of households or percentage of households
    2. Identify an acceptable market level
- H. Marketers can explore psychographic segmentation online through the Internet Values and Lifestyles Web site (http://future.sri.com), a repository of psychological and motivational research originally developed in 1978 by Stanford Research Institute of California
- I. Its hypothesis is that all Americans can self-identify themselves into clusters of lifestyle
    1. Eight segments in the VALS2 categorizations
    2. Ten segments in the iVALS profiles that pertain to recent Internet research
- J. Marketers of consumer products also use behavioral segmentation as a way to divide consumer markets
    1. The rationale is toward linking consumer behavior to usage-light, average, or heavy users
    2. The difficulty in labeling consumers as light or heavy users is that the identification is not constant through the product categories; consumer usage varies according to products

III. Electronic Marketing Tracking Tools

- A. As electronic commerce develops, more and more technology resources will be directed toward identifying and tracking the behavior of online purchasers
- B. Tracking and profiling software, called "cookies", are easily installed, and easily turned off in the individual computer owned by a Web user
- C. Many persons view these electronic tools as marketing surveillance akin to a breach of privacy
- D. Marketers use the information from cookies to track a user's visits to a page and track which advertising banner that user had been viewing so that the site can present a new banner when the user visits next
- E. The marketer is also able to study site navigation from cookies to determine, for instance, what pages are most popular
- F. Clickstream analysis is a study of consumer response data detailing the content and advertising banners that consumers click on during the online navigation process

IV. Art and Science

- A. There are two important areas of judgement in marketing
    1. One area is in the judgement of the creative marketing process in determining whether new sales programs or creative campaigns will "work"
    2. The other area is in market or segment selection in determining who is the appropriate consumer product or service
- B. Employing psychographics is an art that not every marketer has patience for, but it is a longer-lasting strategy for ultimate success

V. The Segmentation Technique of Geographical Mapping

- A. Utilizing geographical database technology is fast becoming a popular tool for marketers
    1. Databases can contain thousands of variables
    2. Each variable may contain the key information required to make a decision

B. The marketer that is using a mapping application can pull the same information from the database and apply it to a map

C. The aspects of mapping include many different levels of geography
   1. Carrier routes
   2. Zip codes
   3. Census tracks
   4. Designated Market Areas (DMAs)
   5. States
   6. Custom created sales territories

D. Benefits of mapping
   1. Organization
   2. Analysis

E. Mapping is a front-end display that tells the story of data that is in the background. The map and database must always correlate

F. It is also critical to have your layers on your map up to date

G. There are three types of database mapping and each function has its benefits to the e-marketer
   1. Site analysis
   2. Territory management
   3. Database plots

Teaching Suggestions

The content of this chapter is an interesting analytical presentation of the choice in using electronic market data tools and also traditional offline materials. The student will perform demographic and psychographic analysis of two metropolitan areas, the Tampa Bay MSA and the metro Orlando MSA to decide where to build the next retail location of a fictitious business. Only one location can be chosen. I'll discuss using the market data contained on the National Decision Systems' CD-ROM shortly.

The chapter begins by explaining the value of market segmentation, dividing the larger market into segments or clusters of persons with like demographics and shared psychographic beliefs. The various methods of segmentation, geographic, demographic, psychographic, behavioral, and benefits sought are explained, and the advantages and disadvantages of each method. For the thick class lecture, I would suggest that the data from the NDS be used to demonstrate the ease and flexibility of using this electronic resource. The Instructor can acquire the two market areas' data by calling 800-866-6510, option #2 for information on the Infomark Express software. This data is free to Instructors; you might check the NDS' Web sites, www.natdecsys.com or www.sitereports.com, for more information on the usage of NDS Full Data Reports or MicroVision Reports.

The Instructor can download the NDS market data software in about 30 minutes at a 28.8 modem connection (faster of course with a cable modem or a 56.6 modem), using a Pentium class computer with at least 16 megs of RAM. Create a file allowing 25 megabytes since the data files are approximately 13 megabytes. I use a Barco projector or similar projectors that are used to display graphics programs such as PowerPoint. The business computing lab maintains the software loaded on a PC cart so that it can be moved from classroom to classroom.

The geo-demographic software is easy to use with Help window instructions available. I open the Orl-Tam MSA file and maximize the window to the full screen. I demonstrate the tool bar features, *Geography* and *Select* to show the flexibility in marketing counties, zip codes, even down to areas as small as Census tracts. If you open or click on too many *Select* check boxes, the screen is filled with Census tract boundaries, highways and roads, names of towns… in other words, too much jumbled information. I do check many boxes just to make that point, that the analyst must know what select information to access or there is information-overload. The best way for the Instructor to become familiar with this program is to investigate the features, such as the Zoom targeting capability for evaluating the radius/radii (up to three distances comparison), the Tag choice for selecting zip codes or Census tracts for comparison, and the Reports that can be generated by this software. After you tag the zip codes, Census tracts, or counties (you can tag multiple areas without processing them one at a time), you can print the data as shown in sampled data sets in Appendix B. There are three reports that will be used in the Geo-demographic exercise, the Full Data Report (demographics), the MicroVision Report (psychographic) and the Retail Trade Potential Report (an estimate of the consumer expenditures spent in the area you selected for a year's period). The retail trade potential report is helpful in comparing dollars spent in various categories such as eating and drinking places, automotive dealers, furniture and home furnishings stores, and other everyday purchases as well as total retail sales for that area; many student projects can incorporate using this type of data in their projects using the Census sources. Even if the student chooses not to use geo-demographic targeting software resources, it is good that he is exposed to its availability and its potential in evaluating market areas across the U.S. and many times far from familiar market geography. These MSA market data disks or hard-copy reports are available for markets throughout the U.S.

Some instructors may be using the U.S. Census Bureau data, (http://www.census.gov), and this site is a wonderful resource for demographic and mapping information. In particular, the TIGER data, Topologically Integrated Geographic Encoding and Referencing system, (http://www.census.gov/geo/www/index.html) on the Geographic Services and Information page demonstrates the market geography mapping and offers products for sale. Other Census sites of value to demonstrate and for students' information are the Data Access Tools (http://www.census.gov/main/www/access.html) and the Government Information Sharing, (http://govinfo.kerr.orst.edu/index.html). The government is continually updating data and adding resources to the Census Bureau site. The appearance may change, but there resides much free and marketing-oriented information.

The geo-demographic exercise requires students to evaluate two data sets to select which market, Tampa (data drawn from a three-mile radius of the University of South Florida) or Orlando (data drawn from a three-mile radius of the University of Central Florida). I have developed demographic and psychographic questions that can be answered by analyzing the data and choosing whether USF or UCF's market area has an advantage over the other. This exercise was designed to help students become familiar with data analysis; students will also learn that some factors are difficult to compare because of unequal population bases. USF in Tampa is a commuter university ranked as 15th largest in the U.S. and UCF is smaller and younger, located in a suburban to rural area. The 1998 estimated number of households in this three-mile radius of USF is 40,449 residences while the same radius surrounding UCF produces 13,856 housing units. USF area households number approximately three times that of UCF. These figures are taken from the 1990 Census modeled to 1998 conditions. So in sheer numbers USF greatly exceeds UCF. Some comparisons the students will uncover puts USF at the same percentage or number as UCF; this might be considered as "no advantage" characteristic.

The front page of the work sheet is closely percentage or amount comparisons such as number of households in each area, the back page is somewhat more subjective, calling for the students to add psychographic clusters' percentages to arrive at a total for each area. The target market is described as "students" and "young singles and couples" for renting furniture and accessories for their living residences, but some characteristics to be profiled such as "medium income," or "medium to high educational" can be subjective in selecting clusters that should be included in the comparison. Many times I tell my classes that there are more than one right answer and that their numeric response, while differing from their classmates, may all produce workable marketing solutions depending on the strength of their marketing plan and marketing execution. Marketing direction and answers can be subjective, and this exercise is a good example of deciding amongst shades of gray.

The chapter ends in a discussion and depiction of segmenting geographical marketing areas by mapping supplied by the direct marketing service, Val-Pak Corporation. The student must realize that knowledge of the market area is necessary to draw boundaries for clusters of like consumers. Direct marketers such as Val-Pak use proprietary databases to assist merchants in defining the demographics of their businesses' trade areas. Illustrations of a typical trade area defined by selections such as household income are included in this section.

Answers to Questions and Exercises

1. You are the owner of an antique phonograph store specializing in collectible 45 and 78 rpm records. To identify your best zip codes for promotional mailings, which segmentation strategy would best suit your merchandise? Who do you think would be collectors of vintage phonographs? Develop a profile of the collector and match it to a segmentation strategy. Write it as a memo to your marketing data representative.

In the field of collectibles or nostalgic merchandise, dealers recognize that these purchases are discretionary wants and not needs. Discretionary purchases require discretionary income. Therefore, the collector can be profiled best by a **psychographic** description attempting to capture his/her lifestyle. The student should research some of the Web sites dedicated to these more esoteric items such as turn-of-the-century Coca-Cola serving trays or movie posters of the 1930s or 40s. The auction sites such as eBay list categories of collectible from rare Pez dispensers to black Americana items such as a 1952 Aunt Jemima griddle might demonstrate the wide variety and interesting oddities people buy and collect.

Collectors of antique photographs might share these characteristics:

- Married men, ages 60 years plus, who remember music from their childhood and who have been collectors of other items such as rare coins or stamps in the past
- Medium to high income, investors in stocks and mutual funds, maintaining more than four checking and savings accounts; frequently owners of small to medium sized businesses
- Owners of a single-family home or condominium worth more than $300,000 with the mortgage paid
- Parents of grown children, probably grandparents themselves
- Often do not play an instrument so recorded music is a pastime
- Many serious collectors do not open the packaging or play the disks; ownership of a rare item is power
- Interested, even expert, in trivia and history
- Most frequently live east of the Mississippi River in metropolitan areas

A possible segmentation strategy could be to select zip codes or Census tracts populated by older males, earning $75,000 plus or possessing income-producing assets as they enjoy retirement; Females, if married, with no children (now grown and living independently); Donors to performing arts organizations or public television and radio; Possesses gold or platinum American Express card; Subscribes to Smithsonian and National Geographic magazines; Donates to environmental protection special interest groups. Educational attainment may not be a factor since many of these men began working in the 1940s and 1950s when affording a college education was considered a luxury. An effective target marketing program can use segmentation according to psychographic characteristics of residence within a given geographical area. Other online marketing might include advertising on the site, Exchange.com, the premier online marketplace hard-to-find recordings and music memorabilia at www.musicfile.com. and for hard-to-find antiquarian and used books at www.bibliofind.com.

2. Research the definitions of undifferentiated marketing and differentiated marketing. Which strategy do you think would be best served by segmentation methods? Write an e-mail to your instructor explaining the differences of the two marketing terms and how segmentation would benefit either one, if any.

By definition, undifferentiated marketing makes no distinction among any segments. Undifferentiated marketing is defined as a strategy in which market segment differences are ignored in only one product or service use distribute to the entire market. So target marketing and undifferentiated marketing are mutually exclusive. Differentiated marketing can be described as a marketing strategy in which a firm offers products or services to one or more segments of the market and develops different marketing strategies for each one. Logically, differentiated marketing programs are produced by segmenting the market into two or more groups.

3. There are inherent advantages and disadvantages using any method of market segmentation. From your readings and experience, make a list of advantages and disadvantages for geographical, demographic, psychographic, iVALS, and behavioral segmentation. Be prepared to discuss these concepts in class.

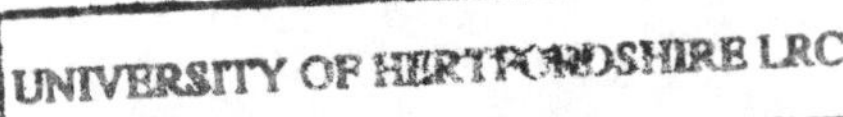
UNIVERSITY OF HERTFORDSHIRE LRC

Segmentation method	Advantages	Disadvantages
Geographical	Simple to establish boundaries	Little selectivity within the geographic area; Many consumer habits contained within one area
Demographic	Information available from Census	Different lifestyle patterns not Recognized
	Expands consumer profile beyond age	Provides little information within age Groups
Psychographic	Focuses on interests, opinions, attitudes; Basis for many emotional campaigns; Appeals suited for brand building	Data more costly to collect and analyze Some suspicion that internal motivations are deep seeded and not valid
iVALS typology	Insight to Internet/Web user	Data more costly to collect and analyze; New research technique to be proved; Limited penetration of Internet access
Behavioral	Excellent identifier of consumption	Some consumers heavy users in one category and light users in others
	Ability to affect attitudes by promotion	Research is costly to develop
	Ability to market to clusters of opinions, rather than todelineated age groups	

4. Access the iVALS site (http://future.sri.com) to take the Internet psychographics test. Print out the cluster matrix, research your projected personality cluster or clusters, and write a memo to your personnel manager stating whether or not you agree with the assessment. Turn the assessment in to your instructor for his analysis.

This is a field exercise and each student's profile and evaluation of the profile should be different.

5. Electronic tracking of consumer usage of the Internet is controversial among various public interests. Privacy interests say there is an invasion of privacy using tools such as cookies. E-merchants counter with an argument that tracking software helps them to become acquainted better with their customers' preferences for online shopping. Some consumers object to devices that record their purchasing habits while others are noncommittal about merchants gathering data on their shopping habits. The government seems to take no stand. Write a letter to the editor of your local newspaper stating an opinion of support for two of these four interest groups. Why are privacy arguments possibly correct? Or why are e-merchants' arguments possibly correct? Follow the same logic if you wish to support or deny e-shoppers. Keep in mind the interests of the government.

- Privacy protection is correct. A frequently asked question is, "where will privacy invasion stop?" Something individuals feel that too much information is kept on them even before online access made tracking easier. Organizations such as the Electronic Frontier Foundation (www.eff.org) take action to bring privacy concerns to the public, whether the public is affected or not. The EFF purpose is to work in protecting free expression, online security, and privacy.
- E-merchants are not invading privacy. The basic premise of marketing is to fulfill customer desires and provide customer satisfaction. The better the marketer knows the customer's wants and the needs, the better he can serve and anticipate those requests. Electronic recording and tracking technology is one way to provide accurate information on consumer habits and behavior.
- Consumers can decide whether or not to protect their privacy. Web browsers have the option for the consumer to turn off cookies, the small programs that record Web usage. Television has long used tracking technology, though much simpler in design with the handwritten diaries, to record customer preferences in television viewing or radio listenership. With the practices of Nielsen or Arbitron, consumers can also choose whether or not to participate.
- The Federal government should protect an individual's privacy. Only the Federal government has the staff and financial resources to police Internet and the traffic therein. Issues of fraud, pornography, or national security are sufficient reasons to have the government monitor traffic for the general protection of society.

- The Federal government should stay out of this issue to let the public decide on privacy. Eventually public sentiment will become solidified, and appropriate legislation if necessary can developed. As has been said, "the best government is that which governs least."

6. Access the site Alexa (www.alexa.com) to report on its methodology of displaying competitive advertising on a selected site. How are competitors' ads displayed on the site? Is this method of profiling a sound business strategy or unfair competition? Write a report on the Alexa process.

Alexa, acquired by Amazon.com in April, 1999, is a tracking system that offers information about competitive sites as the viewer accesses a site of her choice. Alexa developed a free advertising-supported Web navigation service that works with Internet browsers to provide alternative information about the sites being viewed and suggest related sites. Alexa employs a pop-up window displaying information about a competitive product within the same product category as the access site. This is an excellent example of innovative information technology used for marketing purposes. The service is free, the consumer chooses to download Alexa if desired, and the pop-up window can be minimized if the viewer elects. Participating in Alexa's product tracking service is voluntary to the viewer

Should the marketer's product's site be accessed, certainly she wants no competition displayed to cloud the prospect's mind. On the other hand, the marketer of a competitive product is eager to present his product to anyone shopping within the category. The service is advertising supported, and in most similar situations, advertising is an acceptable method of producing product awareness and building purchase preference.

7. Consider geographic mapping as a segmentation method. What are the advantages and disadvantages of this market segmenting process? Write a memo to your advertising manager outlining these points.

The mapping strategy as a segmentation method is based on the assumption that businesses have "retail areas of influence," and that consumers will travel different distances depending on the retail category. With proper knowledge of a geographical area, mapping can be an effective segmentation basis. Different demographic characteristics can be mapped and compared such as household income, population by age, and family households. Mapping is also a more affordable alternative (through U.S. government sources) to costly primary research on psychographic or behavioral factors.

The biggest disadvantage of the mapping segmentation process is that market areas change over time so the marketer is wise to continually review her market's composition and dynamics. A new competitor can upset the retail influence of established businesses. Other geographical changes such as new construction of a freeway or the opening of a new highway can affect traffic and business patterns. Even changing streets to one-way traffic can be detrimental to existing businesses.

8. In Appendix B you will find data reports that pertain to market statistical areas in Florida, the Tampa Bay region and the metro Orlando region. There is an exercise for your analysis of market data information referencing the demographic and psychographic profiles plus retail expenditures for each area. You are the eastern manager of a rental furniture company, Rooms to Rent, and it is your responsibility to conduct a market analysis to select the next location for a store for Rooms to Rent. You can only choose one location between the two; information contained in these data reports from National Decisions Systems will help you make an informed decision.

This is an optional but very educational exercise for the students to familiarize themselves with the concept and application of geo-demographic market data. I have had graduates secure jobs solely on their knowledge of geo-demographic software and its output.

Chapter 9
Integrating the Promotional Mix

Chapter Summary

Historically, marketers have been the first and fastest to grasp new innovations, technical or otherwise, and put them to effective use in the pursuit of sales and profits. In this way, marketers have not changed when presented with the benefits of Internet, World Wide Web, and the expanding electronic environment of today. This chapter builds a case for the value of any organization creating an online awareness as a component of increasing importance in the marketer's toolkit.

The traditional elements of the promotional mix are well suited to online marketing. A review of the advantages and disadvantages of the elements of the promotional mix is accomplished. Their use and application are presented as a complimentary adjunct to the overall process of marketing communications, with emphasis given to their use in an electronic environment for e-commerce. Attention is given to the interactive capability of the Web to enhance each of the five elements of the promotional mix. The overall goal is to create an improved and consumer-friendly promotional program.

Core Concepts

- To explain what the value of an online awareness is and its importance to relationship marketing
- To introduce the elements of the promotional mix as applied to online marketing
- To differentiate the advantages and disadvantages of the promotional mix elements
- To develop a promotional strategy geared toward online marketing

Chapter Outline

I. Developing the Online Awareness
   A. The World Wide Web is exceptionally well suited for the presentation and persuasion aspects of the marketing mix
   B. Capabilities of the Web have matured greatly during the last few years, and marketers are introducing new service applications
      1. Abilities to personalize the user's site and comparison of search engines
      2. Improving the site's navigation
      3. Partnering with complementary products and services
   C. The strategic promotional value of online promotion
      1. The Web should be considered a support media vehicle for most all consumer goods and services with maybe the exception of computer hardware and software marketing
      2. As a support vehicle to print or broadcast, online marketing's function should build on the awareness process because of the unique capability of viewer interaction
      3. For interaction online strategy, the marketer should focus her attention on thinking "external dialog" rather than "internal monologue" since this vehicle provides two-way communication with interested audiences
      4. The marketer must produce appropriate content guided by information rather than exaggeration
      5. The two-way dialog sets the Web apart from traditional media since the majority of mass vehicles direct their messages through one-way dialog
      6. The Web becomes the ideal marketing medium because of its global reach and accessibility as well as its interactive potential for both communicating with the consumer and the business-to-business market
   D. Stages in developing an online awareness
      1. The site will require its own marketing to establish visibility

2. The next stage of building awareness is that of building believability
3. The third step of establishing an online awareness is that of fostering online longevity

II. Commerce and Communications

A. In each step of this awareness strategy, the importance of communications in the electronic exchange process escalates. The marketer should eventually balance commerce with electronic communications

B. Paradigm of the importance of relationship marketing and customer service calls for enterprises to differentiate themselves by constantly providing superior service at every point of contact with the customer

C. Relationship marketing can encompass of influence four opportunities of customer and prospect interaction as formulated by the Gartner Group:
1. Customer acquisition
2. Customer retention
3. Customer extension
4. Customer selection

D. The unique "push" property of the Web
1. The Web was first based on "pull" technology where the client browser must request a Web page before it is sent
2. As a direct marketing vehicle, the Web was thought to be evolving into a "push" medium delivering customized news and advertising to individuals in the workplace

E. Marketers can combine the push interactivity and the promotional program into a push and pull strategy at the same time

III. Formulating the Promotional Strategy

A. The promotional mix consists of advertising, sales promotions, public relations, direct marketing, and personal selling

B. Advertising is any paid form of non-personal message about an organization, product, services, or idea by an identified sponsor directed to a mass audience
1. Advantages
2. Disadvantages of advertising include the following:
   a. The cost of national advertising coverage is expensive as are the production costs for creating the advertisement of commercial
   b. National advertising is not selective in targeting specific target audiences, therefore, creating much wasted coverage or readership
   c. Advertising materials must be produced far in advance and allow little flexibility in making changes to advertisements or commercials quickly
   d. There is much clutter among advertising messages, vehicle promotions, and public service announcements

C. Direct marketing is a promotional element in which organizations communicate directly with the target customers to generate a response or transaction
1. Within recent years, direct marketing has expanded the customary use of direct mail to encompass direct response advertising using television, newspapers, magazines, telemarketing, and the World Wide Web, especially because the Web's direct interrelations with consumers or businesses
2. Advantages of direct marketing:
   a. The ability to target customers via database collection provides high selectivity
   b. Direct marketing pieces can contain large amounts of product or service information
   c. Direct marketing allows for the capability to personalize direct mail, magazine, and Web messages by adding the recipient's name to envelopes, cover letters, e-mails, and Web sites

d. Direct marketing had the ability to send product samples to prospects or targets users of a competing brand
e. Direct marketing to the Web, e-mail campaigns can be cost-efficient
f. There is opportunity for repeated exposure according to the marketer's plan

3. The disadvantages of direct marketing may include the following:
a. Costs of direct marketing using traditional media are high since the message is presented to target groups usually small in number
b. Image problems that are traced to "junk mail"
c. As with advertising, direct marketing fights the clutter problem

D. Sales promotion are those marketing activities that provide extra value or incentives to the sales force, distributors, or to the ultimate consumer

1. Advantages of sales promotion may include the following:
a. Rapid increase in sales activity and volume
b. Attract new buyers to trial purchases
c. Defend an established brand against new competition
d. Reward loyal customers as they continue to be product users
e. Sponsoring specific events can provide additional marketing support

2. Some of the disadvantages of sales promotions include the following:
a. Marketers and retailers can become dependent on sales promotion by "training" their customer to buy only when the product is featured as a special offer
b. Matching competitor's sales promotions can lead to a sales promotion spiral
c. Extensive sales promotion can erode brand perception because of the discount nature of sales promotion
d. There is substantial opportunity for sales promotion abuse such as fraudulent coupon redemption or sweepstakes and contests misrepresentation

E. Public relations and publicity are associated with nonpersonal communications regarding an organization, product, service, or idea not directly paid for or run under identified sponsorship

1. The advantages of public relations may include the following:
a. Public relations can act as an "early warning" system to protect the organization's franchise with the community and with its audience
b. Positive publicity efforts produce an aura of credibility as the media becomes "unbiased, third-part" endorsers
c. A thorough public relations program can earn the company's recognition as a solid community citizen
d. Although considered a short-term tactic, PR is a low-cost, long-term promotional strategy

2. The disadvantages of public relations:
a. Publicity can be positive or negative; negative publicity can do irreparable harm to the organization's reputation and its relationships with its public
b. Public relations programs are not always under the control of the marketer; many programs take months or years to cultivate into positive results
c. Public relations plans are extremely time consuming since PR programs should be developed for each of an organization's constituents; these audiences could number ten or more

F. Personal selling is defined as a form of person-to-person communication in which a seller attempts to persuade a second party to buy, rent, or lease

1. The advantages of personal selling may include the following:
a. Beneficial relationships can be formed and can last for many years
b. Depending on the reaction of the prospect, dyadic communication allows the sender to alter or tailor the message according to the prospect's inquiries; with electronic communications, this would be considered interactivity
c. As in the term, personal selling is a face-to-face experience, disregarding mass media

d. Yields more immediate and precise marketing results

2. The disadvantages of personal selling:

a. Cost of personal sale calls is quite high

b. The reach of personal selling is extremely limited

c. There often is concern among management that the field sales representative is not presenting the product or service with the same and consistent information that the home office intended

d. Many time the purchase cycle can be quite long, perhaps several years in the purchase or repurchase of durable goods

G. With these five building blocks, marketers create new promotional strategies year in and year out and can be applied to consumer and trade promotional programs; local, regional, national international agendas; campaigns for product and services; and promotional efforts for business services or farm products

H. Certain promotional mix elements perform better than others in different categories

1. Startup companies and those in their growth stage, advertising and public relations can build awareness

2. As the product matures, its potential for attracting new customers as well matures, and growth peaks

3. As the product reaches the declining stage of the cycle, to entice retailers and wholesalers to stock the product, money is again shifted from consumer sales promotion to trade sales promotion

4. In the declining stage of the product cycle, personal selling complements the trade sales promotions in pushing sales of the product as long as possible

IV. Developing a Unique Creative Strategy

A. The Web is able to tell the story of the product, and it can react to the impressions or questions that the viewer might have after the online session

B. The process of isolating the unique benefits, sometimes called the "unique selling proposition"

C. Creativity has been defined as the "ability to generate fresh, unique, and appropriate ideas that can be used as solutions to communications problems"

1. Start with a creative platform that delineated the benefits of the product

2. This creative platform is transformed into the creative strategy which is a summary of all the significant research, consumer attitudes, competitor's stances, and client input and directives

3. From these positioning lines, the balance of the campaign can be rendered into the necessary communications tools

D. The marketer should remember why the viewer is using the Web in search of convenience, quality, efficiency, delivery availability, and performance. The home page and subsequent product or service pages should appeal to these influences

E. In developing the creative direction, the marketer should judge the creative solutions as objective as possible

F. Requirements should be mandated in communications materials

1. To include a Web site or e-mail address in all advertising and activity materials

2. Substantial and creative thought to domain names that are immediately recognized as the company "label"

3. Consistency also should be in resemblance of the Web address to a similar e-mail address

G. The way to establish a company's online recognition

1. First investigate the proposed domain name through the interNIC registration site, check the availability of the name, and then proceed with the basic identity items

2. Suggestion is that a company needs no more than one domain name

3. The marketer should inquire with the company's' ISP to ensure the firm's address can accept a non-www subdomain

4. Just as the ISP for an alias to the site's DNS entry point

H. Still appealing to the senses that description that appealed to the senses or the stimuli that trigger sensory reactions, such as smell, taste, touch, sight, and sound could conjure up association with certain product features

I. Assistance from an interactive advertising agency. The Web has conceived a new type of advertising agency and new capabilities that enhance the World Wide Web communications talents. This resource is called an interactive advertising agency, and advertising company that conceives and produces new media campaigns and materials based on electronic vehicles

J. The services of an interactive agency:
   1. It combines state-of-the-art technology with a unique, multidisciplinary approach to business and marketing that effectively helps companies communicate, inform, and sell
   2. Provider of communications and business programs that integrate strategic counsel with traditional marketing disciplines, such as product branding and advertising as well as advanced technology solutions and new media, including Internet and Extranet development, database architecture, and enterprise systems integration
   3. Add dynamic page creation capability to your sites with a relational database
   4. Enable your sites to perform secure electronic commerce and integrate personalized technology for user customization
   5. Streaming media expertise allows your clients to exploit the benefits of Webcasting and high performance Web serving
   6. Office services for the development and production of Interactive Kiosks for Retail and Trade Show applications, Laptop Sales Presentations, and Hybrid CD-ROMS
   7. International expertise for reaching global audiences

K. Staying on top of technology is a full-time job, and again giving the "technological watch" assignments to the marketing staff might keep the company's marketing environment up to date

V. The Components of the Promotional Plan

A. Promotional plan is composed of many process elements, each a small but important link that on completion should result in meeting corporate objectives

B. Elements must be identified and scheduled and then given consideration as to its role in the promotional mix, the message, the media

C. Creative themes, careful planning and execution and creative direction throughout the campaign

D. Elements in a plan for creative development might include:
   1. Source selection
   2. Message selection
   3. Media channels

E. Objective setting is important in measuring the final results of the marketing program

F. Marketer should define what the online communications objectives are planned to be
   1. Will the electronic resources support an introductory mass media product merchandising
   2. Should the electronic marketing resources focus on improving database collection and output analysis?
   3. Will the Web sit be static or will it be a Web-enabled on that can filter and link several databases for relational information?

G. The marketer should extend the marketing plan through online media

H. Do the online capabilities need to support the advertising objectives?

I. Sales promotion is a solid method of introducing new products

J. Sampling strategies are very important in matching the right product to the right prospect in the right place

K. The marketer should define the sales promotion objectives before initiating the sales promotion and to be able to judge whether the goals were met
   1. To accelerate sales to new or existing products
   2. Directed at consumers, but the higher and probably unspoken goal was to placate retailers by increasing the sales traffic to the stores

3. Was the sales promotion an inducement to create higher sales by attracting children or the parents to patronize the fast food restaurant?

L. Sales promotions can fail
   1. An overpowering sales promotion can be as bad as one that flopped
   2. Too successful, the lack of the toys or discounts might disappoint the customer and provoke anger at the company that could lead to accusations of false or misleading advertising
   3. Unsuccessful sales promotions could lead to promotional merchandise that could not sell

M. Sales promotion events can be very entertaining

N. Individuals working within the sales promotion department must possess the same type of creative mind as those in advertising or product development departments

O. Sales promotions can be targeted at internal and external audiences

P. PR depends heavily on publicity, and publicity can be the greatest friend or the greatest enemy to an organization and should be carefully examined and cautiously pursued in generating positive press relations
   1. What could be the appropriate objectives?
   2. The marketer should go through the same process of segmentation to decide which benefits match which segments best

Q. Public relations works best at proactive influencing rather than quickly rushing in a reactive fashion

R. The overriding purpose of a public relations plan is to keep in touch with attitudes and opinions of the various constituencies

Teaching Suggestions

This chapter begins by explaining the capabilities of online promotion. Creating online awareness is a balance of setting the proper communications objectives for recognition purposes: the marketer must cultivate the sequential stages of online visibility, online believability, then online longevity. The rationale and activities for building online awareness are detailed, and the student is advised that these actions require frequent attention and much work, planning, dedication, and persistence. Realistic expectations are also necessary since electronic marketing is not the end-all. Electronic marketing will require integration and support from the traditional promotional mix elements.

The marketer should eventually balance commerce with electronic communications. As a strategy and tactic, electronic marketing tools enhance the relationship between the customer and the marketer. Convenience of speed, accuracy, record-keeping, accessibility, and personalization benefits the usage of the Web by the consumer; within this convenience attribute, the GartnerGroup research firm has developed a paradigm for creating relationship-enhancing Web objectives: customer acquisition, customer retention, customer extension, and customer selection. The text explicates each strategy for customer development using online communications.

An important concept then follows. The rise and fall of push technology is reviewed, with an observation that too complex and compressed digital ads made the push delivery of information too slow in downloading of data. While push technology is currently out of favor, compression technology under development may improve push's desirability as an online promotional vehicle.

The discussion turns examining the last promotional mix P, the traditional promotional elements of advertising, sales promotion, public relations, direct marketing (in which category online marketing falls), and personal selling. The advantages and disadvantages of each activity are explained. Then, the online equivalent is presented such as banner advertising, ads in pop-up windows, or insert ads placed on a larger page all of these alternatives offer the unique quality of interactivity, the two-way dialog between the viewer and the marketer. The text stresses that online promotional efforts can be used and coordinated with traditional promotional tactics for maximum efficiency and effectiveness. As the Web is currently a support medium, its greatest contributions may be in the growth and maturity periods as consumers cultivate relationships with the product and service. This statement relates to the presentation of the product life cycle. Online promotions can assist in the introduction (awareness), growth (reinforcement of message), maturity (emphasis on sales promotion such as online coupons), and decline (less expensive vehicle to publicize auctions of remaining product to targeted liquidators). Different online communications strategies can deal with different products in different stages of the product life cycle; fresh and innovative thinking creates intriguing, customer-oriented promotional activities.

In developing an online creative strategy, many marketers enlist the services of an interactive advertising agency that has staff familiar with electronic marketing tools and are experienced in the workings of consumer and business-to-business E-commerce. Interactive agencies with electronic media expertise have evolved quickly during the late 1990s and appear to be here to stay. Traditional agencies are buying smaller interactive agencies for their knowledge and client base; traditional agencies recognize that it would take years to gain the proper online knowledge, staff, and clients if they want to "grow" their own resources.

The chapter closes with an explanation of the objectives that might be appropriate for creating an online marketing plan such as product or image awareness, introduction of new products or products new to the Web, disseminating press releases over electronic news wire sources. Enhancement of customer service, transaction ordering, and ongoing customer communications will be discussed in Chapter 13. The importance of a marketing plan to designate actions, timing, staff responsibilities, and budgets is also underscored comparing the marketing plan to a road map to follow in arriving at your destination.

Answers to Questions and Exercises

1. Some advertisers use different messages in different media at the same time. Their justification is that they are advertising different products to different markets that have different media habits. How do you counter this statement or do you agree with the advertising strategy? Give some thought to consistency, knowing well the customer, segmentation strategy, and trying to be all things to all people. Write a memo to your advertising manager expressing your opinion on the correct strategy.

Supportingconsistency: Many products are targeted to small market niches so that a uniform message that would include Web communications becomes a reinforcement of the rational or emotional appeal. Changing messages or deviating from the "standard" message could confuse the targeted consumer. Some advertising campaigns are designed to support purchase decisions as the "correct one" by current brand loyalists rather than a design to win new customers or attract old customers who no longer buy the product. These reinforcement announcements can be received by the customer after a purchase and occur during this "post-purchase" period when doubts might linger about buying the appropriate product. This message strategy does not attempt to "be all things to all people."

Supporting differentmessages to thesame market Some advertisers report that special circumstances encourage special advertising responses even though the differing messages are meant for their "core." Perhaps slow sales of a particular automobile model or a year-end clearance of Lincoln Town Cars might spawn a "sale" message rather than advertisements supporting luxury and comfort as producer benefits. Sometimes a marketer will take the same product and "target" it to more than one market. For example, Finnish cellular telephone manufacturer Nokia considered its national market to be businesspeople, aged 30 to 50 years. But as cell phones sold fast to younger people under the age of 25, Nokia took its mainline product and produced hipper "singing woman on the street" commercials, then aired them on MTV. This plan was executed to take advantage of a fortuitous and unforeseen market demand. So in many advertisers' eyes, consistency begins with market conditions.

2. The opening quote of this chapter forecasts larger Web ads. Do you think this occurrence will assist the shopper or alienate the viewer? Is there any happy compromise that would serve both parties? Write a letter to the editor supporting the shopper, or the viewer, or develop a give-and-take proposal for Internet users.

Positive or negative reaction to any advertising usually results from the performance or the delivery of the advertising offer. If Web advertisers conduct honest, value-oriented advertising, online shoppers should be well served. This basic premise of mutually beneficial commerce transcends the question of the size of the advertisement. Hopefully producing "value" ads offering desirable goods or services could attract shoppers because of content rather than size. Remember that not all promotion is advertising; powerful endorsements can be developed through participation in discussion groups, Usenets, conferences, professional writings, and online newsletters.

3. The interactive tracking technology evidenced by Alexa.com seems to be acceptable to many Americans. You are a multinational or global marketer, however, how would this technology fit with more private cultures? Would you have to develop several "privacy policies"? Would your e-marketing policy be global or local? Develop a privacy policy for those cultures or governments who might be offended or that might be considered illegal interactive tracking technology.

Given the levels of suspicion of information technology in many countries, consumer tracking technology would probably be unacceptable in both developing and developed countries. In Chapter 17, there is reference to the protection of privacy for the individual, and this controversy is being debated among the European Union and its trading partners including the United States. Many global marketers are addressing privacy standards by creating different policies for different countries with different levels of online privacy projection. International marketers often profess to adjust their marketing and advertising, and probably now their information technology practices, to fit the laws and customs of the host country in which they are doing business.

For an example of corporate privacy statements visit the Microsoft Corporation web site at www.microsoft.com and view their privacy statement.

4. In your opinion, which of the traditional media mix elements has online communications most affected in the negative sense? Which has online communications strengthened the most? How has interactivity affected each of the five elements? Be prepared to discuss your answers in class.

Probably the media most negatively affected would be print vehicles such as newspapers and magazine because of reaction and publication of news articles. Newspapers have fought back by offering online editions such as the Interactive Edition of the *Wall Street Journal* or Tampa Bay Online presented by the *Tampa Tribune*. Magazines are also trying to compete with online edition such as *Sports Illustrated* or *Time*. These experiments will take time to judge because the print media have always been sources of in-depth information allowing the reader to internally pace the gathering of information (rather than the external pacing as in the control of television and radio). Will online information sources provide sufficient or insufficient depth?

Television viewership has also been reduced as a competitive media vehicle. In recent poll indicated that a majority of people would rather give up their televisions than lose their access to the Internet. Television advertising does have the advantage of sight, sound, motion, and color like the Web but of course lacks the power of interactivity that produces the Web dialog. Radio remains a unique and entertaining media because of its mobility and portability. Future advancements in portable Web appliances may produce another serious challenge to radio listenership as television presented in the early 1950s. Radio recovered its place in the advertising and sales promotion mix approximately 25 years later as FM broadcasting delivered a clearer stereo signal.

The promotional mix element of direct marketing has been strengthened the most. Because of database profiling and accuracy, direct marketers enjoy more efficiency and effectiveness in traditional direct mail activities as well as a new tactical advantage in e-mail campaigns and customer communications. All five of the promotional elements including personal selling have been fortified by incorporating online communications or offering online transaction opportunities. Convenience of competitive shopping, speed of delivery, checking into available inventory or selection without leaving home is each an advantage e-marketing over traditional media capabilities.

5. In your opinion, will any of the five promotional mix elements become less effective or even obsolete in the next fifty years because of advances in electronic communications? Radio suffered as television advertising became more popular, and afternoon and evening editions of daily newspapers folded because of television news programs.

If you think any of the promotional elements might become obsolete, which promotional elements or medium (media) do you think this might happen to? If you do not think any will become obsolete, why not? Write a memo to the head of strategies planning.
Fifty years will need to pass to judge this question accurately. Current generations' media habits will continue, and at least two generations raised under new media must go by to establish their own patterns of usage. Of the five elements (advertising, sales promotion, public relations, direct marketing, and personal selling), most observers see each becoming stronger because of online resources and communications. Each of these elements has a different purpose and execution for persuading purchasers. Advertising can create long-term brand image or fill a store with customers in one day. Sales promotion offers the buyer added incentive to purchase immediately. Public relations and publicity are credible endorsements by the media and these endorsements can produce both long-term and short-term benefits. We have discussed the strengthening of direct marketing by the online capability of interactivity. Personal selling efforts have added information resources with Web access, fax back, or proprietary intranets or extranets. Consumer or business-to-business audiences can be targeted by any, or all, of these promotional tactics.

6. Under what circumstances do you feel it is appropriate to mass e-mail various groups of e-mail users, such as Usenet groups as DejaNews? Or a listserv, such as Online ads? Or a "proprietary" e-mail address list, such as the entire employee group of a private company? Or a government organization? Or the entire faculty of a University? Write an unsolicited e-mail policy paragraph for each group mentioned.

As a general rule, any list that you can sign on to is often available for unsolicited e-mail. The lists that you are automatically included in, with little option for unsubscribing such as employee lists, are inappropriate for unsolicited e-mail usually referred to as "spam." Examples of spamming can be:

- *E-mail to listservs.* Voluntary subscription so unsolicited messages are acceptable
- *Newsgroup e-mailings.* No mass e-mails to newsgroups or "communities" unless allowed by the newsgroup
- *Chat e-mailings.* Voluntary participation so unsolicited messages are accepted
- *Proprietary list for private company.* Involuntary subscription so unsolicited e-mail prohibited
- *Proprietary list for government organization* Involuntary subscription so unsolicited e-mail prohibited
- *Proprietary list of public university.* Involuntary subscription so unsolicited e-mail prohibited

7. Concerning the design of your company's domain name, surf the Web to locate ten domain names that you consider memorable, creative or both. After each name, write a paragraph explaining why you think it is special. Humorous, double entendre? A unique meaning or a unique initial?

This is a field exercise, each student's list and explanation of the curious or interesting domain name will be different.

8. You are the media liaison for a large public utility. You are new in your position, but you have experience as an assistant public relations director. The first task you decide upon is to organize your customer constituencies according to special interests. You begin to develop e-mail lists for news releases. What would be the e-mail list that should be directed to each of your market interests? Different groups may require different news releases or announcement slants: what information would you need directed to each customer constituency? Write an outline listing each group and type of information you would release to them.

Large public or private companies serve a wide variety of customers, suppliers, and other constituencies. A public utility usually answers to or serves many of the following groups:

- Energy or water customers: news on new facilities or services to improve productivity or save money. Perhaps news on charitable activities.
- Stockholders: news on earnings, employee efficiency or achievements, new facilities and why they are important to the stockholder
- Employees: news on improved wages or benefits, employee achievements, safety or job postings
- Local government officials: news on improved services, future expansion plans, new jobs
- State or Federal regulators: news on improved services, customer satisfaction levels, safety
- Financial analysts and the securities community: news on earnings, new stock or bond issues
- Suppliers or stakeholders: news on new facilities or services to productivity or service availability, news on the general health of the organization

- The community at large: news on the general health of the organization, new services
- The news media: news on company events, improvements and outages, employee achievements
- Local schools and community special interest groups: special programs to explain the public utility's purpose and position in the community

Depending on the importance of the constituency, specially prepared electronic news releases or press kits can tell powerful stories about a company.

9. Many times (almost always) sales promotions that award prizes ask for the contestant's e-mail address. Why? E-newsletters also request e-mail addresses for the obvious reason of delivering the newsletter online. Why? Why is sales promotion so popular among marketers dealing with consumers and businesses alike? Write an e-mail to your marketing manager suggesting a sales promotion for your class project's product or service citing these reasons.

Collecting mailing and e-mail addresses can be managed and segmented into various customer clusters to be matched to products or services attractive to the group. E-mail newsletters can contain special offers to "premium" customers, and e-mail communications are proving extremely economical. Mailing in envelopes entails postage, materials, and labor. The student group should suggest a sales promotion that contains an electronic resource component and an explanation why e-mailing to customers or prospects is more efficient than postal mail.

10. From the list of strategic and tactical promotional media tools, collect samples of each and place them on pages in a portfolio. The items you might find are magazine or newspaper ads, signs or billboards (photograph any that apply), brochures or flyers, publicity articles, packaging from products, and, of course, printed Web pages.

There is an extensive list of traditional and electronic promotional materials that the student or group can collect, photograph or print out supporting one brand or company. This is a field exercise; each collection may be different if the Instructor specifies no product or service duplication. This exercise also helps the marketing or communications student learn to assemble an attractive portfolio as a prototype for eventual job interviews. The Instructor should also provide tips and instructions for the portfolio appearance.

Chapter 10
Using the Internet

Chapter Summary

To any observer of the changes in information technology, it is clear to see that the Web has undergone dramatic changes in an extremely short time. One major shift has been in moving from an exclusively text-based format in the early years of its existence to one that is highly graphic and loaded with movement. These technological advances have easily moved the Web site from that of a static source of information to a dynamic sales and marketing tool. With what may be seen as an almost infinite array of information sources, it is crucial for the marketer to determine what is the "right" information to find. Marketers must start by differentiating between "what would be nice to know" and "what do I need to know." Clearly, to effectively manipulate the vastness of the Web to one's advantage requires a clear definition of the information needs of specific markets in question. All of these concepts are covered in this chapter.

Also, chapter material includes an explanation of the wide array of marketing information the Web can provide. It gives a distinction between consumer marketing and business-to-business marketing on the Web, and stresses the differences in message content required by each. Techniques for product sampling are also introduced. As a follow-up, empirical data is presented on people's attitudes and perceptions to Web shopping.

The importance of knowing which search engines customers prefer is addressed and presented in the context of their ease of use. A ranking of search engine popularity is provided, as well as research data on consumer's Web use habits and preferences in use. Strategies and tactics for building Web audience loyalty, stimulating and building Web site involvement, and creating use policies are outlined.

Core Concepts

- To understand what sources of marketing information are available on the Internet and discuss the applications in various examples
- To differentiate between the personal can commercial use of the World Wide Web
- To introduce the special culture of the Internet and its code conduct

Chapter Outline

I. Just What Can you Get from the World Wide Web?
   A. The marketer should be aware of the content available via the Web and be able to judge whether information is appropriate for his industry and of use to his customers
   B. One of the best marketing tools in examining the different retailer offerings to their customers is to look at a competitor's Web page
      1. "Search Products"
      2. "Customer Service"
      3. "Virtual shopping cart"
      4. Color photographs of popular merchandise
      5. Hyperlink "More Featured Items"
      6. "Company", is a formal corporate presentation
      7. "Newsroom", for press releases and articles
      8. "Career Opportunities", the employment page
      9. "Store Locator"
   C. Among high-tech companies, the content is very informational, stressing technical support and downloading capabilities
   D. If the firm sells commodities such finished hardware, the content of the site is informational reassurance toward the inventory availability, delivery, quality and price

II. Personal Use of the Web
   A. As retailers devise ways to satisfy the consumer's purchases on the Web, partners are wise to understand the reasons for the purchasers' personally using the Web
      1. Convenience (65%)
      2. Availability of vendor information (60%)
      3. No pressure from sales people (55%)
      4. Saving time (53%)
      5. Males and females both ranked convenience first
      6. Female users valued the notion of no pressure from salespeople (54%) slightly over vendor information (51%
   B. There is another "personal" side for an individual to use the Web, that of being able to personalize the browser's home page to retrieve information from specific Web resources

III. Consumer Habits Are Being Formed
   A. Consumers are welcoming the power and variety of the Web's treasury of information, and users are adapting their daily activities to accommodate their online practices
   B. Being appraised of the search engine of choice is an important factor for the marketer to know for two reasons
      1. First is on the consumer side, the software developer can create sites designed to the "lowest common denominator" the most persons have the ability to access the site and its appearance is attractive without losing any copy or graphics because of inconsistencies among browsers
      2. The second critical decision concerns search engine popularity, the marketer should register the Web site with the most popular search engines
   C. Can the marketer know too much about her market's want, need expectations, or preferences?
      1. Knowing customer's constraints (as well as the customers' plateau of patience or frustration) is most valuable in "giving the customer what she wants"
      2. Knowing these searching habits is essential to building a responsive, content-laden, and interactive Web site that draws the surfer into the merchandise or material without obfuscating the e-commerce experience
      3. Consider the "hit ratio" the number of searches that produce successful results
   D. Besides understanding how your markets gather information, it is necessary to try to learn what they do with this information
   E. Two of the best resources of customer opinions
      1. Consumers' expressing their opinions about product experiences both positive and negative usage
      2. Voicing what products or product features are missing in the marketplace
         a. Deja News (www.deja.com), the home of hundreds of discussions about various topics of interest to their participants
         b. The marketer can start her own discussion group, monitor consumer comments or attitudes expressed on the discussion, and interject or counter written opinions concerning her product or service

IV. Browsers-Specialty among Equals
   A. While browsers manufacturers promise equal performance in retrieving information, some browsers handle different search engines differently
   B. Web surfers are turning to Meta search sites, which blast your request to numerous search engines then create one huge list of hits
   C. Searching on the Web can be quite sophisticated if you use the proper search strategy
      1. Boolean searches are created using operators that tell the search engines what terms must be on the page or what terms must not be on the page

V. The Culture of the Internet
   A. It is odd that the Internet is considered for its commercial purpose because its origin was far from that
   B. As the Internet was born of the academic research and communications, a culture of freely sharing and non-commercial usage flourished among the gatekeepers of the Internet
   C. The academic intention to be viewed differently with the introduction of color, graphics, and augmented text in 1993 to the Internet; this enhanced research vehicle became an attractive and persuasive commercial medium as the elements matured and more people, other than researchers and educators, discovered the boundless holdings
   D. In following the traditions of the Internet, the marketer should try to extend this cultural style and perceptiveness of his site
   E. The ideal business on the Internet would build a loyal audience by providing an attractive environment in which users could discuss matters of common interest with one another and with experts
   F. Depending on your business model, you could aim to build a global virtual community of people with common interest-staking out your subject matter niche-or you could use this medium to forge closer ties with your local, physical community

VI. Learning Proper Netiquette
   A. Quite simply, "Netiquette" is Internet etiquette, the informal rules of behavior of the Internet
   B. Organizations develop their own "Acceptable Use Policies" (AUPs), a set of rules specifically for an organization's network
   C. There are Netiquette guidelines for most Internet resources
      1. E-mail
      2. Mailing lists
      3. News groups
      4. Telnet
      5. FTP's
   D. E-mail, mailing lists, and Usenet newsgroup Netiquette
      1. Use normal upper and lower case letters. Avoid using all capital letters in a message' this is know as shouting and is generally frowned upon
      2. Careful use of emoticons can help get your emotional point across clearly
         a. Smile (humor, happy, encouragement)
         b. Frown (sad, disapproval)
         c. Wink (kidding, joking)
      3. Avoid "flaming" (inflammatory or antagonistic criticism), or sending insulting, abusive, or threatening remarks
      4. Remember that e-mail is not necessarily private
      5. When replying to a news group posting, be sure to include the portion of the original message that your are responding to
      6. Always identify yourself and keep messages as brief and to the point as possible
      7. Avoid "spamming"
      8. When sending or posting to multiple mailing lists or news groups, indicate that you have done so
   E. Telnet also has a set of unwritten rules that need to be followed when you use it
      1. Do not stay logged in to a terminal longer than necessary
      2. "Help" pages are provided at a Telnet site, download them to you local terminal and read them after logging off
   F. File Transfer Protocol "FTP" Netiquette is important to understand as much of the problems it can cause the effect of slowing down the network
      1. Try not download large files (larger than one megabyte) until after normal business hours
      2. Use the time zone that applies for the FTP server that you are accessing, not your local time

3. Users are responsible for checking copyright or licensing agreements for the files that they download
4. If downloading shareware, be sure to pay the appropriate fees

G. Messages are so sterile in black and white text displayed on a flat unemotional monitor. To add some animation and some unspoken depth to messages and conversation, "emoticons" or "smileys" found their way into online dialog

Teaching Suggestions

This chapter acquaints the student with more of the capabilities and hidden talents of the Web. The Instructor probably has some favorite Web sites that demonstrate the different purposes for Web usage. I access popular home pages of familiar companies such as Wal-Mart, T.J.Maxx, the Gap, retailers the students recognize or have emotional attachments to. These home pages contain a plethora of information not just about merchandise for sale but also job opportunities, company history and philanthropy activities, investor news, store locations, and various links unique to each retailer. After the consumer pages are discussed, a business-to-business site, usually IBM or Oracle, is reviewed in order to show what information is displayed for business interests. Oracle maintains a deep but friendly site that is constantly changing. The home page features special promotions, offers, and conferences much like a retailer would present to stir up interest.

The chapter continues by sharing information on consumer usage of the Web. More and more individuals are creating personal Web pages, and consumer habits are developing in Web operation just as consumers engage television viewing or newspaper reading habits. The point is made that the marketer is wise to investigate online media habits such as national news, sports, special interest pages, search engines chosen...in other words, to which Web tools and information resources are online consumers drawn? With this knowledge, e-marketers can better communicate on the consumer's level of Internet usage and services.

The chapter concludes with examinations of hints on how to search more effectively for information topics to be found by search engines. Boolean limiters (and, or, not) are explained as well as the +, -, and * (the wild card expansion) search conventions. The student should master searches to reduce the research time during the situation analysis. In proper use of the Internet, an invisible set of rules should be followed in communicating with the various communities that use the Internet. These rules as a whole are called "Netquette," and breaches in this conduct can evoke loud and pointed responses called "flames" directed to the offender. The student should be aware that there is a technical, as well as cultural and social environment to the Internet.

Answers to Questions and Exercises

1. In this chapter, methods to retrieve marketing information on the Web were discussed. Make a list and define those electronic tools that assist in locating and narrowing information searches.

- Search engines on Web pages (searches by question, phrase, name, title, URL, so forth)
- "Answer" resources on Web pages such as Ask Jeeves or Answers.com (searches by question)
- Shopping bots (usually searches by titles or names)
- Database inquiries (usually specific commands in proprietary records)
- Boolean search techniques (searches by using and, or, or combinations)
- Matching search string techniques (searches by using +, -, t, u, * or combinations)

2. Through this chapter's discussion you observed that much competitive information can be gathered by studying a rival company's Web site. Pick a retailer's Web site home page of your choice and explain the elements. What are the elements displayed? What information can you gain from the products or services listed on the site? Print out the Web pages you are commenting on and include them with your written report.

This is a field exercise; information gathered by the student will differ according to the company Web site selected.

3. Probably more specific information can be obtained from a business's Web site. Pick a business to business Web site home page of your choice and again explain the elements. What are the elements displayed? What do you know about the businesses? What information can you gain from the products or services listed on the site? Print out the Web pages you are commenting on and include them in your written report.

This is a field exercise; information gathered by the student will differ according to the company Web site selected.

4. Why do the design and content of a business-to-business Web site differ from a consumer retailer's site? What elements might appear on the business site absent from the consumer site? Write a four-paragraph memo to the Web master in your company. Print out examples to demonstrate your points.

This question can be answered primarily in two ways. The business-to-business organization may not have a marketing orientation in dealing with its customers. Management may not know the customer well therefore, marketers may not care or know what content to share. Perhaps the Web site has been recently created so its appearance of insufficiency is a reflection of a work in progress. As far as content overlooked by businesses, the elements are numerous: no manner for e-mail contact, confusing navigation, too little information or too much information, no online transactions capability, no e-mail directory, no information search engine, no company history, or identification where the company is located. The list of absent features can go on. Even more serious is when site pages will not load or the hyperlinks crash the site. These are omens of negative impressions; the company would be better off without this Web presence.

The student might offer an alternative answer. Business design and content are beginning to differ very little from consumer Web site design and content because business-to-business marketers are adopting communications strategies similar to those of the consumer marketer. Strategic emphasis is placed on customer satisfaction with content such as easy to read product information, easy navigation, product search engines, well constructed FAQs, company job opportunities, mission statements, and other knowledge that the company wants to share with the consumer, prospect, or stakeholder. A well-planned and constructed business Web site is a user-friendly Web site

5. What is the leading reason for consumers to use the World Wide Web when personal shopping is the objective? Give three examples of your choices and write an e-mail to your marketing manger suggesting that a Web site would be appreciated by your customers.

The recent GVU Tenth User Study has an extensive survey on Web purchasing/intention to purchase; surveys are posted for U.S. respondents, European respondents, and other world respondents. The information is located at: http://www.gvu.gatech.edu/user_surveys/survey-1998-10/graphs/shopping/professional/q220.htm.

The five major reasons cited by Americans for personal shopping on the World Wide Web were listed as follows:

Convenience	83.3%
Save time	74.0%
Vendor information	72.2%
No pressure	64.6%
Reviews	33.0%

6. Web sites should be designed to the lowest denominator for browser display. What does this statement mean? There are so many attention-getting applications for sound, movement, and other surprises, why should a Web site be limited in its memorability and appeal? Be prepared to discuss this concept with your Web designer.

Web browsers have been in use for less than a decade, but browser manufacturers have created a great competition in races for the best features for viewing the World Wide Web. New, "improved" editions called releases are introduced almost annually, and these new releases incorporate features that older versions lack. Besides upgrading Internet access and e-mail capabilities, the newest releases handle sophisticated graphics and sound plug-ins best that older versions of Web browsers, both Netscape and Internet Explorer are incapable of displaying or playing.

This variety of versions presents a problem to the marketer and Web designer. Viewers may still be using Version 2.0 or 3.0 to access and surf the Web; they have not upgraded to the most currently available release. Therefore, an elaborate Web site cannot be viewed with all graphics, motion, or sound applications functioning. Many elaborate sites actually "break down" and appear incomplete, unattractive, or produce a bad impression. There are several reasons why people use outdated releases. Perhaps the viewer is familiar with a certain browser and chooses not to learn a more complicated one, or chooses not to move all e-mail functions or files to a newer browser because of the trouble. Maybe he has an older, underpowered computer that can't run newer browsers because of RAM limitations. Often the user works in an educational or governmental setting, and funds are not released to upgrade information technology equipment. Sometimes users merely do not want to waste the time to download the newer browser even though the software is free.

The marketer is wise to design the Web site to be accessible and operative to the greatest number of browsers, thus expanding her e-marketing programs to the widest audience. Site designers may feel their creativity is limited by designing for older browsers, but if the viewer cannot view, the entire marketing message and exposure will be lost to a significant portion of customers and prospects.

7. Using a search resource such as Deja.com , produce three posts each on the following subjects:
   a) sports injuries such as tendonitis or a shoulder separation
   b) the occult such as where practitioners buy their ingredients for spells or potions
   c) creative writing tips for writing Gothic novels
   d) blues music concerts reviews for the artist Roxy Perry, New York Blues Queen

This is a field exercise; information gathered by the student will differ according to the subject and post dates selected.

8. If you were building "Internet communities" how would you start? Most marketers build a hierarchy of constituencies such as current customers, past customers, so forth. How would you rank eight groups of special interest? Describe these groups and what content you would place on your Web site.

The marketer needs to consider several factors in building an Internet community for his product or service. First consider the vehicle as the mechanism for interested constituencies to sign on as members. A convenient and economical mechanism is organizing discussion groups with sites such as eGroups.com or Deja.com. These sites offer convenient forms to establish the discussion group and methods for member posts. There are several options in constructing the group messaging structure such as moderated or unmoderated discussions or postings visible only to members or visible to members and guests.

The marketer should then segment his constituencies and decide if each would use or benefit from targeted communications about the company, product or service, or usage experiences. The interested communities may number fewer than expected: customers looking for advice, prospects looking for information, and product usage experiences probably both positive and negative. The more specialized or prestigious the product, the more users can be expected to become members of the discussion group.

Monitoring these discussion groups will assist the marketer in shaping content for the product or company Web site. Many customers will make positive suggestions for using the product, and more will be posted if incentives are given to the best posts of the week or month depending on discussion activity. Negative comments should be addressed immediately, and product or operational shortcomings should be fixed.

Chapter 11
Web Page Design

Chapter Summary

The visual and interactive components of a Web site are critical in attracting a viewer's attention, tempting them to bookmark the site, recommending the site to others, and returning to it at a later time. This chapter gives a detailed introduction to the principles of Web site development from both of the perspectives of technical development (writing the code) and the aesthetics of layout and stylistic design. It explains the three stages of Web site design (analysis, design, and construction), and takes the reader through the stages of building a Web site step-by-step. In addition to the technical side of site development, a solid emphasis is placed on the graphical elements and style comprising a "good" site. The code used in the creation of HTML documents is presented in detail, yet in a manner that guides the reader through the technical development of a Web site.

Core Concepts

- To establish the groundwork for developing Web-based communications
- To provide the knowledge necessary for the marketing student to create a business or personal Web site
- To define what elements should be included on every Web page

Chapter Outline

I. Web Site Design Both Simple and Complex
   A. A Web site is a file of information residing on a server connected by an address to the World Wide Web, and a Web site may include text, photographs, illustrations, music, or other computer programs
   B. On the Web site are smaller files called Web pages that are accessed by clicking on hyperlinks, usually colored text, pictures, or icons of instructions directing the computer to other pages on the Web site or the other sites on the World Wide Web
   C. The marketer must be prepared to answer questions such as:
      1. What is the purpose of the Web site?
      2. Is it a primary or supporting vehicle
      3. Should it provide exposure, house publicity articles, or support retailers or field sales representatives? Who will be reading your pages?
      4. Should the graphics be fast-paced for a younger market or more conservatives for a middle-aged viewer?
      5. Should you include sound or motion?
      6. What types of computers will the typical user be using?
      7. What browser software will they have access to and how fast are their connections to the Internet?
      8. What search engines does your market prefer?
      9. Will they be viewing your site with a color or black and white monitor?
      10. What size of monitor will they be using?
   D. Once these types of questions have been answered, a design should be created for a working plan
   E. Web pages are created with a very simple, text-based scripting language called Hypertext Markup Language (HTML)

II. Issues of Web Site Design
   A. There are basically three stages to the design of a Web site
      1. Analysis phase
      2. Design phase

3. Building phase

B. The analysis phase is important in the development process because it provides the designer with the proper background in setting the site up correctly for the audience, without forgetting the purpose of the site itself
   1. You must identify the audience
   2. Types of technology this audience is most likely to have should be determined
   3. Settle on the media elements that can or should be included in the Web site
   4. What do you want to accomplish with your Web site?
      a. Do you want to provide information?
      b. Do you want to collect information?
      c. Do you want to communicate with your audience in other ways?
      d. What marketing purpose is this Web site going to serve?

C. The actions of the design phase
   1. Make an outline of the topics that you might like to include
   2. Determine what information you need to gather
   3. Determine the order in which it is to be presented
   4. Decide what items or information are most important to your market and present that information first or display it prominently

D. The next aspect of the design is, plan how you intend to structure the Web site. Think efficiency
   1. Do not require the user to click too many times
   2. Decide if you want to keep your site simple with a few textual links to create a graphical interface that uses buttons and icons to navigate throughout
   3. The flow of you Web site will be crucial in keeping your audience interested and connected
   4. Limit graphical elements on the opening Web page to "one screen"
   5. Extra media elements such as graphics, movies, sounds, and animation will make your site larger, more unwieldy, and harder for someone with a slow connection to use
   6. Choose graphics, sounds, and motions only if they are appropriate to your market and make the site stronger

E. When you begin to develop the actual appearance and feel of your site, there are many thing that you need to consider
   1. What skill level do you need the consumer to learn in order to navigate your site?
   2. How will your site grab the attention of the consumer?
   3. How will your site intrigue the consumer to see, do , or buy what your site is offering

F. Flow is a function of control, content, and motivational characteristics of a Web site
   1. Consumer is "hooked" and wants to continue investigating the site that has caught his attention
   2. Interactivity is the key. Intimacy with your consumer grows through interactivity

G. Attract the consumers attention by creating a site that is:
   1. Easy to use and understand
   2. Fun and fast
   3. Personalized
   4. Comprehensive
   5. Highly visual
   6. Easy to navigate

H. You can catch the consumer's attention with content that is well structured and enticing

I. Hyperlinks make interacting with a Web site easy

III. Creating HTML Documents; the Language of the Web

A. Hypertext Markup Language (HTML) is the scripting language in which documents seen on the Web are written

B. Web documents contain content that is then interpreted by Web browsers such as Netscape and Internet Explorer

C. The content consists of codes called "tags" or "elements" with "attributes" that tell the computer what to show on the screen
D. HTML editors are available to make the job of creating a Web page much easier
E. In addition to full HTML editing programs, many word processors and other software programs now have the ability to "Save As HTML"

IV. HTML Standards and Practices
A. If these standards and practices of HTML are followed, the Web pages will work with most of the current Web browsers
B. Good HTML follows the current version of HTML, as specified in the HTML DTD (Document Type Definition)
C. "Bad" HTML is considered to be documents that ignore these standard practices
D. Tags are the instructions that the computer is looking for in order to decipher what the code is telling it
E. There are different types of tags or elements, but they all have one or two basic structures
   1. Container tags
   2. Tags that stand on their own
F. Now that your are getting the idea of how things work, you need to be aware of what should be included in every Web page
   1. Head section
   2. Page title
   3. Signature or contact information
G. The title is the Universal Resource Locator that is the address of your page on the Web
H. Memorable titles serve three major purposes:
   1. Titles are used by application such as searches and indexes to identify your page
   2. Titles act as indicators of what to expect
   3. Titles are at the top of the HTML document giving you an easy visual clue to identify the source files quickly when you need to make changes or corrections
I. A signature, usually at the end of the document but before the </HTML> tag
J. The <HEAD> section; making it searchable
   1. The Head section defines the function of the document and adds a quick reference for Web browsers
   2. The <META> tag contains information about the document, such as keywords, expiration dates, author, page generation, software used, and many other document-specific items and is important when you want your document to be found in a search of certain keywords
K. The <BODY> section; holding it all together
   1. The body of the HTML document contains the majority of your information
   2. The body tags form a container that encloses the content of your HTML document
L. Formatting the page; making it look good
   1. HTML provides many tags that can be used to format text to allow for uniqueness and creativity
   2. Text level formatting can occur in two ways
      a. Using HTML, you can format the actual font properties, or you can describe how the text is being used
      b. Additional formatting of text can be accomplished in a block-level format
      c. To get even more fancy in your text layout, you could use formatting styles for lists and table
      d. If you are trying to get a certain effect, you will need to test your pages on multiple browsers; this a good way to double check the functionality of your Web site
M. Definition lists provide for a dictionary entry-like format
N. The caption tag is a container tag that specifies a caption for the table

O. Hyperlinks let you move from one place to another on the Internet or within a Web site by maneuvering the mouse

P. To add the visual appeal necessary to make your site attractive to your audience, you can use images and image maps

Q. An image map consists of four basic components
  1. An image map program that resides on the server in the cgi-bin directory
  2. A graphic image file saved in a gif format for the user to click on
  3. A map file to give information that will convert points on the image into URLs
  4. An HTML file to link the image and the map file

R. Image maps come in two flavors:
  1. Server side
  2. Client side

S. When a user clicks on a server-side image map, the server interprets the coordinates that the browser sends using a program on the server

T. With client-side image maps, the browser processes the information from the user's click instead of sending it to the server for interpretation

U. For lessons in what not to do in Web page design, this site with an attitude is Web Pages That Suck (www.webpagesthatsuck.com)

V. Test the Web site in different environments and for different browsers
  1. The first step to testing your Web pages is to view them yourself in all browsers that you have available and in all platforms that your consumers will be using
  2. Test the HTML code that you have written to see if they are standardized and are working correctly

W. Check for the proper use of the tag to make sure it is working

X. Notify the world that you are online

Y. Be sure to register your site
  1. Hire a service to register the site, since there are more than two hundred search engines to consider
  2. Pick and choose the search engines by doing the registration yourself with InterNIC

Teaching Suggestions

Many Instructors have learned and mastered the coding language of HTML and will feel confident teaching HTML tags and Web page design and construction. Those that are not confident in this subject material should invite a guest lecturer to teach this material. I contact the Academic Computing department and they supply a graduate trainer who teaches a basic HTML class. You may find assistance at your institution in the MIS or IT department, Academic Computing, or within the Business Technology Lab. The objective of these classes is to familiarize the students so that they can design and build a consumer or business-to business e-commerce Web page.

I conduct coaching sessions approximately three times during the term to inspect the progress the student groups are making on the project assignment. After I approve their product or service concept, I share my thinking on the objective for the Web site (usually sales-oriented site or information-dispensing resource such as a public service site). Some student groups choose to develop a Web site for existing companies, possibly a family or friend's company. I've found these "real" projects are stifling to the creativity placed into the students' concepts and limiting to the potential scope of the assignment.

I also share my spur-of-the-moment thoughts on Web site elements, such as hyperlinks to appropriate resources germane to the project topic, subjects for pages such as "testimonials," "about us," "history of the company or industry," specialty pages such as recipes, golf tips, motorcycle maintenance, the activity of wine tasting, FAQs, or other relevant tidbits. The group needs direction to begin the project and then they begin to think like marketers. I recommend meeting with each group privately to monitor progress and give them some advice on making the project interesting, persuasive, and organized.

Answers to Questions and Exercises

1. The Web can be a powerful form of communication between the consumer and the marketer. It can be used to gather vast amounts of useful and useless information. In order to develop good Web-based communication, the tools of the trade must be studied and understood. Both the limitations and the reach of these tools must be considered to effectively communicate with the consumer. How can a marketer better ensure effective Web-based communications? List methods or actions that should improve your company's Web design performance. Write an e-mail to your interactive advertising agency to explore these areas.

A Web site can collect customer or project opinions; a strategic memo from the advertising agency might include these points:

From: Marketing Director
To: Advertising Agency
Subject: Effective Web-based Communications

In order for Web-based communications with our customers to be most effective, we would like to ensure the following methods are being properly explored. First it is imperative that each of our pages contain an e-mail link which allows for quick access to questions and feedback which should be easy to find and easy to use. This can be facilitated using a good Web-based form in conjunction with information on how to use more traditional channels such as our 1-800 number and postal mail. We may also wish to consider designing some form of Web-based, on-going discussion with those who are interested via a bulletin board, news group or a listserv. Methods for consumers to solicit customer service requests must be prominent and easy to use. The requests must be forwarded immediately to appropriate personnel and an initial reply should be automated which includes an estimated response time. In order to facilitate ease of use on our site, we need to ensure we have clear and appropriate navigation, a good site map would increase this effectively. These ideas are just starting points and we will be happy to entertain any additional ideas that you may find useful. Please get back to me with a response to these proposed methods and actions at your earliest convenience.

2. Why is HTML called "platform independent" and how is this important in marketing on the Internet? Be prepared to explain this concept in a class discussion.

HTML is written in plain text not a binary computer code. It does not need to be compiled for the computer to understand it and it is readable by humans. Because of this feature, it is possible for it to be platform independent. By platform independent, we mean that any computer can read the HTML files without having to convert it to a different form. An HTML file can be seen on a PC, a Macintosh, or a Unix machine without having to be in multiple formats. For marketing purposes this is important because you do not need to worry as much which platforms your audience is using and you need not create multiple versions of your site for different customers.

3. Over the years, browser manufacturers have declined in number. Today, the browser battle seems to be dwindling to two major players: Microsoft Internet Explorer and Netscape Navigator/Communicator. From a consumer standpoint, is this lack of competition healthy or unhealthy in the marketplace? Write an opinion in a proposed letter to the Federal Trade Commission on the subject of justifying your stand.

A well constructed support letter might contain these thoughts:

May 26, XXXX

Federal Trade Commission
123 ABC Drive
Washington, DC. 12345

Dear Sir or Madam:

In the last few years, the competition in the Web browser market has declined to the point that only two major players are still in the running, Microsoft Internet Explorer and Netscape Navigator/Communicator. Under normal circumstances, a non-competitive market such as this would be an unhealthy situation for consumers, as it would drive up prices and not offer additional choices. However, in my opinion, this is not the case in the current Web browser arena.

Considering that both browsers are currently being freely distributed, there is no supply and demand to drive the competition and pricing. Therefore, it is better for consumers to have fewer decisions to make and more standardization. This will reduce the learning curve and allow more users to get online easier and faster.

For the marketer, this improves the audience stability and allows for less testing of their sites. After looking at their site statistics, it will become clear that most of their users are using one of the two main browsers and they can simplify their design and testing accordingly.

Sincerely,

Shauna Schullo
Marketing Director, ABC Design

4. The Web is a picture window for consumers to compare one company to another and one offering to another. Go to the Web and find other companies that are similar to your company, supposing you own a company or work for one. How do their sites compare to your ideas? If you were a potential customer, what would be the content elements (such as price or store location convenience) that you would be looking for? Make a list of decision elements to compare and contrast two different companies in the same industry.

Students will choose varying sites depending on the company they have developed. Here is an example of decision elements placed on the home page of a business- to-business site such as the Xerox home page (www.xerox.com).

- a statement of mission for the page
- product photography or illustration; in this case, a rendering of the logotype
- a menu list of products or services hyperlinks
- a site map or other site navigation element
- an internal site search engine
- categories of hyperlinked information such as "News Room," "About Xerox," Get help fast," Search Worldwide", a search engine that combs Xerox resources worldwide. There can be myriad other information offerings or combination of these company or product features. They are arranged according to the importance the company places on these features.
- Another hyperlink is the option to "Order Online," a customer service for the busy executive purchasing agent.

For comparison of the Web pages, the Instructor might choose a competing company such as Canon (www.canon.co.jp.com) for copiers (www.photorealism.com) and other financial, information, or computer products or Mita, (www.mita.com) multi-product companies that also manufacture copiers. Both of these competitors organize their Web home pages as regions of the world with a hyperlinked globe.

5. In learning HTML, the marketer encounters many new terms that she should be familiar with; define in writing the following words or concepts:

Meta tag - This tag contains important information to those viewing its source and is used for search purposes. It can contain elements such as; NAME="name" which holds the name of the information, and CONTENT="content" which holds the actual content, such as a list of keywords for searching.

Stand alone tag - Stand alone tags do not need to be paired with a closing tag. A good example is a tag to create a line feed (<BR>). This tag would not need an ending because the computer needs only one command, go to the next line.
Container tag - Container tags need an ending tag to inform the computer it is OK to turn off what ever was turned on. A good example of this would be a tag to make text bold (<B>). If you only wanted a few words bold for emphasis, you would need to turn off the bold tag (/<B>) when you were ready for regular text again. Therefore, the text you want to have bolded is "contained" within the two parts of the container tag.

Site map - A structural representation of the Web site. This can be done using graphics or text. It provides the designer and the user with a "map" for navigating the site.

An Anchor tag (<A>) - The anchor tag is used to create a link or an anchor declaration. The best example is the code to create a hyperlink; (<A HREF="URL"> </A>) the first part of the tag contains the actual URL, everything between the opening and closing of an A tag is "clickable". Another example is a target; (TARGET="windowname") which loads a page into the frame of a window named windowname. The anchor declaration (<A HREF="#bookmark">) for same-page links created by linking a HREF using a # in the beginning of the name.

A .gif extension - The extension on a graphic image file, which has been saved in a gif format. This is one of two graphic formats that are common for use on the Web.

6. Address, in writing, the difference between <P> and <BR> tags. Define a <HR> tag. What is the purpose of the </HTML> tag? What is the difference between the <TR> and <TD> tag? What is the function of the tag, <HEAD>?

The paragraph tag (<P>) denotes the beginning of a paragraph. This tag adds one extra line of vertical space after the original line feed. Most browsers ignore the use of multiple paragraph tags to increase the amount of vertical space in a document.

The break tag (<BR>) inserts a break in the document. It is similar to a line break or carriage return in a word processor. Carriage returns are not recognized as line breaks on the screen in HTML unless the break tag is used. The break tag adds no additional vertical space after the break.

The <HR> tag uses a horizontal line to separate paragraphs of text. This tag places a fixed weight, shaded line across the width of the viewer. It does not require an ending tag and places a paragraph break before and after the line.

The </HTML> tag is the closing part of what is called an HTML container, meaning it contains information between two tags. It must be present at the end of the document in order to complete the HTML container code.

The main definition of a table in HTML is accomplished using the table row (<TR>) and table data (<TD>) tags. Each time a new row is needed in the table, the <TR> tag should be used. To separate cells, the <TD> tag should be used.

The <HEAD> tag defines the head section of the HTML document, which makes it searchable. Most good HTML documents contain a header that provides additional information to the browser. The Head section defines the function of the document and adds a quick reference for WWW browsers. Although information contained in the Head section is not visible to the consumer looking at your page, it supplies the document title and establishes a relationship between HTML documents and directories. It can also signal WWW browsers to index the document. The head section can be complicated, but it is an important piece in making sure your Web page will be found when people are looking. The head element encloses the head section. It is a container and therefore requires two tags, one at the beginning (<HEAD>) and one at the end (</HEAD>).

7. As more and more people access the Web, users of different physical capabilities are part of the population. How can a marketer's Web site accommodate persons with visual impairments or speech impairments? Write an e-mail to your human resources director suggesting how these accommodations will be beneficial to your company and its constituencies.

The information in this chapter has been expounded on in the answer to this question. Without additional information or directions to go out and find a more extensive answer, the student may provide only the information about the use of alt elements in the <img src> tag. The additional information is found in the new specifications for HTML 4.0.

****

From: Marketing Director
To: Human Resource Director
Subject: Access to our Web site for consumers with disabilities

In the United States, Title III of the Americans with Disabilities Act of 1990, a civil rights law for people with disabilities, states that all newly constructed places of public accommodation and commercial facilities must be accessible to individuals with disabilities to the extent that it is not structurally impracticable.

This has been well implemented in the physical world, but how are we to implement it in the virtual world? The Internet is no exception. It, too, should be a public space available to all. The people who write the specifications for HTML hope to make it universally accessible by making a few changes in the HTML specifications. In this e-mail I hope to explain how we can immediately implement some changes that will help and also how the HTML specifications are currently being altered to answer this problem for the future.

There are thousands of hardware and software products for computer users with physical disabilities. Yet, with current standards, it is not necessary to become an expert in assistive technologies to create an accessible Web site. All you have to do is one thing: make your documents navigable by textual browsers.

The majority of assistive technologies - screen readers, voice-recognition software, touchscreens, Braille readers, and speech synthesizers can read basic ASCII characters. This is due to the fact that most of these technologies were developed before the Graphical User Interface (GUI). So for the most part, these devices work well with HTML. At this time, the easiest way to make our pages work with a text-only browser is to use the alt element of the <img src> tag properly. Many people include alt text without thinking about what it's actually for and how we can begin to make our pages accessible.

To solve many of the challenges of universal access, those setting the standards are choosing to make HTML less about document presentation and more about document structure. This choice is leading not only to new tags but also to the "deprecation," of some features. The WAI went back over the HTML specifications and made recommendations for deprecating tags that function as visual layout tools, advising that style sheets be used for this purpose instead. Here are a few of the items being discussed for HTML 4.0 specifications, which would facilitate the use of the Web by those with disabilities.

- ACCESSKEY Increases navigation by allowing single keystroke manipulation rather than using the mouse.
- ID Provides information to screen readers about table heading and cells.
- SCOPE Similar to ID except explains an entire row, column or group of cells.
- AXIS Allows for potential queries of all labeled table data.
- OBJECT Cleaner way to provide textual descriptions of images, imagemaps instead of using the ALT tag.
- D-link An interim solution that allows a screen reader to surf from D to D to find out about the images.
- LONGDESC A better solution to replace the D-link. Will allow for long descriptions.

If this is not enough information for us to begin working on improving our site, you can find additional information in a workshop on HTML by WebMonkey. Just go to this site http://www.hotwired.com/Webmonkey/ and search for HTML and disabilities.

8. According to the text, every Web page should contain four elements. What are these four elements, and why is each important from either an information or marketing standpoint? Write a four-paragraph explanation to turn in to your instructor.

According to the text, there are four important tags containing important attributes that need to be included for the creation of good Web pages. These are a head section, a page title, a signature or contact information, and code comments. Below is a description of each of these components and why they are important from an information and marketing standpoint.

A head section of the HTML document makes Web pages searchable. It defines the function of the document and adds a quick reference for WWW browsers. Although information contained in the Head section is not visible to the consumer looking at your page, it supplies the document title and establishes a relationship between HTML documents and directories. It can also signal Web browsers to index the document. The head section can be complicated, but it is an important piece in making sure your Web page will be found when people are looking.

The title tag names your document by identifying a string of text that is the title of your page. This tag is interpreted differently by different platform browsers. Usually it is only seen in the title bar at the top of the window, so it should be brief. Meaningful titles should be used as they are what a user will see in his bookmark list when he saves the URL. Titles serve three major purposes of importance to marketing and information: titles are used by applications such as searches and indexes to identify pages, they act as indicators of what to expect, and titles are at the top of the HTML document giving you an easy visual clue when you need to make changes or corrections.

One of the most important elements is a prominent signature or contact information on each page. The signature allows the consumer to contact the company. A signature can be handled in many different ways. A Web page can list the contact information for the company, the contact information for the Web master, and/or the contact information for the page author. Whatever information is supplied should be easy for the consumer to find and use. One of the easiest ways to add a signature to a page is to have a hyperlink that will allow the consumer to send e-mail to someone responsible for answering question pertaining to the page and its contents.

Comments are important and all good programmers comment their code and so should everyone who writes HTML code. Comments allow for updating the code easier because you have left yourself notes and hints to work with in a few months when you have forgotten what you had in mind. A comment that you do not want the browser to show, but you would like to have in the source code for clarification can be placed between these codes.

9. As with most marketing materials, the more experienced Web designer will have accumulated more skills and tools in providing solutions to Web site or page designs. A more advanced designer might use tables and frames. What is the difference between the two elements, and what does each do for the appearance of a Web page? Prepare an outline to be orally delivered to a high school electronic graphics class.

Here are some guidelines that will lead in evaluating the answers students might provide to this question. There are other possibilities, but these are some of the main points that should be covered.

I) Tables
- a) Organize and format content
- b) Made up of rows and cells
- c) Easy to use and are often used for formatting and layout of content
- d) Move with the page when user scrolls
- e) Widely accepted as a standard in most browsers

II) Frames
- a) Organizes content and navigation
- b) Separate page content can be used in each frame
- c) Often used for navigational purposes
  - i) Can call new content to a different frame on the page using navigation
  - ii) Remains stationary when user scrolls main page
- d) Harder to understand and code properly
- e) Beginning to be widely accepted as a standard in browsers but not as much as tables

10. This chapter discussed learning the basics of HTML editing and compared this knowledge to learning an alphabet to create words and sentences for communications. HTML editors that "automatically" format typed sentences into HTML code have also been described. Why is it advised for the marketer, designer, or even the viewer, to learn the basic tags, attributes, functions, or other conventions of HTML rather than rely solely on an HTML editor? What are the benefits of understanding HTML code? Be prepared to discuss this question in class.

HTML editors provide a familiar document interface with menu options and button bars inserting HTML tags at your command. They are useful tools for creating HTML documents with little or no knowledge of HTML tags or elements. However, they seldom create clean HTML code and often leave things looking not quite like you had planned. For this reason, it is important to know how to fix what the editor messes up. If you are familiar with the HTML code, you may be able to get the exact effect you are looking for in a much shorter amount of time. Learning HTML can also allow you the freedom to create Web pages with very limited resources. All you need is a computer and a basic text editor such as Notepad or SimpleText and you are on your way to great Web pages.

Chapter 12
Capturing Customer Profiles and Data Management

Chapter Summary

Marketing has come full circle, from personal service provided by small village shops of centuries ago through the recent apathetic world of mass media and merchandising. The new information age has allowed the completion of this cycle by encouraging a highly personalized, one customer relationship at a time outlook. It is to the advantage of the marketer to learn about customer data collection, database storage, and customer data retrieval to out-service the competition. This chapter will take a look at these concepts and discuss the new marketing technologies involved in database management.

The business of data management is viewed from the perspective of marketing and business in general, laying down a foundation that can be built upon. The collection of data and the necessary thought process for developing a useful database is covered and includes issues of transactional databases, compiled databases and proprietary databases.

The next section covers the aspects necessary to build a database for the use of marketing. What software is necessary? Which type is available? Explanations of each part of a database will be reviewed with discussion on the use and significance of each piece in the overall puzzle of data management.

Lastly, step by step instructions for building a database in Microsoft Access are provided. This instructional process should make it possible for students to construct their own Access database for the purposes of the course marketing project.

Core Concepts

- To introduce the marketing database and its importance in organizing the characteristics of market segments
- To demonstrate how a database can be constructed using Microsoft Access software
- To plan and build a simple marketing-oriented database using Access

Chapter Outline

I. Keeping the Data House in Order is Critical to Database Development and Management
    A. Good marketing programs are built around good information, and good information is collected, categorized, and saved for future analysis and usage
        1. Databases are formed from purchase transactions and possibly, customer surveys
        2. Databases can be searched by people or computers
        3. The marketer should never underestimate the value of data collection
    B. Businesses began to formulate their database system in the late sixties and early seventies, and what was very complex at the time, in the nineties become much more manageable, quicker to sort and retrieve, and more powerful
    C. Database structure
        1. Every item has a record within the database
        2. These data are then linked in a hierarchical manner to the top of the table
        3. The table is the main entity within a database that holds the fields and records of the database
    D. The conceptual elements of database design
        1. Data
        2. Technology
        3. Research technique
    E. Once the database application is developed, the ongoing communications program to query current customers or prospective ones can be initiated

(2)

II. Measuring the Value of the Database
   A. Accountability can be derived by giving specific attention to the data within any database
   B. Customized products, new distribution and communications channels, and multiple pricing options will drive 70% of enterprises to reengineer and automate their marketing process
   C. Already traditional metrics are proving inadequate in measuring marketing activities across multiple-product categories, diverse placement channels, and constantly changing retailer discount and consumer sale price points
   D. New fact-based metrics will let enterprises dynamically allocate marketing resources to the activities with the best return on investment (ROI)
   E. Technology and automation will be the key in managing these new marketing processes
   F. Vast amount of detailed data that must be collected and analyzed to make effective decisions in this environment will task information systems

III. Building a Transactional Database
   A. The best database for e-commerce is the transactional database, which is assembled by on ongoing transaction with customers
   B. With a transactional database that has an enabled or linked data capture system, a marketer's company is able to keep track of customers' transactions or purchases
   C. The transactional database is considered superior to public databases because the customer is already buying from the marketer's company

IV. The Compiled Database
   A. The marketer may opt to use a compiled database, which is a collection of public records such as drivers' licenses, birth records, hunting and fishing licenses, automobile registrations, or marriage licenses
   B. The marketer should decide how the company's database is to be assembled:
      1. Compiling customers' profiles by demographic and geographic information
      2. Compiling preferences by psychographic profiles
      3. Creating a proprietary database from the data of the company's activities with either consumer or business-to-business customers
         a. Return of warranty cards
         b. E-mail inquiries
         c. Customer service data input
   C. As a plan for data management, the design of the tracking system must be considered as well

V. Designing a Proprietary Marketing Database
   A. The marketer is wise to have a system input from other departments, which might be integrated into the customer or prospect databases
   B. The importance of integrating special data collection features in the planning stages will make the system development a much smoother, "no-surprises" production
   C. These questions, "who, what, when, where, and why" form the basis for all database ventures
   D. At the planning stage, thought should be given to the report formats that are derived from the data collection
      1. What are the important figures that drive the marketer's department?
      2. What is the measurement of consequence?
      3. What are different expectations of efficiency?

VI. Software Systems for Traffic Measurement to Web Sites
   A. As other components of the marketing process are measured, so should the performance of a Web site for attracting viewers and encouraging longer visits to the site
   B. There are several areas of accountability that bring objectives and results into better focus
      1. Counting unique visits (one person one visit)
      2. The number of hyperlinks visited
      3. Recording the domain extension of the visitor (.com, .edu, .gov, so forth)
      4. Keeping track of hourly, daily, and monthly visits
   C. Key Web marketing terms:

1. “Hit” is a request for a file
2. “Visitors” are the number of unique persons accessing a site
3. “Session” is a series of uninterrupted mouse clicks from a visitor

D. Like frequent customers, a repeat visitor is probably more valuable to the site

E. Ways to estimate visitors:
1. Issue “cookies”
2. Require session identification
3. Registrations
4. Statistical software packages try to filter the true numbers of page views
5. Clickstream and analysis

VII. A Quick Overview of Database Definitions

A. A database is a collection of information related to a particular subject or purpose and data can be:
1. Stored
2. Manipulated
3. Used in many ways

B. A database file is simply a container for your data with many small partitions dividing it into logical parts

C. To store your data logically, one table for each type of information you wish to track should be created
1. The first step in the process is to define relationships between your tables
2. You can create queries, forms, and reports to display information from several tables at once
   a. A form, report, or query may include information from any number of tables

D. What exactly does “relational” mean and how does it work?
1. A relationship works by matching data in key fields with the same name
2. Matching fields are the “primary key” from one table, which provides a unique identifier for each record, and a “foreign key” in the other table

E. Type of data relationships:
1. One-to-many relationship
2. Many-to-many relationships

VIII. Understanding the Database Elements

A. A table is a collection of data about a specific topic, such as products or suppliers
1. Tables organize data into columns, which are called fields and rows that are known as records

B. You can use forms for a variety of purposes
1. Create a switch-board or starting form opt open other forms or reports
2. Create a data entry form to enter data into a table
3. Create a custom dialog box to accept user input, then carry out an action based on that input

C. Parameters that will be stored in the form’s design rather than a table
1. Descriptive text
2. Graphic elements
3. Expressions for calculations

D. Items stored in an underlying record source are your data

E. Forms can be divided into sections to increase the effectiveness
1. Detail section
2. Form header
3. Page header
4. Page footer
5. Form footer section
6. Sections in a sub-forms, or forms within forms

F. Tips on gathering information over the Internet
1. Limit information requests to a form that can be completed in three to five minutes
2. Do not ask for information that requires the user to leave her workstation

3. Limit response options per question
4. Use open-ended questions when quantitative response measurements are not necessary
5. Build in questions that separate surfers from customers and prospects

G. Queries are the most mysterious of the database elements
1. You can use queries to view change, and analyze data in many different ways
2. They can also be the source of records for forms and reports
3. The most common type of query is a select query, that retrieves data from one or more table using criteria you specify and then displays it in the order you want
4. Queries are created using a wizard or are created from scratch in a query design view
5. A join line tells your database program how data in one table or query relates to data in another query or table
6. Another type of query is a crosstab query

H. A report is an effective way to present your data in a printed format
1. The information in a report comes from an underlying table, query, or SQL (Select Query Language) statement, which is the source of the report's data
2. Reports can be customized in the same manner as forms
3. Each section has a specific purpose and prints in a predictable order on the page in the report
   a. Report header
   b. Page header
   c. Detail section
   d. Page footer
   e. Report footer

IX. Database Design

A. A good design is the foundation for creating a database that accomplishes your goals effectively, accurately, and efficiently

B. The seven basic steps in designing a database are:
1. Establish the purpose of your database
2. Decide what tables you need in the database to accomplish this task
3. Determine what data will be collected and placed as fields in your tables
4. Identify these fields with unique values
5. Determine how the table will relate to each other, review and refine your design to be sure it accomplishes the goals in step1
6. Enter a sampling of data and create any other database objects that are needed
7. Design and implement your interfaces using forms, reports, and queries to make the database easy to use and productive

X. Creating a Database in Microsoft Access

Teaching Suggestions

Using a database software package such as Microsoft® Access has served well for almost three years in my Electronic Marketing course because it is widely used and is part of the Office 97 Suite that many students own or have access to in their computer labs. If the instructor is unfamiliar or rusty using the Access program, perhaps a guest instructor can be secured to teach this two-session class. If your institution has a business technology staff, or an Academic Computing department, these may be good sources for the guest speaker. I have gone into the business community to secure qualified speakers depending on their area of expertise. All speakers are pleased to help and have exposure to college classes. Some are interested in knowing what is being taught at the university; others consider the session as a recruiting opportunity for their own firms.

I typically use a scenario of creating a database for a video rental store. The demonstration includes planning the database (such as names, addresses, payment, credit card expiration date, genre of movie usually rented, etc.) to allow for about 12 to 15 profile characteristics. Field characteristics are decided and the database is constructed. The session ends with a demonstration of how the query operation is performed.

It is important for the student to have an understanding of building a marketing database. We will discuss customer identification further in Chapter 13, the overview of customer service communications. The better the marketer understand various market segments, the better marketing programs will perform.

Answers to Questions and Exercises

1. Perhaps your company is very small with few, but very active, customers. You have analyzed the electronic database method, but you feel that it will be too costly and time consuming to track your customers via an Access database. What would be your alternative keeping accurate records on your customers' purchases and preferences? Make a list of the types of data that you feel is important for ongoing customer knowledge and how you would record this information. Direct your list to your purchasing or inventory staff in a memo form.

As quoted from the textbook - unless you are selling a single low price, low usage product with very limited LCV, your company can and should make full use of the database a vital of your sales strategy. A fictitious memo could read:

INTEROFFICE MEMO

To: Purchasing Staff
From: Marketing Manager
Date: May 31, XXXX
Subject: Important Data Collection Types

Below you will find a list of data types that are important to our on-going customer knowledge. Please review the list and be prepared to discuss it at our next staff meeting. The purpose of this list is to brainstorm on ideas for collecting the information we need to keep up our customer knowledge. On that note, you will also find some preliminary ideas on ways that this information can be collected and organized within our company.

Contact information: name, address, phone, email, fax

Household Information: household income, household decision maker, household purchase maker, number of children, age of members of household pets, etc.

Personal Preferences and Purchasing history: number of times customer has contacted company, number of times customer has ordered, types of products customer orders, most Recent order information to be flagged if not recent, are coupons used or products purchased when on sale? Is there a buying habit of purchasing when there is no particular promotion is going on, is their a particular promotion that they purchase on repeatedly?

If there is ever too small a company to use a database system to collect important information on customers, then here are some alternatives that might be possible in the interim: a simple web counter, a spreadsheet system (ie. Excel), a book keeping software (ie. Quick Books), and lists of customer information that can be used for mail merges and searched.

2. Different businesses use the database function for different purposes. Make a list of twenty business or industries and speculate what each would use database management for. Compare your list to other members of your group.

Below you will find a list of suggestions for results to this question. Students answers will vary and there are few incorrect answers. Databases have a wide variety of uses in many different industries and business.

Retail industry

Video rental
- $ Tracking sales and inventory, promotional marketing, customer database

Clothing store
- $ Tracking sales and inventory, promotional marketing, customer database, on-line order requests and processing, on-line catalog (ie. Nordstrums.com)

Record store
- $ Tracking sales and inventory, promotional marketing, customer database

Bookstore
- $ Tracking sales and inventory, promotional marketing, customer database

- $ On-line sales
- $ On-line searchable catalog (ie. Amazon.com)

Grocery Store
- $ Tracking sales and inventory, promotional marketing, customer database
- $ Coupon matching for purchases

Automobile Dealer
- $ Building your perfect car (ie. Saturn.com)
- $ Tracking sales and inventory, promotional marketing, customer database

Computer Sales
- $ Tracking sales and inventory, promotional marketing, customer database
- $ Purchase options and technical support via the Internet (ie. Dell.com)

Wholesale Industry

Computer Sales
- $ Contract pricing
- $ Sales force training and communication
- $ Inventory control
- $ Information for sales force

Grocery Wholesaler
- $ Market research
- $ Customer research
- $ Customer Service (ie. nabisco.com, kraftfoods.com)

Automobile Wholesaler
- $ Market research (ie. volskwagen.com)
- $ Customer database
- $ Customer service
- $ Problems database

Services Industry
- $ Technical Support
- $ Consulting
- $ Marketing

Education
- $ Registration
- $ Recruitment
- $ On-line Courses

Organizations
- $ Information
- $ Recruitment
- $ Sales

Governmental
- $ Data warehousing
- $ Public Awareness
- $ Governmental Documentation

3. What is the difference between transactional and relational databases? Define the two and give examples of the usage of each one. What types of businesses would use one or the other, or both? Prepare a memo on the concept for submission to a retail client you are servicing.

Relational Database -database in which data is stored in multiple tables, these tables then relate to one another to make up the entire database. The basic collection of data in a relational database is usually represented as a rectangular array of data, in which each row is a collection of data about one entity. This database is designed to alleviate redundancy and collect related data. An example of a relational database would be a product catalog, ordering and inventory system in which data can be pulled from multiple tables to represent the order and inventory process.

Transactional Database database that changes as each transaction occurs. A real time database in which the fundamental unit of change; the real-life event, is modeled by the changes to the database. For example a transactional database could track the type of condiments that the patron of Pizza Hut orders on his pizza, which location he buys from, and the time or day of the week. Or this consumer might be purchasing sporting goods, and the company marketing manager may be preparing a profile of

persons who buy scuba and other water sports equipment.

Most supplier or wholesaler type companies would probably use a relational database rather than a transactional database. Those dealing with consumers such as retail or service companies may benefit more from a transactional database, but they could also use a relational database for much of their data collection and management.

4. What is the difference between many-to-many database relationships and one-to-many database relationships? What types of businesses or suppliers would use one or the other? Write an e-mail to your instructor defining the concepts.

Many-to-many relationship -One or more rows in one relation may be related to one or more rows in a second relation by a common value of a join attribute. This implies that each value of the join attribute may appear any number of times in either table or in both. This type of relationship is only possible by defining a third table (called a junction table) whose primary key consists of two foreign keys from both Tables. Therefore, a many-to-many relationship is really two one-to-many relationships with a third table. Many-to-many relationships are not used frequently, however one could use a many to many relationship to create an Order Details Table. To do this, an Orders table and a Products table can have a many-to-many relationship that's defined by creating two one-to-many relationships in the Order Details table.

One-to-many relationship - Exactly one row in one relation is related by a common join attribute to many rows in another relation. This implies that each value of the join attribute is unique in the first relation but not necessarily unique in the second.

Most databases are based on one-to-many relationships. An example is a customer order database where a customer has *one* set of personal information in one table yet can make *many* purchases which are recorded in the order table.

5. Define in writing the following words or concepts:

All the words or concepts discussed here are defined in the glossary at the back of the book. However, students should be given the leeway to define them on their own as long as the basic concept is grasped.

6. Define in writing the following words or concepts:

All the words or concepts discussed here are defined in the glossary at the back of the book. However, students should be given the lea way to define them on their own as long as the basic concept is grasped.

7. What is the definition of a "primary key"? The definition of a "foreign key"? Write an explanation of the two and how each would be used in database activities.

Primary or Unique key -The mandatory column or columns used to enforce the uniqueness of rows in a table. This is normally the most frequent means by which rows are accessed. While primarily referring to tables, Primary Keys can also pertain to entities and help maintain referential integrity. This is normally the most frequent means by which rows are accessed.

Foreign key - One or more columns in a table whose values must match the values in the primary key of the referenced table. The columns in the foreign key typically reference the primary key of another table but may reference the same table. This mechanism allows two tables to be joined together.

An example of how these work is provided in the chapter. The example talks about the relationship a product from the product table with an order from the order table. Another likely example would be the relationship between a customer order with the customer's information. Each answer should contain a schema similar to this: A customer number is the primary key in the customer table and a foreign key in the order table. This allows each customer's order in the order table to be connected to the customer's information in the customer table.

8. Microsoft Access is very flexible in the implementation of database design; there are several ways to perform the same function, such as designing a table. What are the four ways to create a blank (empty) table in Access? List and explain the four methods.

-Use the Database Wizard. This is a completely automatic process that asks a few questions and creates all the tables, forms, and reports required for an entire database., but it can not be used to add tables, etc. to an existing database.

- **Use the Table Wizard.** This method allows you to choose the fields for your table from a variety of predefined tables such as business contacts, household inventory, or medical records.
- **Enter data directly into a blank data sheet.** A more flexible method, but not quite as easy an approach. When you save the new data sheet, Microsoft Access will analyze your data and automatically assign the appropriate data type and format for each field
- **Use design view to specify all of your table details from scratch**. Regardless of which method you choose to create a table, you can always use table Design View at any time to customize your table further with options such as adding new fields, setting default values, or creating input masks.

9. The text discussed two major ways for designing and executing a database table, either using a Design Wizard or creating it from scratch. Explain the differences between these two methods. In what situations is the marketer better served from one or the other method? Give examples of business situation that apply to each. Be prepared to discuss this design concept in class.

Using Design View. The good thing about Design View is that Access will help you. Access assigns data types to each field (column) based on the kind of data you entered. If you want to customize a field's definition further, for example, to change its data type, or define a validation rule, you need to use Design view. In addition to renaming and inserting columns, you can delete or reorder columns at any time, before or after saving your new data sheet. However, you can not enter your data in the Design View. This view might be used to set up your initial database design or to make changes in the format of the columns. It is a good starting point for database design.

Using the DataSheet View or from Ascratch. You can also use the DataSheet View to design your database tables (it is a bit harder). Here you are required to determine what type of data you are going to enter beforehand and how it is to be formatted. This works like a spreadsheet where you need to name your columns and enter your data. The main difference is that this is not as easy to use for formatting your design, but this is a good place for the marketer to enter data directly in the database. Another solution would be to create a data entry form. Data entered into the DataSheet View is similar to entering data in a spreadsheet, but calculations would need to be setup in the Design View.

10. Using the suggestions developed by the text and help screens in Microsoft Access, prepare a simple marketing database for a video rental store. What would you as a marketing manager wish to know about your customers' characteristics. Make a table of twelve to fifteen personal items (first name, last name, street address and so forth) that could be unique to each customer. Create the table and enter six real or fictitious persons. Print the database and turn it in to you instructor. If you need assistance, call the computing department at your University or perhaps the help lab at your business school for more information on Microsoft Access.

Below you will find an example (not a print out) of a resulting table from an Access Database for a Video Rental Store. It contains the personal information of six fictitious customers. Students will of course have many different variations on this table, but this is a good start. If desired, this section could be enhanced by requiring students to create a report highlighting this data.

#	First	Last	Address	City	State	Zip	Phone	e-mail	Fax	Preference	Age	Kids Age	Marital Status
1	Jane	Doe	123 ABC St.	Walla Walla	WA	99362	(509) 123-4568	jdoe@mom.com	5091234563	Childrens	35	2, 6, 10	Divorced
2	John	Smith	2732 Baker	Walla Walla	WA	99361	(509) 234-5678	jsmith@dad.com	5092345673	Educational	54	10, 15	Married
3	Happy	Gilmore	120 Hanover Sq.	Walla Walla	WA	99362	(508) 567-8932	gilmore@comedyhouse.com	5085678932	Comedy	23		Single
4	Lucy	Ball	12 Orchestra Terrace	Walla Walla	WA	99363	(509) 546-7894	lucy@laughs.com	5095467845	Comedy	60	25	Married
5	Daniel	Boone	89 Chiaroscuro Rd.	Walla Walla	WA	99362	(508) 456-1234	boone@adventures.org	5084561235	Adventure	40		Single
6	Humphrey	Bogart	P.O. Box 555	Walla Walla	WA	99360	(507) 654-9873	bogart@kid.edu	5076549871	Drama	80		Divorced

Chapter 13
Considerations for Ongoing Customer Communications

Chapter Summary

Customer service aims to assist the customer in receiving the ultimate product utility and satisfaction. In this process, the marketer must know how and when to act by improving service delivery, by introducing new products or services, and by monitoring customer communications. Several methods can be employed to communicate with the customer. As we have discussed in many chapters of this book, electronic marketing tools are well suited to provide timely and accurate information to the marketer to promote a better customer-company relationship. In this chapter, the basic premises of monitoring customer services as well as Web-enabled instruments and their construction using an HTML editor have been discussed. Surveys, forms, polls, and similar reporting devices can be built into Web sites. This information is provided directly by the consumer of the services or products without filters to modify the meaning and urgency of reform. Excellent customer service programs enhance repeat purchasing as recurring revenues are the most profitable of all commerce, electronic or otherwise.

This chapter will discuss the value of repeat customers and how marketers can help create an atmosphere that will encourage them to come back. Issues of good customer service programs will be examined and examples provided to drive the lesson home. Intertwined with customer service is customer communication, which plays a major role in the image a company portrays. We will look at some of the issues surrounding customer communication, electronic customer service programs, and feedback provided by and to the customer.

The chapter will also delve into the realm of delivery services as a high priority in maintaining a positive company reputation and repeat business. How to make this work in the new era of fast paced electronic communication is examined and new tools are discussed to make it easier to track these issues. The process of creating a Web based form and how it works will help to bring the concepts discussed in this chapter to fruition. The instructional aim is learning to create forms for the Web links customer communication and feedback with marketing and the Internet in a way that will prove useful to the student in the real world.

Core Concepts

- To demonstrate how the Web can be used to facilitate customer service
- To present techniques to encourage customer response, the two-way communications benefit of the Web
- To show how HTML can be used to construct customer and prospect survey instruments

Chapter Outline

I. The Value of Repeat Customers
   - A. Retailers and wholesalers along with their suppliers are looking for new customers and trying to determine what these new customers like
   - B. It is the retailer or service's responsibility to produce products and services attractive to a niche market and then retain these customers through product satisfaction and customer service
   - C. Marketers should consider spending a fraction of this amount to satisfy and enhance the goods' performance and services' delivery to past customers who are satisfied with the product or service
   - D. Electronic marketing provides excellent tools for focusing efforts on fewer persons, attempting to achieve a mutually beneficial relationship
   - E. The Web's capabilities can:
     1. Be programmed to deliver gratitude
     2. Congratulations
     3. Confirmations to existing clients
     4. Provide technical support for new product users
     5. Conduct surveys inquiring what changes the customer would like to see

6. Expand communications to outside suppliers and the general community
7. Supply associates with the latest company news first

II. Where Do You Stand?
A. It is best to learn what customers think about a product or service before the marketer launches new, ambitious customer service programs
B. The Web is well suited for conducting prospect and customer, supplier, and ex-customer opinions
C. Many companies today strive for value-added customer service strategy
D. Electronic marketing tools allow the customer extensive knowledge about a product or about a company through information on a company's Web site or through hyperlinks on the Web site
E. The marketer should develop a full customer service plan and test it before putting it on the company's Web page
F. Customer response or opinion polls can be conducted on Web sites or by e-mail to determine advantages or disadvantages of the performance of an existing product's Web site to gain feedback on proposed new product concepts
G. Companies are finding substantial cost savings in information transfer between offices that have heavy paperwork involving high sales volume tied to customer service records
H. Companies with extensive human resources records also benefit from electronic tools

III. Should It Be Called Customer Communications?
A. The value of positive customer communications is glaringly apparent from this consumer research finding
1. Two-thirds of the reasons for the customer displeasure were breakdowns in communications
2. One-third was attributable to actual product failure or poor service
B. Customer relationships are vital for long-term benefits of both parties, and never before has customer communications been as expedited and rich as with today's electronic vehicles
C. Studies have shown that dissatisfied customers will tell at least ten other people about their bad experience (which, of course, is bad advertising for the company)
D. However, with the Internet, that figure could potentially be multiplied by thousands
E. Sites should develop or utilize some form of "auto-knowledge" features that responds to all incoming reports stating that the question was received and estimates a time frame for how long it will take to respond to the question
F. It is the marketer's job, therefore, to initiate, nurture, and improve the customer service process

IV. Establishing the Electronic Customer Service Program
A. You might begin establishing your electronic customer service program by asking yourself, "How would I like to be treated if I were the customer?"
B. You might then investigate competitor's customer service pages and programs, particularly the successful competitors

V. Evaluating the Sources of Feedback
A. In any plan for commerce, online or traditional, these "listening posts" must be identified and ranked so that appropriate communications mechanisms can be set to gather opinions-positive and negative
1. Source 1: Customer complaints
2. Source 2: Direct customer contact
3. Source 3: Your own e-mail
4. Source 4: The formal customer survey
5. Source 5: Suppliers and manufacturers
6. Source 6: Employee and associates sessions
7. Source 7: Your neighborhood
8. Source 8: Community involvement
9. Source 9: The online community involvement
B. Delivering services as the number one priority
C. Sometimes the only concrete proof of an e-commerce firm is its performance in customer service

D. In organizing a customer service program, two ingredients create a winning program
   1. First, the marketer must insist on hiring excellent representatives
   2. Secondly, superior training of these representatives must be undertaken
E. These two steps can be followed up with the other portions of the customer service program:
   1. Setting standards for customer service
   2. Time-lapse elements
   3. Activities schedule to solve problems

VI. Make Web Forms
A. Forms are one of the most popular features on the Web for conducting business
   1. They can add a flexible dimension of interactivity to your Web documents by allowing you to conduct surveys, take orders, sign up users, gather feedback, even administer tests
   2. Forms can be very simple or highly complex
B. A form is a graphical user interface that uses text entry fields and areas, buttons, check boxes, pull-down menus, scrolling lists, and other specialized graphics
C. The ACTIONS attribute, points the form to a URL that will accept the form's information and do something with it
D. The form script is typically called a CGI (Community Gateway Interface) script or a CGI program
E. The CGI script performs some manipulations of the data and composes a response that is typically sent back to the user's browser as an HTML page
F. The METHOD attribute tells the form how to send its information back to the script
   1. The most common type of method is POST, which sends all the information from the form separately from the URL
   2. The other option for METHOD is GET, which tracks the information from the form to the end of the URL
G. INPUT is single tag option for gathering information
H. Different input types can vary so much and are so important to creating the perfect form
   1. Most input types require a NAME attribute that sets a unique name for the information being passed to the server
   2. Input tags also use the VALUE attribute to assign an original or default value to the input
   3. TEXT type displays a simple line of text
   4. TEXT can use the LENGTH attribute to specify how many characters will show in the input box
   5. MAXLENGTH can limit the number of characters that can be entered by the users
   6. The VALUE option would be used to provide text present in the field initially
   7. The PASSWORD type is a modified text field displaying bullets instead of the characters actually typed
   8. The HIDDEN type attribute uses NAME and VALUE
   9. The CHECKBOX type is a valuable resource for surveys and order forms
   10. Radio buttons are grouped together using the NAME option
   11. FILE type provides a file upload feature
       a. The FILE type uses the NAME, VALUE, ACCEPT, and DISABLE attributes
   12. The IMAGE type is used to create an image-based button
   13. The SRC attribute tells the browser where it can find the source image file for the button similar to the SRC attribute in the IMG tag
   14. The ALT attribute provides a textual alternative to the image in case the user does not have a graphical browser
   15. ALIGN can be used to control how the image is aligned on the page
   16. USEMAP can be used as it is in a regular image map
   17. DISABLED will disable the button
   18. The VALUE attribute specifies the text that will be on the button face
   19. The ONCLICK attribute is set equal to the name of the script to be executed
   20. The SUBMIT type displays a push button with the present function of sending data from the form to the server
   21. VALUE can be used to change the text on the button

22. The RESET type displays a push button with the present function of clearing data from the form to the original values
23. VALUE can be used to change the text on the button
24. If DISABLED is used, the buttons will be turned off
25. TEXTAREA tag allows you to provide an area for multiple-line text entry
26. The SELECT tag shows a list of choices in either a pop-up menu or a scrollable list

VII. How to Make CGI Scripts Work
   A. For the forms that you create to work, each must have an accompanying script or small program that deals with the information to and from the form
   B. This script is placed in a cgi-bin directory on the Web server
   C. A script for forms is usually created in a programming language
   D. Your script and your form must match up in order for the script to handle the information the form is passing

Teaching Suggestions

The learning material in this chapter, the presentation of forms and surveys, involves specialized knowledge in advance HTML. The Instructor might again want to call upon an Academic Trainer to lead the class. The online output is the creation and implementation of forms for customer service or product ordering and covers form elements such as dropdown lists, radio buttons, check boxes, and dialog boxes for customer input. Forms tags and other response elements are built from HTML, and the students are much more familiar now with the language. Students ask if they are allowed to use HTML editors that are included in Netscape Navigator® and Microsoft Explorer® browsers. My response is affirmative because at this point in the electronic marketing course, the student should be comfortable with computer and browser operation. The "alphabet" of HTML should have been learned, and browser editors save the composer much time.

If the student group has been keeping up with the assignments, many assignments can be applied to their project. The simple construction of the demonstration Web site can be expanded to accommodate their product or service, and other hands-on class lectures such as the database collection plan and form and this lecture, forms design for customer service response and online ordering, produces elements applicable to the project. There may be time for the trainer to cover the topics of colors, tables, frames, sound, or video clips inclusion. Most of these topics will be used by a Web master in implementing a professional Web site.

The Instructor might inquire about his/her institution's training capabilities for after class hours tutoring or expansion of Web and HTML capabilities. At our library, the trainers schedule classes in basic and advanced HTML, tables, forms, frames, and colors that the students eagerly attend. I award extra credit for attending these after hours classes because this additional learning will drill the concepts and lead to a better group project.

Answers to Questions and Exercises

1. In your opinion, what is the most effective way to deliver responsive customer service? What is the most inefficient way? Compare the advantages and disadvantages of each method. Write and outline of your thoughts to your customer service manager.

The answers to this question may vary since the opinions of the students may vary, however, one good answer to this question might come in the following form.

In the many opinions of customer service experts, " Self Service Customer Service via the Web" can be additionally supported by e-mail or phone customer service options if the volume of contact is extremely high (ie. www.ford.com and www.americanexpress.com), is currently the most effective way to deliver responsive customer service. Here are some of the elements that a responsive customer communications service might contain. Communications in a timely manner is the key to good customer service.

Features/advantages

$ Searchable company information on the Web

- $ Searchable product information on the Web
- $ Web site coupled with telephone sales or online sales
- $ E-mail contact points for questions and solutions that entail immediate auto-responders and minimal response times for actual feedback to the customer.
- $ Including additional methods of contacting telephone and postal mail with a supporting customer database

The least effective way is by offering only one customer service approach. Today people do not want to wait for answers, or be on hold, or even worse to leave a telephone message in an unfamiliar voice mailbox. The customer never knows if the message is received or acted upon.

2. Describe the various benefits of a strong, consumer-oriented customer service program as a strategy to build a program of relationship marketing? Write an e-mail of suggestions to your customer service manager in London.

A strong customer-oriented service program can create relationships with longevity if they are correctly designed. The most promising customer service program will encourage positive word of mouth "advertising," provide a good company or product image, as well as boost brand loyalty. The following is an example of an e-mail that a student might write in response to this question.

To: Customer Service Manager
From: Marketing Manager
Subject: Customer-Oriented Service Program

John,

Here are just a few ideas that I think might help to enhance our customer service program and provide our company with a stronger customer-oriented approach. As you know, this would help to enhance our customer relationships and hopefully increase our image and our profits. Communications in a timely manner is the key to good customer service. How can we achieve this?

I think we need to implement more customer communication options on our Web site. Here are a few ideas to get us started:

- $ A searchable *About Our Company* page providing useful information for consumers about our company including contact information both via the Internet and via the regular channels.
- $ A more useable *Product information* site that allow customers to search for product information and order online, by e-mail or by telephone.
- $ A formal customer survey should be part of our Web site to poll our customers' opinions and suggestions.
- $ E-mail contact points for questions and solutions. These should have a way of automatically responding to the customer with information on how long a customer may have to wait before getting an answer.
- $ Make it a very high priority that each customer contact is responded to in a minimal time frame. We do not want to leave them hanging long, or they may go elsewhere. I would say no more than 24 hours if possible should be our goal here. This should be achievable with our e-mail capabilities.
- $ For those visiting our site with no desire for electronic communication, there should be an outlet for human contact. This would route them to our existing communication resources of telephone or postal mail which will have a lighter load and can be more responsive.
- $ All the above customer-company transactions should be recorded in the customer database for us to review when making additional improvements to the system.

Let me know what your thoughts and ideas are on this subject.

3. Does automated response and robot e-mail systems constitute a workable customer service program? Do they represent a responsive customer service program? Do they deliver a gratifying customer service program? Write a memo justifying the aspects of each system consequence, workable versus responsive versus gratifying customer service experience.

INTEROFFICE MEMO
To: Customer Service Manager
From: Marketing Manager
Date: May 31, XXXX
Subject: Automated response and robot e-mail systems

Jan,

The following is a short exposition on how I think automated response systems would be useful in our customer service organization. Please review the material and let's discuss at your earliest convenience.

In my opinion, automated response and robot e-mail systems cannot make a workable customer service program on their own. However, they can make a difference in how our customer service program works. In order for automatic responses to help with the customers we service via the Web, it is necessary to couple these quick response tools with timely follow-up making the customers feelings that they are being heard.

These types of systems are only a starting point for a workable system that provides a certain aspect of responsiveness. They make the customer feel that at least their question is being reviewed and someone will be getting back to them. It is similar to letting them know where they stand in the telephone system backlog instead of just saying "all operators are currently busy; please hold."

The automated systems will not produce customer gratification. In order to provide customer gratification, communication will need to be efficient, problems will need to be solved, and answers will need to be provided in all situations. This is the way we can create the atmosphere for repeat and satisfied customers. In order to have a workable, responsive and gratifying system, all possible communication channels should be open and well designed.

4. As electronic customer service becomes more widespread, the capabilities of this electronic marketing resource are also becoming more flexible. Its benefits are primarily speed, accuracy and convenience. Which of these three benefits do you consider most important in serving your customer groups? Be prepared to justify your opinion in a class discussion.

The main goal of this question is to have the students realize that the answer depends on their customer group. The decision on customer service standards should come from...who else? The marketer's customers. They should dictate what their expectations on timing or accuracy should be. They need to look at their market audience and determine which benefit the customer is looking for. This answer will need to be evaluated on an individual basis depending on the market…some will demand speed to match their busy lives. Some will be looking for accuracy such as banking services. Others will search for convenience as in home delivery of dry cleaning. There is not one answer to fit all audiences.

5. Define in writing the following words or concepts:

a.) Natural language understanding - An artificial intelligence computer program designed for understanding human languages through speech recognition, written input, and other methods.

b.) robots - A program that automatically explores the World Wide Web by retrieving a document and recursively retrieving some or all the documents that are referenced in it. See also crawler, or spider. Robot shipping agents are a form of robots that can perform shipping functions.

c.) cgi-bin - The directory on the server where most system administrators keep CGI scripts. This directory is usually not accessible to the normal user. CGI is an abbreviation for "community gateway interface."

d.) CGI scripts - Small software programs for transferring information between a Web server and a CGI program. This program is designed to accept and return data that conforms to CGI specifications.

e.) Alistening posts – An information gathering system of opinion retrieval, usually in a casual sitting. Some examples are Customer Complaints, Direct Customer Contact, your own e-mail, the formal Customer Survey, Suppliers and Manufacturers, Employee and Associates Sessions, your neighborhood, and the Online community.

f.) Matt Wright's Archives - A Web site (http://www.worldwidemart.com/scripts/) that contains scripts that can be downloaded and edited for use on Web sites. One of the best collections of scripts available on the Internet.

6. Define in writing the following words or concepts:

a.) The purpose of the METHOD attribute - The METHOD attribute instructs a Web-based form how to send its information back to the script for processing.

b.) The purpose of the POST attribute - The most common is type of method is POST, which sends all the information from the form separately from the URL.

c.) The purpose of the ALIGN attribute - ALIGN is used to control how an image is positioned on a Web page.

d.) The purpose of the SUBMIT attribute - The SUBMIT type displays a push button on a Web form with the preset function of sending data from the form to the server. VALUE can be used to change the text on the button.

e.) The purpose of the ACTION attribute - The ACTION attribute, points the form to a URL that will accept the form's information and process it. If you don't specify an ACTION, the server sends the information back to the same URL the page came from.

f.) The purpose of the INPUT attribute - The most versatile tag used in a form is the INPUT attribute. INPUT is a single tag option for gathering information, which contains other options for gathering information. It is the most versatile HTML tag because it has many different options and many attributes.

7. In developing surveys and other types of forms, the respondent might not wish to have her responses easily read by some parties. How would the form maker solve this problem? What parts do the attributes PASSWORD and HIDDEN play in this situation? Write an e-mail to your director of security explaining this issue of privacy and cite some examples of this scenario.

To: Director of Security
From: Marketing Manager
Subject: Issues of Security in Use of Web Forms

Bill,

The need to maintain customer privacy is of high concern to many that use our Web site. For this reason I would like to explain a little about how certain parameters of a Web form function to increase security for the individual and for us. These are minor features of security for both our customers and us. However, at a later date we may want to discuss other security options using more pro-active measures. These options would need to be discusses with the system administrator of our servers. In the mean time, here is a short description of some options available when creating forms. Please review them and let's discuss it at your earliest convenience.

The PASSWORD type is a modified text field displaying bullets instead of the characters actually typed. This is used to protect the customer's password from watching eyes but does not encrypt the password when it is sent to the server.

Hidden fields are used when you want to send a value to the server, but do not necessarily want the customer to see it. As the user will not actually see this input, you must pass the value you wish it to contain to the server in the form code.

8. Access a consumer survey form on any Web site and click on the View option on the browser. Then locate the View Source button to see the HTML code displayed. Select a half-page section and explain the various tags and attributes of the form. Prepare a written explanation and include the section of code you selected. Turn your report in to your instructor at the next class.

The following is a survey found at http://www.onlinesurveys.com/interests/signup.htm. It is very in depth and should cover most elements that your students discuss in this exercise.

Chapter 14
Establishing and Promoting the Virtual Store

Chapter Summary

This chapter takes an in-depth look at the procedures the e-marketer will go through in developing the virtual store. The foundation of virtual store development is based on the integration of three fundamental areas for e-success: financing required for the purchase of hardware and software, establishing an office, and arranging for personnel and business materials. In developing the online storefront, the advantages and disadvantages of hiring a developer versus "doing it yourself" are explored. The physical requirements for hardware are outlined, as well as the ancillary services of telephone, ISP, and Web master.

The final design of the Web site must follow the marketing plan in order to meet marketing objectives. A checklist of questions to attain this goal is presented. The question of joining a Cybermall or remaining a stand-alone site is explored as a component of strategic planning for site development. Suggestions for promoting and marketing the Web site are presented to understand the techniques typically used be e-marketers to attract visitors to the Web site. After the site is online, it is critical to generate repeat site visit and techniques for this are presented. The chapter concludes with statistics reviewing of the present state of online commerce.

Core Concepts

- To explain the online responsibilities in opening a virtual store
- To identify the suppliers and resources necessary in opening a virtual store
- To introduce promotional strategies and explain how these strategies work to gain awareness for the virtual store

Chapter Outline

I. In Creating the Virtual Store, the Best Advice is "Go Slow"
  A. The marketer as the merchant should investigate the pitfalls before he begins to extol the potentials of e-commerce and become blinded by its advantages
  B. To avoid "commerce overconfidence," the general strategy of setting up commercial units by function should not be any different for e-commerce activities
  C. Traditional organizational responsibilities for establishing financial affairs, production concerns, and marketing actions should be determined in the same manner for virtual commerce companies

II. The Triad in Action
  A. The virtual marketer must arrange for financing to purchase hardware and software material
  B. Establish an office
  C. Arrange for personnel and business necessities
  D. Rounding out the triangle of finance and operations is the marketing function working to investigate customer wants and the proper, highly-exposed delivery process for these bundles of benefits

III. Do It Yourself or Hire a Developer
  A. One of the biggest decisions, particularly for the small company or individual, is how to set up its online storefront
  B. The decision usually revolves around the answers to the following two questions:
    1. How experienced in business is the person responsible for setting up the online storefront?
    2. How technology-savvy is this individual?
  C. Intangible qualities in establishing a virtual storefront
    1. Finding a niche to fill

   2. Attracting and training good people
   3. Creating an attractive company culture
- D. To establish an electronic presence, it will also require some tangible equipment to access the Web
- E. Whether or not the e-marketer employs a developer or does it herself, the storefront must have reliable access to the Web as well as these elements
   1. Virtual store-building software
   2. Virtual online information sources
   3. A 300MHz or faster PC
   4. A large hard disk, perhaps 4 gigabytes or memory or larger
   5. Sixteen or more megs of ROM memory
   6. A large color monitor
   7. 56.6 baud modem if possible, 28.8 at minimum
   8. A browser
   9. Printers
   10. Scanners
   11. Telephone service and Internet service provider

IV. Engaging a Storefront Developer
- A. Service companies have evolved to produce the entire virtual storefront in a turnkey fashion
   1. The marketer supplies the developer with marketing plan
   2. He directs the company according to his understanding of the target market
   3. The developer would design the site for the most popular browsers and specify the necessary equipment to implement the design on the Web
- B. It is easy to be dazzled by graphics, however, the marketer must ask himself the following questions:
   1. Does the design and copy fit the objectives for the online marketing?
   2. Is the design attractive, memorable, and motivating
   3. Does the design ask or require the viewer to do something, such as click through the site, register for a promotion, and visit a dealership or retail store?
   4. Is the site reflective of other company marketing materials?
   5. Can the site be produced for the budget allotted and within the time frame allowed?
   6. Do the site strategies match the corporate strategies of the company?

V. Joining a Cybermall?
- A. After the site is created and the metatags are tested, the next decision for the marketer is how to maintain an optimal awareness for the site
   1. Step one in this process is to register with the variety of search engines so that the consumer can locate your offerings
   2. Step two might be an assessment in maintaining a stand-alone site as opposed to participating in the “bundling” of cybermall retailers
- B. The cybermall is a virtual collection of sites, usually bringing financial, insurance, or automobile sites together, that offer the shopper many hyperlinked addresses to follow from one page
- C. The major benefits of signing on with a cybermall are:
   1. Expanded exposure over and above the efforts of a single site
   2. The selection to be found at the cybermall’s address
   3. The site maintenance services by the cybermall operator
- D. The major disadvantages are:
   1. The cost of joining and “renting” space monthly
   2. Heavy competition

VI. The Marketing Duties of a Web Site Manager
- A. What are the necessary elements to begin setting up an online presence?
   1. A detailed study of the Internet and the Web as well as the peripheral promotions and communications capabilities nested on the company desktop
   2. Proficiency at a word processing program
   3. An understanding of advertising procedures, graphics, and copy is also helpful
   4. Communicating effectively with advertising suppliers

5. Be cognizant of technology changes, in hardware and software
6. Be able to judge if new equipment or applications would improve the site's performance
7. Familiarity of HTML editing, linking hyperlinks, and acquaintance with frames and tables page construction
8. An appreciation of customer service and conflict resolution are pluses
9. A general proficiency in basic communication

B. The Web master has many duties in maintaining the e-commerce site, and a sense of organization is absolutely necessary

VII. Choosing an Internet Service Provider

A. An ISP is a company that can provide you with a connection to the Internet as well other Internet-based services

B. There are also many types and levels of ISPs
  1. ISPs can be part-time hobbyists who are inexpensive-but also not well equipped to handle a business Web site
  2. Some ISPs are small businesses that are quite successful and can be well equipped to handle a business Web site that gets moderate traffic
  3. Large ISPs often provide many services to businesses and have in-house technical support
     a. The downfall to using large ISP is that they may not be as flexible
     b. Large providers will most likely have the best equipment and fastest connections to the Internet

C. A commercial provider such as AOL, CompuServ, MSN, and Prodigy
  1. Theses services may not be flexible enough to run your business the way you want and within your budget

D. To find an ISP:
  1. Search on the Web
  2. Ask others in your area
  3. Look in the yellow pages
  4. Check an ISP reference service

E. Considerations when investigating which one to use will depend primarily on why you want an ISP
  1. If you want one for personal use, a local small business might be better as they may be more helpful
  2. If you want one for business purposes, reliable service is going to be a major issue

F. Some questions that you might ask when looking at ISPs:
  1. Are you able to communicate with the service representative of the ISP?
  2. Are your personal and business goals understood?
  3. Check their references
  4. Are you able to do everything that you want with this ISP?
     a. E-mail access
     b. Host Web sites
     c. News groups
     d. Scripting
  5. What is the pricing structure?
  6. What type of connection does the ISP provide?
  7. What software is provided by the ISP?
  8. Who will service your account?
  9. What type of technical support is available?
     a. Make sure support is available when and how you need it
     b. See if they offer on-site support

G. Once you have chose an ISP to host your Web pages, there are still a few things you need to be aware of
  1. What are the limitations set by the ISP on the size of the Web site?
  2. If you plan to have a site that is accessed often, check for limitations and additional fees for excess hits on your pages

3. How will your files be transferred to the ISP and what type of access will you have for editing those pages one they are in place?
4. See if scripts are allowed, or if they are provided by the ISP themselves
5. Is the provider capable of handling the security necessary for your type of site
6. What statistics are available from your ISP, how easy are they to obtain and in what form will they be provided?
7. Make sure that you have ownership of the design and content of your pages and that you have thoroughly read the contract your ISP should happily provide you

VIII. Promoting the Web Site
   A. The twist in online promotion is that no one has a long history doing it right and doing it well, so much experimentation in promotion is ongoing
   B. The confusion in promotions is that the Web:
      1. "Reads" like a newspaper, but it is not
      2. The Web is like television, but where are the programs?
      3. It has sounds like the radio, but where is the music?
      4. Promoters of Web advertising speak of billboards, but try to find one of the huge structures along the information highway

IX. Planning and Organization
   A. Prepare a solid marketing plan focusing on the promotional element to expose the product and display the discipline to follow it
   B. What are the elements of the online communications marketing plan (your road map to marketing on the Web)?
      1. Online marketing plan
      2. Online promotional program
   C. Identify your consumer or business-to-business targets

X. Tactical Online Targeting
   A. The means by which you will use to communicate with your primary targets are established online vehicles such as e-mail and discussion groups
      1. Mail servers and e-mail
      2. Electronic or virtual storefronts
      3. Advertising
      4. Electronic publishing
      5. Hard copy publishing
      6. Conferences venues
      7. "Cookies"
      8. Sig files
      9. FAQs
      10. Usenet Newsgroups
      11. "Cross fertilization" between your Web site and your traditional marketing media to increase the success of your Web presence
   B. The marketer can increase visibility through the following actions:
      1. Register you site with Web search engines, listings, and catalogs
      2. Participate in discussion lists and Usenet newsgroups and the use of informative .sig files
      3. Make online announcements and use news releases
      4. Study FAQs
      5. Use cross-linking of your page to other relevant pages

XI. How Can You Get Web Surfers Hooked?
   A. After the initial visits, activity and interactivity will encourage your visitor to return to your site
      1. Curiosity
      2. Item turnover
      3. Indispensable tool or resource
      4. Unique event or resource

B. Explore sources for professional net advertising information

XII. The Present State of Online Commerce
- A. What are the dynamics of consumers actually buying online?
  1. 76.2% of the GVU Ninth WWW User Survey respondents reported that they have "ordered a product or service by filling out a form on the Web"
  2. Respondents were usually U.S. males familiar with the Internet activities
  3. 1.9% actually had a bad experience with online purchasing
  4. Only 4.5% found the process too complicated or thought the process would be too complicated
  5. Almost 40% of online purchases were software
- B. What are the trends in consumer purchases that e-businesses selling online should be aware of for the immediate future?
  1. Computer and accessories
  2. Entertainment
  3. Securities trading services

Teaching Suggestions

Much of the student learning is implemented in this chapter. The marketing process has been investigated and planned for the nonexistent product or service project. The capabilities and output of the tools of electronic marketing resources have been explained and demonstrated in class sessions. Prototype Web sites have been designed with customer-oriented elements such as product information, online ordering forms, and mechanisms for customer response or feedback. Perhaps performance tools such as Web statistical packages have been included. Now is the time that a "real" Web vehicle would go live. Or would it?

This chapter explains the decisions to be made in implementing the site. Assembling all of the elements above into a coherent and persuasive site requires marketing decision making. Class discussion should revolve around the availability of the marketer's time and talents for his/her own execution of the electronic tools. The text poses simple but critical questions: "Should your site be a do-it-yourself assignment?" "Should you hire a Web master for internal development?" "Should you hire a Web developer to produce the site?" "Should your site join a cybermall complemented by other cybermerchants?" Depending on the desirability and demand for your product, do you need viewing traffic or will your site supply it? The answer to this question is important and might figure into your cybermall contract negotiations.

The Instructor should demonstrate sites for the do-it-yourself Web site builder. One solid primer has been created by my colleague, Dr. Clive Sanford of the USF's Department of Management Information and Decision Science (http://www.sanford.com/ism4480/). This site contains explanations and tutorials on the construction of Web resources. Search for the key terms, "Web master" or "Webmaster", to see what resources are retrieved. Then search for the key terms, "storefront developer," "virtual storefront," "cybermall developer," and "cybermall". Many helpful and imaginative sites will help you differentiate these services.

After the Web site is placed on the Web, promotional efforts must begin. The chapter contains explanations of the key promotional actions such as registering the site with the important search engines, considering the decision to advertise the site contents and URL, using PR and publicity to create exposure and knowledge of the site. Many promotional elements such as press archives, online advertising, and discussion groups on allied subjects assist the students in learning the promotions' applications.

Answers to Questions and Exercises

1. Describe the tasks and responsibilities of the e-marketer concerning establishing and promoting the new e-commerce Web site. In one sentence, explain the tasks in order and give an example of each. Prepare a written outline to give to your Web designer.

The marketer takes responsibility for researching, supervising the design, implementation, and maintenance of the e-commerce Web site; the student's answers will vary depending on the product or service featured on the Web site. Work to achieve a memorable and creative domain name and Web address. Create a distinctive .sig file for company e-mail usage. Schedule speaking engagements with local business organizations, university classes, and civic groups on the topic of e-commerce or e-marketing. Some online exposure efforts could include registering the site using a service such as DoubleClick.com, create a discussion group about your product or your industry category, issue online news releases about your product, product trivia, company performance, employee profile, or community involvement. Plan sales promotions to benefit community projects such as building homes for Habitat for Humanity or children/family issues.

This exercise is to challenge clear thinking by the student to focus on the purpose of the Web page. Examples of promoting the e-commerce Web site will vary.

2. You are developing a Web site for your own business, and you are concerned about selecting the right ISP. Make a list of the services and equipment you want to rent from the ISP you choose. Compile the list of items and write a letter to your partner who is supplying the money for your venture. Explain why you need each item.

Careful consideration in selecting this crucial partner might include decision points such as these:

- Is the ISP running a full-time or part-time business?
- What level of technical support is offered…low or high service?
- Is the connection able to handle heavy traffic and define heavy traffic?
- What is the type of equipment and connection to the Internet?
- What use the pricing structure and amount of access numbers?
- Can you communicate easily with the ISP management?
- What is the ISP's reputation and reliability; contact current users of the service to ask these questions.
- What services are offered such as e-mail, scripting.
- Who will service your account?
- Is there redundant equipment in case of outages or failures
- But is the space limitation on the server?
- What is the level and procedures for security?
- Can traffic statistics be gathered and reported on?
- Who owns the domain name and the site?

3. There are advantages and disadvantages in preparing the Web site yourself or in hiring a storefront developer for the assignment. Suppose you are planning to open an online store that is a full-service iguana shop. You will carry a complete line of iguana supplies. Prepare a list of the top five advantages and the top five disadvantages of hiring an outside source to create the site. The list is for your own planning purposes.

Advantages of hiring an outside resource:

- Lesser time commitment, someone else is doing the work
- No learning curve, someone else has learned HTML and other Web conventions
- Supplier experience, the supplier has prepared other Web resources and can incorporate knowledge
- Probably a better product because you are using a n specialist
- Faster time to market

Disadvantages of hiring outside resource

- Cost of hiring outside supplier
- Uncertainty of finished product and its functionality
- Little control over supplier's time and priorities
- Having to teach supplier the pet store business
- Unsure ability to communicate with supplier

After interviewing Web storefront developers, make a list of your priority questions to investigate.

4. Contact a storefront developer and interview the company to understand what services they provide to the online merchant. Give the representative a product or service scenario, and write a one-page report on your interview.

This is a field exercise; students' interviews and responses should vary according to the companies contacted.

5. In your opinion, what are the advantages and disadvantages in operating both a traditional retailing location and an online store? Prepare a list of advantages and disadvantages of operating each at the same time. Be prepared to discuss your opinions at the next class meeting.

Advantages of operating both the traditional store and the online channel

- The expanded reach that the online store gives, nationally and internationally
- potentially larger display of selection with online catalog
- Expanded channels of sales with little increase of overhead
- Ability to operate and sell 24-hours each day
- Convenience for customers to shop in either method
- Ability to contact customers with special offers rather than to wait until they contact the merchant
- Ability to respond faster to customer inquiries

Disadvantages of operating both the traditional store and the online channel

- Added cost of operating both facilities
- Requires expertise of online marketer for maximum benefit
- Requires alteration of operating procedures because of 24-hour service
- Requires constant management of online communications, inventory status and inventory status
- Possibility that merchant will not be paid
- Requires revision of payment systems to allow inclusion of digital certificates

6. Write an e-mail to a storefront developer requesting a proposal for the design and implementation of a virtual store. In the e-mail list what services you are looking for and what specifications there are for the hardware to operate your site. Be detailed in your instructions.

This list must be detailed for an accurate quotation of the specifications for retailing services' capabilities. The student should surf other developers' sites to gather the technology for retailing services that she wants. This is a field exercise so the e-mail list will vary according to the student's product and level of service.

7. Of the promotional tactics listed in the text, which three do you feel will be most effective for building initial awareness of a consumer-oriented virtual store? Of a business-to-business virtual store? Justify your thinking in support of these three awareness elements and prepare your thoughts as a speech outline to be delivered before a college business fraternity.

Building initial awareness of a consumer-oriented store

1) General image advertising in traditional media such as television, newspaper, magazine, and radio
2) E-mail announcement of online newsletter pertaining to the store's merchandise category such as science fiction literature or Gothic novels
3) Online advertising on search engines or Web pages of sites that could deliver exposure to be market segment
4) Electronic news releases to general interest newspapers and magazines
5) Announcements and advertising to discussion groups about the store's merchandise category memo

Building initial awareness of a business-oriented store

1) Specific benefits advertising in trade magazines and newsletters that target the industry's category
2) Sales promotions sweepstakes on the new Web page targeted to business prospects' interests
3) Online advertising on Web pages of sites that could deliver exposure to the business target market
4) Traditional direct mail to business SIC designations
5) Electronic news releases to trade or business-oriented newspapers and magazines

8. .Sig files can create a personalized signature for your correspondence. Write your own .sig file for your e-mails and use characters, numbers, letters, or designs that you think are distinctive to your personality. E-mail your instructor with an e-mail displaying the .sig file.

This is a field exercise to challenge the student's creativity.

9. What catches your attention on commercial Web sites as you surf? Select six Web sites you believe are creative or memorable and write a paragraph on each stating reasons each caught your eye. Print each Web site out to accompany your report. Assume this is research to assist your Web designer in developing a site for your company.

This is another field exercise to encourage the student to be alert to other sites' content and execution. Explaining why the Web sides are memorable also aids the student's writing communications.

10. You are planning a Web site to support your virtual storefront that specializes in sports pins commemorating sporting events. They were originally made to be worn, but a collectors' hobby has emerged. In planning your site, you are considering incorporating the following items; make a list of the advantages and disadvantages of each element:

a) color photography of each pin for sale or trade
b) sound bites of sports music
c) sound effects to match the category of sports pins
d) video clips of famous moments in sports
e) Java script of sports teams' logos in motion
f) Site search engine
g) Trivia test page
h) Offer to subscribe to Sports Pins Collectors' Newsletter, a text-based online newsletter you write and e-mail each month

In the context of the online medium, there are many features that can be added for interest and for distraction. Students must think about the market they are trying to communicate with. Are any of these embellishments distracting? Consider the students' evaluations and make comments or suggestions that could be incorporated into their projects. Hard Rock Café sells collectors pins; you might demonstrate that Web site as an example. An old advertising adage is "to include everyday is to include nothing." Be flexible, be cautious, and be empathetic to your market's desires.

Chapter 15
Security on the E-Commerce Site

Chapter Summary

This chapter presents an in-depth exploration of the role of security and privacy in e-commerce. The basis of e-security is Cryptography. Cryptographic systems are discussed in detail and the introduction of technological developments to improve their effectiveness is presented in a chronological manner to display "state of the art" electronic security. The process of securing electronic credit card payments for e-purchases from the points of view of buyer, bank, and seller are outlined. This chapter is technical in nature.

Core Concepts

- To explore the basics of cryptography and its role in e-commerce
- To investigate the digital certificate, the foundation for payment systems
- To discuss methods of security, Secure Sockets Layer versus Secure Electronic Transaction protocols

Chapter Outline

I. A Survey of Cryptography
   A. Cryptography results in the creation of cryptographic methods, known as cryptosystems
      1. Symmetric cryptosystems use the same key, or the secret key, to encrypt, or scramble, and decrypt, or unscramble a message
      2. Asymmetric cryptosystems, on the other hand, use one key to encrypt a message and a different key to decrypt it
         a. Asymmetric cryptosystems are also called public key cryptosystems, and rely on technology in which two keys, the public key and the private key, are used to encrypt or decrypt data
   B. Symmetric cryptosystems are the easier of the two implement, since only one key is required

II. Digital Certificate
   A. Authentication is the digital process of verifying that people or entities are whom or what they claim to be
   B. Digital certificates are in effect virtual fingerprints, or retinal scans that authenticate the identity of a person or thing in a concrete, verifiable way
   C. A typical digital certificate is a data file of information, digitally signed and sealed by the encrypted using RSA encryption techniques, that can be verified by anyone and includes:
      1. The name of the holder and other identification information, such as e-mail address
      2. A public key, which can be used to verify the digital signature of a message sender previously signed with the matching mathematically unique private key
      3. The name of the issuer, or Certificate Authority
      4. The certificate's validity period
   D. To create a digital certificate for an individual, the identity of the person, device, or entity that requests a certificate must be confirmed. This is typically accomplished through a combination of the following:
      1. Personal presence
      2. Identification documents
   E. Digital certificates may be distributed online. Typical means of distributing certificates include:
      1. Certificate accompanying signature
      2. Directory service
   F. The decision to revoke a certificate is the responsibility of the issuing company

III. Secure Sockets Layer (SSL)

A. SSL was introduced in 1995 by Netscape as a component of its popular Navigator browser and as a means of providing privacy with respect to information being transmitted between a user's browser and the target server, typically that of a merchant

B. SSL establishes a secure session between a browser and a server

C. A channel is the two-way communication stream established between the browser and the server, and the definition of channel security indicates three basic requirements:
   1. The channel is reliable
   2. The channel is private
   3. The channel is authenticated

D. By virtue of SSL's requirement of Transmission Control Protocol (TCP) as the transport mechanism, channel reliability is inherent

E. This encryption is preceded by a "data handshake" and has two major phases:
   1. The first phase is used to establish private communications, and uses the key-agreement algorithm
   2. The second phase is used for client authentication

F. Limits of SSL
   1. While the possibility is very slight, successful cryptographic attacks made against these technologies can render SSL insecure

III. Secure Electronic Transaction (SET)

A. On February 1, 1996, MasterCard International and Visa International announced the development of a single technical standard for safeguarding payment card purchases made over open networks called Secure Electronic Transaction (SET)

B. SET seek to bolster confidence in the payment process by ensuring that merchants are authorized to accept credit card payments, this reducing risks associated with merchant fraud, and ensuring that the purchaser is an authorized user of the payment card

C. SET protocol was created to bolster the confidence of the online consumer by mitigating the security risks in SSL

D. While the goal of SSL is to reduce the likelihood communication interception, the goal of SET is to reduce the likelihood of fraud

E. SET provides the special security needs of electronic commerce with the following:
   1. Privacy of payment data and confidentiality of order information transmission
   2. Authentication of a cardholder for a branded bank card account
   3. Authentication of the merchant to accept credit card payments

F. The purchasing process
   1. A merchant applies for , and receives, an account with an issuing bank, just as they would apply for a normal credit card merchant account
   2. A consumer makes an application to an issuing bank for a digital credit card, which is a digital certificate that has been personalized for the credit card-holder
   3. After the consumer receives her digital credit card, she adds it to her browser wallet
   4. The consumer browses the Web at a particular site
   5. At checkout time, the Web site asks for the shopper's credit card
   6. Instead of typing in the credit card number, the browser wallet is queried by the Web sit SET software and, following selection of the appropriate credit card and entry of its password by the consumer, the bank-issued digital credit card is submitted to the merchant
   7. The merchant receives the digital credit card in a digital envelope
   8. The merchant software then sends the SET transaction to a credit card processor (also known as a "payment gateway application" or "acquire") for verification
   9. The financial institutions performs functions including authorization, credit, and capture (voiding and refund) reversals on the transaction, and following successful processing, the merchant, cardholder, and credit card processors are all advised electronically that the purchase has been approved
   10. Following this notification, the cardholder is debited and the merchant is paid through subsequent payment capture transactions

11. The merchant can then ship the merchandise, knowing that the customer transaction is approved

G. Limitations of SET and SSL
1. A downside of both SSL and SET protocols is that they both require the use of cryptographic algorithms that place significant loads on the computer systems involved in the commerce transaction
2. For the low and medium e-commerce applications, there is no additional server cost to support SET over SSL
3. For the large e-commerce server application, support of SET requires additional hardware acceleration in the medium term resulting in a 5 to 6% difference in server cost
4. In the medium term, this payment gateway application will require additional hardware acceleration to support SET resulting in a 5% increase in server cost

H. Thus, the conclusion is that SET as an emerging technology has a definitive security component that very clearly represents an advance in technology over SSL, and that any deficits that may be related to performance will quickly be rendered minor as hardware-based processing technology rapidly advances

Teaching Suggestions

Most of these exchange concepts are new to traditional marketers because of the digital technology involved. The instruction in this chapter is best presented as a class lecture which will require familiarization of the tools used for online transactions. You might visit some of the electronic security sites such as Verisign (www.verisign.com) to become acquainted with the services and how the electronic security systems present themselves. Financial services such as Visa or MasterCard also are sources of general information about securing financial transactions.

Answers to Questions and Exercises

1. You are the marketing department's liaison to the IS department of your company. The company operates in 15 countries, and is setting up an e-commerce site to sell rare Beanie Baby collectibles. You are on the committee evaluating software, and the subject of cryptography has come up. Name three factors regarding cryptography that would guide your recommendations, and your caveats with respect to each one.

a. *Length of Key*. Within the US, longer keys are allowed, so if the traffic is within the US, then large-key encryption would serve, but for traffic where any leg of the journey is outside the US, then only small-key encryption would be allowed. Therefore, any encryption product and plan using that product must factor this in.
b. *What has to be encrypted?* If it is the traffic, then I would go with public-key encryption. But if it's the data, for example within a database, then consider symmetric cryptosystems since they don't require the creation of public and private keys.
c. *How sensitive is the data and what is the budget?* Remembering that cryptography requires substantial computing power, it would be important to isolate those areas most likely to benefit from encryption, and budget appropriate resources to ensure that the effort to encrypt the data or traffic does not bring the systems to their knees, and thereby alienating potential customers.

2. At your company, where you have worked for the last five years, you have this gnawing feeling that your career is at a standstill. So you decide it's time to hit the road, and go on your own. You want to start an auction Web site to allow your friends (and extended family) to auction everything *including* the kitchen sink. But, you're collecting sensitive information about your customers. How will you assure your customers that their information is safe? Create a document which names three possible security problems and how you intent to allay potential fears about them.

a. *Traffic Snoopers*. You tout your "Secure Web Site" featuring the use of SSL and how the customer can tell if secure information is being sent through the lock and key symbols of their browser.
b. *Access by unauthorized individuals*. You provide a page on your site that describes how you protect their privacy by preventing unauthorized access (which is different from secure communications).
c. *Dissemination of personal information to outsiders.* Join an organization such as TRUSTe. These are typically watchdog organizations that make sure that any member organization is taking the proper precautions and safeguards to

protect personal information. Make sure that you display the logo prominently on the site and provide a link back to the organization where the customer can learn more about their function.

3. You have been notified that you must attend a meeting with the security auditor of your firm. The audit in question concerns the new international e-commerce site that you've helped to steer through to implementation. What aspects of site security will you research to prepare for the audit? Write a three-page position paper outlining a strategy to ensure that proper security measures have been taken with respect to your customer's confidential data.

a. Protect against unauthorized access.
b. Make sure that passwords are changed frequently.
c. Make sure that servers are not touched by unauthorized persons prior to, during, or after implementation.
d. Ensure that servers are kept in secure rooms and that access to these rooms is carefully controlled.
e. Use SSL for all communications e-commerce traffic.
f. Make sure that all countries participating in the site are at the exact same levels of security compliance, both with respect to the laws and regulations of the country as well as the standards and practices of the participating e-commerce personnel.

4. As the assistant to the CEO of a small company (20 employees) that does business in four countries, the CEO has charged you with helping to establish an online presence. The company is implementing an extranet that will allow the company's clients to get product marketing literature. What security controls will you recommend? Defend your decision from a marketing, finance and IS point of view.

a. Register as a digital certificate holder, but allow the Certificate Authority to handle routine certificate administration tasks. This would free your organization from having to maintain these tasks yourselves.
b. Require each client to register with the Certificate Authority to get access to your system, and require your system to use digital certificates before providing sensitive information.
c. Marketing. Get the word out to your clients that you give the same level of commitment to the protection of their data that you do to theirs.
d. Finance. Total security, beats the cost of losing (or compromising) your data.
e. IS. With digital certificates, you can be assured of proper authentication, and relieved of the burden of supporting a large infrastructure to maintain security.

5. While preparing for your new entrepreneurial venture, you realize that you will need digital certificates to establish the security of your SSL-based site. Create a memo to your prospective partners that outlines why you need digital certificates and what the requirements will be to obtain them, paying particular attention to the timelines for your company's legal incorporation, plus the implementation and subsequent marketing of your online presence.

a. According to Netscape's Security Center, "E-commerce sites secured by [VeriSign] digital certificates will be able to authenticate themselves to visitors and conduct encrypted transactions, including the exchange of [Visa] credit card numbers, enabling online customer to shop with confidence."
b. A digital certificate cannot be issued until the legal incorporation has been executed, since the entity requesting a digital certificate must be a valid company, university, or government organization. Therefore, incorporation and the timelines required in accomplishing submission of the Business License must be followed closely in executing the business plan.
c. As a startup company, your financial credibility is crucial, and use of digital certificates will be necessary to conduct business with your potential partners.
d. Financial systems' security is also critical, both for internal and external reassurance.
e. Should your business include international marketing, financial transactions will be facilitated

6. You are the marketing director of a small company (50 employees) with offices in Europe and the U.S. What factors would you take into account in determining the number of digital certificates you will need for your two new mirrored sites in London and New York?

a. Number of employees.
b. Number of sites.
c. Number of external certificate holders.
d. Level of security. Domestic US is the only place where you can use 64-bit or higher encryption, and therefore you would need to know how much security is enough for you, and whether employees would require one or two keys (for international or domestic use).

7. As the assistant to the CIO of a Fortune 500 company, the CIO has been given the task of creating a Web site to sell products currently being sold through the direct-market catalog business. Furthermore, the decision has been made that the site will take credit card payments. The CIO has asked you for information that would help him make some decisions. What factors would you use to determine whether the site should use SSL or SET? Prepare a one-page discussion of the merits of each protocol and the factors that would come into play in making a recommendation.

a. SSL or SET: What level of security is desired? If it's transmission of secure information only, then SSL. If it's non-repudiation, authentication, and a range of security required to perform a secure transaction, then use SET.
b. Machine Power. SSL requires much less power on the server side to accomplish.
c. Money. SET costs much more to implement.
d. Time to implement. SSL can be implemented more quickly than SET.
e. Administration. Remember that SET is a complicated, end-to-end solution, while SSL represents the solution to secure the transmission of information.

8. As an assistant director of the marketing department of a medium-sized company (400 employees) creating a new campaign to promote your new secure online catalog, give three security-related advantages that you would promote. In addition, prepare a one-page strategy memo that you would create to communicate your marketing campaign with the Information Systems department that will implement it, showing them that you are sensitive to their needs while being just as sensitive to the needs of your intended customers.

a. Complete privacy of data.
b. Secure communications.
c. Prevention of unauthorized access.
d. Strategy: You will defer to the judgment of the IS department as to whether they will hire an outside contractor to provide the SET-based system, or do it themselves. In addition, you will recommend that if they are having trouble providing their own resources, then you will provide your own, and ask them to offer an IS liaison to make sure that their needs are being met along with yours. In addition, you will provide funds from your budget for this project that will go toward implementation of IS-initiated e-commerce projects that they may be planning.

9. You are a marketing consultant for a research firm. Your client has asked for your opinion about whether they should use SSL or SET as the basic protocol for their online catalog. The reason they want your advice is that they want to make that decision part of their marketing plan. What information would you request from them?

a. Why are they thinking about it?
b. What is their budget, and what is their liability or exposure with respect to customer data?
c. What do they know about SSL and SET?
d. Will they take payments directly from the system?
e. Are they set up to accept credit cards?
f. Is their current bank registered to allow SET?
g. What kinds of systems, Internet-connected or otherwise, do they support within their organization?
h. Do they currently use SSL or SET in their organization?
i. Are they registered as digital certificate holders? If so, do they administer their certificates or contract that out?
j. Do they have an Information Systems infrastructure?
k. How do they secure their current systems?
l. Do they have a security officer?

10. Based on what you've read in this chapter, would you use a digital credit card? Why or why not? Prepare a one-page document explaining your position.

A typical answer might include these points. Consumers would probably use it because it is completely secure, it is easy, and the organizations that support it must be registered themselves. They should be careful, however, to be sure that the financial institution are not only keeping the transactions secure, but that the card issuer is not distributing consumers' confidential information about spending patterns, habits or dollar value purchases. They should only spend with recognized firms, since the tendency has been for firms to change their policies, and even large corporations such as Microsoft have been found to break the rules on privacy of data which they themselves have set and fostered.

Chapter 16
Special Opportunities for Business-to-Business Situations

Chapter Summary

This chapter introduces the concepts of e-commerce and e marketing in the business-to-business sector. It is critical for the student to understand the role of e-marketing since it is predicted that this sector will have the largest growth potential in the next few years. Statistics for current usage as well as projections for its growth are presented. Techniques for developing and implementing e-marketing in business-to-business situations are outlined. The values of e-business to the marketer are described and presented as fundamental to building and managing business growth in cyberspace. Techniques for selling products and services in an electronic environment, as well as the impacts of competition on e-commerce, are discussed in detail.

Core Concepts

- To document the factors why business-to-business marketers are shifting sales efforts to online activities
- To demonstrate how the business-to-business organization integrates online marketing with its traditional sales activities
- To present the trends in business and consumer demographics and product sales projections around which business-to-business enterprises can be directed

Chapter Outline

I. The Brave, New World of the Web
   A. For competitive pressures, business management is looking inward to evaluate its own strengths and weaknesses, defining the corporate competencies and shoring up or outsourcing its deficiencies
   B. A minimum of 32 million business users worldwide account for at least 46% of the total traffic volume
   C. Additional findings:
      1. The business universe-according to *RelevantKnowledge*, 34% of all Web users fit the definition of an "active business user"
      2. Current estimate of 93.8 million Internet users worldwide, that would amount to some 32 million business users worldwide
      3. Site universe-Dun & Bradstreet reports that more than 40 million companies are listed on its worldwide database
      4. Web usage-a recent *Thomas Register* and Visa USA online survey of 2000 American and Canadian businesses (out of a possible 155,000 *Register*-listed companies) shows that 40% say they used the Web at least once in the past month, primarily for quick research
      5. Fortune 500 sites-in October, 1997, IDC showed a chart that estimated that 80% of all Fortune 500 companies had Web sites in 1996
      6. Small/medium/large segmentation-In 1997, IDC estimated that small business users made up 17% of "total Net use," while businesses with more than one hundred employees made up 28%
         a. Worldwide, IDC estimates that medium and large business will account for 49 million users by 2000
      7. Small business-According to *Cyber Dialogue's* U.S. Small Business Interview Survey, which was based on interviews with one thousand U.S. businesses with less than one hundred employees, 37% are online equivalent to 2.6 million small business employees out of a 7 million universe
      8. Volumetrics-Media Metrics reports that business users devote 65% more time on the Web than home users

II. The Logic of Web Usage by Business-to-Business Organizations
   A. The way commercial enterprises conduct business has changed drastically through the nineties, and few managers, marketing included, could have foretold how technology would entangle itself in the Web of business
   B. Marketers recognize the greatest benefit of the Web to the business sector is its efficiency
      1. Products can be rushed to the market
      2. Production costs can be reduced by computer-aided design and computer-aided manufacturing
      3. The marketing process can be made more efficient with electronic resources
      4. Targeting prospects can be enhanced with Web sites, listservs, or Usenet discussion groups, which are directed specifically to electronic commerce support, entrepreneurial, or venture capital funds
      5. Advertising messages can seek out viewers chosen by these viewers site selections and search engine choices; electronic publicity releases covering business topics find their ways to news wires
   C. Businesses are finding methods to adjust their business practices in the Information Economy

III. The Opportunities for Electronic Marketing Resources in Business-to-Business Transactions
   A. The first order of e-business for many companies was toward automated procurement because much of the material handling involved numbers easily recognized by computer interfaces
   B. Open Buying on the Internet (OBI) became the standard way for exchanging and trading information
   C. Values delivered by e-business as described by PricewaterhouseCoopers
      1. Achieve market leadership
      2. Reach new markets
      3. Create new products and services
      4. Build customer loyalty
      5. Optimize business processes
      6. Enhance human capital
      7. Harness technology
      8. Manage risk and compliance
   D. Information is the key commodity in business-to-business transactions
   E. E-business strategies are selling products and services
      1. E-business is conducive for presentation through the catalog medium
      2. The Web serves the catalog medium well
      3. Listings, color photographs, diagrams, prices, and details subject to quickly change are popular product specifications
      4. Web site selling keeps product information updated
   F. Management and advisory services are other forms of worthwhile information gaining awareness and sales momentum on the Web
      1. Consultative selling, situations where the outside representative becomes a trusted team member of the client's management team and the salesperson's input is highly valued, is a most profitable activity
      2. IBM has created a "virtual seminar for e-business"
   G. The electronic marketing resources for e-business
      1. Commercial auctions to sell surpluses carried with "live price boards" for common knowledge, either buyer or seller
      2. Virtual consulting using videoconferencing or virtual reality Web sites
      3. Speech recognition for routing telephone sales inquiries and security authentication
      4. Automated kiosks for guard-less entry of lodging facilities after hours, retail order-taking by push key, or printed or graphical information dispensing such as maps or brochures
      5. Automated procurement and reordering
      6. Robot shopping for availability of item and best price
      7. Delivery tracking
      8. Customer and prospect profiling for company preferences and buying patterns
         a. Inventory control and balancing

b. Custom communications networks
c. Supplier extranets for partnering and collaboration
d. EDI for fast and efficient passing of large amounts of data
e. Company marketing presence via Web advertising and customer communications and Web-enabled product and service ordering
f. Customer service e-mail and call routing systems for customer communications

9. Virtual seminars and CD-ROM training of personnel
10. Partnering with specialized companies to strengthen all technology and service areas of an e-commerce organization
11. On many Web sites the user will find search engines that are time-savers in locating information contained within the site

IV. Internal Considerations for Business Operations
A. Businesses should always be searching for the best methods for doing business
B. Competitive forces are pushing many companies to assess the Internet as a competitive tool

V. Disadvantages of Online Business-to-Business Commerce
A. While the strength of e-business is streamlined efficiency, companies employing e-business lose contact with their distribution channels and sales personnel
B. The biggest disadvantage is the threat of alienating distributors and therefore loss of physical distribution points
C. Different companies are trying different strategies to address the distributor or salesperson displeasure
1. Compaq had introduced its own Web commerce site, selling computers at rock-bottom prices directly to small business and individuals
2. IBM has tried using their Internet sites mainly to direct prospects to online ordering sites operated by long-established dealers
3. Radius, Inc. began online sales of its software for handling digital photos
4. Many other industries have been long partnering with distributors or third-party resellers, and e-business marketing strategies should be set with the prospect of gaining or losing key personnel or distribution outlets at any time

D. Some companies abhor the prospect of limiting its sales over the Internet
1. 3M lists hundreds of its products on its Web site, but generally does not provide a way to order these products directly from the company

VI. E-Business Sales Forecasts by Industry
A. The e-commerce specialist, Forrester Research, expects business-to-business e-commerce revenues to jump from $109 billion in 1999 to $1.3 trillion by 2003
B. In making your marketing decisions and plans, you should probably adopt a conservative strategy, projecting your industry's sales volume and your company's market share and volume no further than two years hence
C. Study the industry projections to see which you find reasonable for the environmental conditions of today and hopefully of tomorrow

Teaching Suggestions

Research tells us that 80 percent of online purchases are business generated so attention should be given to the role and application of the World Wide Web as an enabler of business-to-business commerce. The Instructor should demonstrate several business sites of choice to "dissect" the objectives and elements of the business Web site. In many cases the business site is much more sophisticated in serving its visitors' needs: easy navigation, legible linking buttons, prominent product specials, technical support at hand, as well as customer service assistance by e-mail, FAQ, telephone, audiotext, and in many cities, trained technical personnel available to provide service at your office. Is this focus on business customer service happening because companies can pay and the margins are larger? Probably. But the business marketer discovered this profit model herself and shaped the customer satisfaction systems to suit businesses' demands.

Answers to Questions and Exercises

1. As we discussed in this chapter, the business-to-business environment has changed rapidly in the last twenty years. List five factors in the business-to-business sector that have produced drastic change. What are the advantages and disadvantages affected with each change? Write an e-mail to the company's director of strategic planning naming these changes and their expected consequences.

Consolidations and mergers	Advantages	More efficient operations and higher return on assets
		Smaller staff that is technology enabled
	Disadvantages	Wasteful destruction of valuable assets
		Toll in human capital
Information technology	Advantages	Greater productivity
		Smaller staff that is technology enabled
		Furthers reach to global capability
	Disadvantages	Generally expensive endeavor
		Requires extensive training in usage, costly endeavor
		Can quickly become obsolete
Speed of change	Advantages	Can be considered a competitive advantage
	Disadvantages	Company fortunes can be quickly reversed
		Management problems in coping with changes
Fierce/global competition	Advantages	Expands markets through innovation and marketing
		Can create operations such as EU or NAFTA
	Disadvantages	Traditional markets can be wiped out
World stock markets/finances	Advantages	Expands business opportunities
	Disadvantages	World economies interlocked; emergencies globally
		Disparity between developed and underdeveloped countries

These factors lead to great uncertainty in the operation, financial, and marketing functions of a company; management should be observant of change and ways to manage change such as information technology.

2. In comparing online versus traditional business-to-business marketing, efficiency has become a highly prized competency. Name five electronic marketing resources that have improved efficiency in e-business activities. Write a letter of inquiry to IBM e-commerce calling out these resources and specifying the benefits of each resource. Ask for a sales representative to make an e-business presentation to you.

a) An electronic messaging system for internal communications, either for national or international business marketing
b) Electronic Data Transfer, for faster data exchange between offices or countries
c) Extranet networks, for collaborating and partnering among business entities
d) Online marketing resources such as a sales-oriented Web site, a virtual storefront, or the cybermall
e) Database storage and manipulation, for recording customer transactions and information
f) Fax technology for answering repetitive inquiries
g) Sophisticated software systems for distribution routing or design/manufacturing applications

If the sales representative won't present to the class, a second choice of information is to request hard copy brochures, PowerPoint presentations, or other e-commerce sales materials.

3. Access the e-commerce pages of the IBM Web site and critique the services that are offered. If you were starting your own business, which of these services would be of most importance to you? List and rank six of the services and explain why each is so important to your business. Write a memo as part of your "business plan" for interviewing potential marketing consultants.

The IBM home page is a treasury of advice, resources, and hyperlinks to other valuable information. It is changed frequently, but on the date I reviewed the page, many topics were of e-commerce and small business development.

a) The major pages were titled News, Products, Services, Solutions, About IBM, Shop IBM, Support, Download
b) The left menu bar was labeled, "Resources," and of particular interest, hyperlinks to "Business partners," "home/home office," and "small business." All of these subjects should be investigated by the startup businessperson.
c) On clicking the hyperlink, "small business," intriguing subjects such as "small business solutions," "find a business partner," "interest groups," "women-owned businesses," "expert advice," "promotions," and "industry focus," to name a few gems, were the content of the day. Products directed toward small business solutions were IBM client servers, IBM Internet

solutions, IBM computer telephony business solutions, IBM SureOne Point of Sales Terminal, and other IBM business solutions. Each product contained a hyperlink, "Find out more."

d) One headline was entitled, "Price Advantage." To the small businessperson, this offer could be powerful.
e) Also strong was the headline entitled, "Promotions," that featured equipment and accessories at special discounted prices.
f) On the home page were several stories of value to the small business; one offered information on data mining. The article hyperlink read, "Beyond Computing: Is Anything Wrong with Data Mining?" This is an important technique for understanding customer happens.

4. Using the Deja.com Usenet, locate a business-to-business discussion group or groups (probably listed under alt.business or misc.business) that are discussing Web activities in e-business. Find five recent posts, print each out, and summarize the questions and responses. If any. What was the tone of the message? Are people confident in e-commerce?

This is a field exercise and will depend on the subject chosen by the student concerning Web activities in e-business. The Instructor should check the reports for accurate summation, the tone of the report, its negative or positive spin, and an answer to the question, "Are people confident in e-commerce?"

5. Review the list of opportunities presented by PricewaterhouseCoopers. From all of these objectives for implementing electronic marketing resources, which four opportunities would be most important to an automobile dealership specializing in fleet sales? A professional basketball team? A regional chain of lumber yards? A national chain of office building maintenance and cleaning services? Explain your logic in an e-mail to your PricewaterhouseCooper manager, who is also your instructor.

PricewaterhouseCoopers has taken a strong stand on e-business and how it can help shape relationships with customers. It provides opportunities such as:

- Building customer loyalty
- Reaching new markets
- Creating new products and services
- Achieving market leadership
- Optimizing business processes
- Enhancing human capital
- Harnessing technology
- Creating new products and services
- Managing risk and compliance

The objectives for implementing electronic marketing resources could be ranked for these disparate industries as follows:

Automobile dealership specializing in fleet sales:

- Building customer loyalty
- Reaching new markets
- Achieving market leadership
- Optimizing business processes

A professional basketball team:

- Building customer loyalty
- Managing risk and compliance
- Enhancing human capital
- Reaching new markets

A regional chain of lumber yards:

- Building customer loyalty
- Creating new products and services
- Reaching new markets
- Optimizing business processes

A national chain of office building maintenance and cleaning services:

- Building customer loyalty

- Creating new products and services
- Managing risk and compliance
- Optimizing business processes

The student and Instructor may judge different objectives for e-business, but the important point is that e-business capabilities change with each industry and each company. There is no one paradigm to follow.

6. You are the marketing manager for an automotive parts supply organization that has recently moved to direct customer sales (such as individuals, service stations, and automotive service centers) via a Web site ordering system. This change in your company's forty-year relationships with exclusive distributors is an uncertain risk. What marketing actions and resources can you implement to placate both long-term independent-contractor sales staff and your automotive parts distributors? Create a list of distributor relations and outside salesperson relation activities designed to support your company's reputation of being a trusted partner. Submit a one-page outline of ideas to your CEO.

Activities that the marketing manager might consider for the independent-contractor sales staff might include:
- Allowing the salesperson to "protect" five accounts permanently, thus earning the commission on sales
- Locating new lines of automotive products that the salesperson can have first choice at
- Earning 50 percent commission on all new Web customers
- Allowing the salesperson to take on new automotive lines that do not conflict with the automotive parts supply company's lines or services
- The parts supply company will pay for computer training of the independent-contractor sales staff

For the distributor company, activities could include:
- Allowing the distributor to take on new automotive lines that do not conflict with the automotive parts supply company's lines or services
- Earning 50 percent commission on all new Web customers

The student should realize that Web sales reach and ordering capabilities are changing traditional distribution arrangements and should be sensitive to this issue of altering the longstanding wholesale relationship. Perhaps the student or Instructor will have additional suggestions on balancing the compensation from Web transactions.

7. What are the advantages and disadvantages of an exclusive distribution agreement with a manufacturer? What are the advantages and disadvantages of multiple distribution channels including the Web for the same manufacturer? Select a product to describe these two scenarios. Write a one-page memo to your logistics manager explaining the situations and make a recommendation for future company channel management.

If the product is scarce, desirable, fashionable or crucial to a business process such as a burnt-out circuit board that stops production, then being a sole supplier as an exclusive distribution source can be very lucrative. Other advantages might include the prestige of carrying the line or first right of refusal for ensuing products made by the manufacturer such as a distributor of Armani or Hugo Boss. Hot-selling toys or video games and players are popular children's gifts during the holidays; often availability is scarce. The disadvantages of an exclusive distribution agreement can control product ability, possibly affect pricing (often the distributor will skim prices), and can lead to black market activities. Counterfeiting of watches, designer handbags or CDs and video tapes cost artists, manufacturers, and distributors millions of dollars in sales each year. Trademarks and copyrights are protected by intellectual property laws and manufacturers should take legal action against makers of pirated goods. However many of these protected products are manufactured overseas and are difficult to prosecute; we will discuss the ethics of e-marketing in Chapter 18.

8. Discuss the concept of partnering with other e-businesses. Explain what situations might arise as you serve a large oil company that has charged you with assessing, designing, and implementing a new private e-mail communications system. What would be the steps that you plan for the assignment, and what types of specialized partners would you recommend to the CEO of the oil company? Prepare outlines of the steps to the planning process and of the technology suppliers describing their roles in the construction of the e-mail system.

Many business and project decisions will be made in an assignment such as this. An excellent example of planning a business process, those series of steps and decisions that leads to the attainment of a larger goal. Management experts call for anticipating plans for product, personnel and processes. The project execution process of evaluation, planning, and execution provides a framework for studied and efficient determination of the workflow. While the evaluation and planning stages require flexibility and creativity in defining the problem and listing possible solutions (no two projects are ever exactly alike), the implementation stage can be structured into more anticipated labor.

A large oil company probably wouldn't charge any single person with assessing, designing, and implementing a new private e-mail communications system; the project would be way too big for one person. However, charging an individual with "coordinating the project" or "heading up the project," where s/he doesn't need to have technical knowledge in all areas is another matter. It is just too complex for a single person. But, having said that, the following responses would be part of the solution:

Is this going to be out-sourced or deployed in-house? Is this new or an upgrade to an existing system? How is e-mail currently being done (departmentally, personally, Yahoo!, Hotmail)? How many total users are there? What is the geographic distribution of the users? What type of network is currently in place? What is the network protocol? What desktops are running (UNIX, Macintosh, Win31/95/NT)? What are the current network failover mechanisms? How many servers currently exist and what are their geographic distributions? How many countries will be included in the initial rollout?

Then, designate the team:

i) Project Manager. Responsible for general coordination of the project.

ii) Technology Analyst. Responsible for review and selection of the proper e-mail system (i.e. Lotus Notes, MS-Exchange) within the framework of the existing corporate infrastructure.

iii) E-Mail Architect. Expert on the selected email system, with particular knowledge of load balancing, e-mail replication, failover mechanisms, multi-domain considerations, multi-company synchronization, etc.

iv) Network Team (Architecture, Implementation, Support). This team would be responsible for the design of the enterprise network and related tasks.

v) Security Team (Architect, Implementation, Support). This team would handle access control, security, authentication, enterprise-level user lock-out, etc.

vi) Hardware Team (Research, Planning, Implementation, Support). Experts on server, Backup Systems, routers, wiring and other physical infrastructure components.

vii) Training Team (Design, Planning, Implementation). Experts on how to train users on the new system by grouping common knowledge and skills by geographic area. This team would also have specific knowledge of language barriers and constraints within a global enterprise.

viii) E-mail Support Team (Post-install administration). This includes everything from desktop support to server support, including networking and security.

Next steps include allocating resources, developing the prototype and testing with small but representative user group, implementation of the system, the rollout to the desktops and train end-users, and, finally, the maintenance and administration the system. Of course, the marketer could ask IBM, Hewlett-Packard and Microsoft to give her a complete proposal, and then she would select a single vendor to do the whole thing.

9. There are parallels between traditional media and online media such as preparing a publicity program in which news releases on company activities are to be disseminated to the press. Some will be sent through U.S. mail to various news outlets while some will be posted to electronic news services such as Business Wire. Why should you use both traditional and e-marketing vehicles? Would you expect overlap of distribution employing both? What about traditional advertising and Web advertising? Are these duplications of efforts and audience exposures cost effective? Write your opinion on this topic and e-mail your response to a class member who will send you her opinion. Turn the two e-mails in to your instructor.

There is not sufficient reach to all of the business contacts that might be used in this dissemination program. Some traditional vehicles might not use the e-mail resources such as Business Wire or PR Newswire, major outlets that carry electronic news. Because of these uncertain business practices, the overlap is a necessary waste of resources. The same factors must be addressed in traditional advertising and Web advertising to consumers. No medium enjoys a hundred percent penetration of mass or targeted audiences therefore, message duplication is a necessary and wasteful evil, certainly not cost effective.

10. At the end of the chapter, e-business sales projections were presented for several years. Would you expect these projections to be accurate, plus or minus a 10 percent variation? What are five environmental factors that could upset these projections greatly? List the five factors and explain how these conditions could stop or limit the realization of these projections. Which industries do you feel are most vulnerable? Prepare your thoughts for a discussion in class.

Judging as how young the electronic commerce industry is, there is no history and no certainty that these figures will be close or even closely resemble the actual figures. Students should realize that estimates are guesses of future, unpredictable events; the wise marketer will review and evaluate economic projections. Then he will develop an optimal marketing program backed up by two or three contingency programs.

So many environmental factors (or combination of factors) could upset any one projection. If businesses are the drivers of online commerce, then I would look to economic forces affecting business purchasing or is this expansion as most likely to upset these projections. Negative business factors (listed in no particular order) could include:

- Increasing interest rates and rates of inflation
- Governments instability or ineffectual management of the economy
- Uncertainty of new political unions such as the EU
- Rising imported goods purchasing leading to trade imbalances
- U.S. government budget surpluses or deficits
- The performance of the U.S. stock market, particularly the technology issues

Some of the mentioned are causes and some are effects. As we have posited, marketers are becoming information technologists; worthwhile knowledge is also of the economic and market forces operating domestically and abroad.

Chapter 17
Implications to the International Marketing Program

Chapter Summary

E-commerce is ideal for expanding domestic operations into international markets. This chapter explores the opportunities, as well as the barriers, that must be overcome to market internationally in an electronic environment. The differences between marketing domestically and internationally in an electronic environment are discussed in detail. Questions and issues to address in determining foreign market potential are presented in a logical manner, which typically leads the marketer to the ultimate "go-no-go" decision on foreign market entry. The resultant information is then translated into techniques for the development of e-marketing programs that will provide entry in to foreign e-markets. Sources for international demographic and market information are discussed. In addition to opportunities for international e-commerce, the problems of international e-commerce, which the international marketer must overcome, are presented.

Students familiar with concepts of International Business should find this chapter both interesting and a natural extension of their knowledge of International Business practices.

Core Concepts

- To examine the similarities and dissimilarities of the international electronic marketing process
  To investigate the demographics and preferences of international Web users
  To explore the potential of e-commerce in various parts of the world

Chapter Outline

I. Analyzing the International Markets by Geography
   A. Evaluating the international marketing process and potential is the same thorough investigation conducted through situation conducted through situation analysis, marketing planning, and marketing implementation in domestic challenges
   B. The market research might be more sensitive to differences in product usage, product perceptions, and cultural diversities
   C. Domestic marketers will be wise to carefully scrutinize important practices that might be taken for granted in the U.S.
   Stipulations on systems' privacy
   Distribution of personal data
   Taxation
   Consumer protection laws
   D. International e-commerce is a complex endeavor through such things as:
      1. Monitoring currency fluctuations on the value of digital certificates
      2. Varying country regulations on Web site content
      3. Allowable types of advertising claims or sales promotions
      4. Levels of literacy among developing countries
   E. For assessing international e-commerce potential, a marketer should be alert to several conditions
      1. Web user profiles, hopefully on a country to country review
      2. Web usage profiles and Internet home penetration
      3. Levels of interest in online shopping and projected purchasing by category and country
      4. Trends in Web communications appliances
      5. Costs of access time and computer/appliance equipment
      6. Products and services usage and online purchase propensity
      7. Sensitivity to cultural influences that might negatively affect your product's association with the Internet, its content, or its technology in contemporary society
   F. The worst mistakes marketers make are failing to investigate the markets dynamics:

What consumers are wanting and buying
The level of category competition
The differences between each market

G. The marketer should also investigate the country's or region's infrastructure including:
Transportation for distribution
Traditional media outlets for primary message delivery
Standards of living
Strength of financial systems
Availability of reliable credit sources
Acceptance of credit cards for online shopping
Sophistication and availability of communications networks
Levels of discretionary income
National and local taxes

H. Using the Web's research sites, government transactions and records, even inquiring in Usenet news groups or listservs, the marketer can develop competitive intelligence, country by country

I. The Iconocast report is a good source of information on the specifics of European countries

J. You might wish to engage a market research firm as you would in the U.S.

K. There is an international address code that identifies every country of origin

L. The Internet Society has assigned letter country codes to countries

II. General Demographics Information on European and World Markets

A. Sources of international demographic information are:
United Nations' resources
U.S. Department of Commerce's trade records
International Chamber of Commerce's services
Private sources such as the Internationalist (www.internationalist.com), a web site for international business information

B. In the GVU Eighth User Survey, it was revealed that :

1. Respondents from Europe are more likely to have been online one to three years, while respondents from the U.S. are more likely to have started on the Internet within the last year
2. 46% of all ten thousand interviewees have created a Web page
3. European respondents (67%) were more likely to have created a Web page than U.S. respondents (43%)

C. "Europe [is] a beehive of Internet activity with some countries having as much as 21% Internet penetration

D. Online penetration is important in deciding country selection and segmentation

E. An international marketer should examine proposed markets for familiarity with Web usage and other online technologies before launching ambitious e-marketing programs

F. What may be familiar and second-nature to most Americans may be complicated and unclear to consumers of other nations

III. Patience Will Be Required

A. International marketing is unsettling and uncertain for many persons

B. People may be uncomfortable amid unfamiliar cultures or environments

C. Sound judgement is acquired through experience, and success or failure will be faced in local, national, or international assignments, even with the best research or advisers

IV. Internet Appliances in Europe

A. In Europe there are many options being developed separate from the PC

B. "Among the best array of non-PC Internet appliance emerging in Europe, Jupiter Communications research projects that smart phones will be the market leader, with over 12.9 million users access Internet content in 2002"

C. "While Internet appliances will not display Web sites, they will access specially filtered content from existing Web servers"

D. Web sites designed for international markets should be "sanitized," dropping American jargon, flags, or pop symbols that might only be recognized in the U.S.

E. A more graphic approach is recommended since photographs or illustrations can be processed visually for consumer or business-to-business information

F. Consider electronic marketing tools with simpler, more evident operation for your customer's convenience, particularly when he might be using an unfamiliar language

V. The Other Problems of International E-commerce

Be cognizant of the impact that the Internet has on nations and their social and government structures

Different countries view the effects of the Internet with different values in protecting their citizens, their economies, their national security, and their cultures

International e-commerce practices such as taxation, consumer protection, consumer data collection, and fraudulent operations mitigation are all new experiences and will take years to balance

Marketers are presently assuming a self-regulating stance and will adjust their practices on e-commerce and online communication to fit the country's laws that they are doing business with

Top executives of Internet, media, and telecommunications have begun an industry-live campaign, called the Global Business Dialogue on E-commerce, which is focusing initially on online privacy, taxation, and consumer confidence

The Global Business Dialogue is particularly concerned about the so-called EU Directive, a European Union policy that forbids companies from sending personal information out of Europe unless the destination country has certain privacy protections

Many U.S. businesses feel the directive is too restrictive

The GBD goal is to generate industry-led solutions to issues affecting electronic commerce. The nine areas that the group will focus on are:

1. Taxation
2. Data security
3. Online privacy
4. Liability for online content
5. Intellectual property-rights protection
6. Technical concerns about the Internet
7. Controversial content such as pornography
8. Who has jurisdiction over Internet transactions
9. Consumer confidence in e-commerce transactions

G. If any laws are to be enacted, international businesses want to be a part of the decision-making process

Teaching Suggestions

The topic of international marketing via the Web is an interesting one; its potential for opening international markets seems unmatched, but early into online marketing activities, the tactic has been largely ignored by consumer and business practitioners. The neglect can probably be traced to three major factors. First marketers have been busy sorting out strategies and systems directed toward domestic prospects and products; after all, the U.S. is the leader in networked communications for consumers and businesses. Secondly, the U.S. online penetration of the World Wide Web is the highest of any country. Thirdly overseas marketing research has been difficult to conduct or locate to the detail that American marketers have grown used to for reasonable decision making. The learning in this chapter is largely a presentation of the market situations in Europe and Latin America with comparisons to network status and Internet appliances. Much more effort in developing the Internet infrastructure and access, the number of Web users, and appropriate international or country-specific merchandise will be required before businesses will reap major sales from countries other than their own.

The text presents current problems and uncertainties in conducting e-marketing and e-commerce internationally. The Internet knows no boundaries but already faces barriers such as jurisdictions for commerce taxation, standards for privacy, legal content, and varying interpretations of liability. The content in this chapter is a work in progress like most of the online enterprise; the Instructor should supplement the learning by reading and viewing business news Web sites and business periodicals.

Answers to Questions and Exercises

1. Do the customs and assumed behavior actually affect a company's view of the Internet? Surf the Web for three international Web sites that you consider to be uncharacteristic, distasteful, or non-traditional as compared to "American" values or norms. Print each out and explain why you think these messages, graphics, or offers would not be well received by an average American shopper. Write a letter to each company making suggestions or changes to the site that would be more appealing to the average American consumer.

This is a field exercise that different students will investigate and demonstrate differently. The Instructor might give the students a hint by using the search engines' foreign language search capability to input key terms such as "German hygiene" or "Russian condoms." Differences in cultural sensitivity, consumer behavior, and consumer perceptions should be discussed.

2. Of the various demographics and economic factors that were discussed in preparing a situation analysis, which two do you consider most important conditions for entering an overseas market? Are they demographic, economic, cultural, or legal/regulatory conditions? Write a memo to your boss explaining your thoughts on the correct indicators for marketing exploration in a host country.

Economic infrastructure certainly would be a key factor in judging online penetration and capabilities for financial ability to consume with product distribution network. Probably the second most situation factor would be the legal/regulatory setting in that the foreign governments would allow the retailer to operate in the host country. In a populated country, consumer behavior due to demographics would probably allow for sufficient supply and demand, and because of needs and wants, products and services could be tailored for consumption. Cultural influences could also be accounted for by market research and marketing to appropriate segments.

3. What would you do if your boss gave you that LatAm assignment? How would you approach your decision? What would be your deciding factors to take the assignment and what would be your strategy in turning a market around? Say your company is an international chain of radio stations, which country would you select and why? Prepare an outline of your strategic plan for your company's vice president of international marketing.

In most marketing situations, domestic or international, marketers will find good and bad news; this LatAm proposition is no different. Analyzing the economic factors, GDP of Argentina, Brazil and Mexico is unexpected to grow therefore it is reasonable to expect inflation and interest rates to remain constant. Unstable local currencies certainly are problematic, but perhaps currency hedges could be secured against the currency of the nation in which the investment is made. At a zero growth rate of the GDP, buying business assets could be timely and possibly considered undervalued. Given that this situation prevails upon the three countries, business assets could be considered equivalent. If the parent company wishes to expand its radio station holdings, the decision factors may be drawn to the consumption levels of the general population, media habits, and the communications (for Internet expansion) infrastructure. The company purchase's of existing radio properties can provide a base for ongoing operations and cash flow while building a prospect base of future Internet users. The four to five-year waiting period for developing the Internet project might be a blessing in disguise as other infrastructures and market conditions mature. The Instructor may have to lead the logic of the business strategy for the class.

4. In comparing the international electronic marketing process to the traditional marketing process, what are the similarities and the dissimilarities of each practice? Select the three most similar and the three most dissimilar points and explain your thoughts. Write an e-mail to an associate who is opening a branch office of an internationally-known stock brokerage in Asia. Since this is her first overseas assignment and you have opened branch offices in South America, give her advice on the marketing process' similarities and differences.

The three most similar practices or elements shared by both the traditional marketing process and the international e-marketing process are: the vehicle (the Web), the consumer (wants and needs motivations), and the concept of marketing facilitating commerce (the exchange process). But, the traditional and the international e-marketing's most similar elements are: consumers' wants and needs, a method of communications, and the practice of the marketing mix. Products may change according to national tastes and ability to consume. Distribution methods also vary according to the level of development of the country. Price strategy will fluctuate depending on the market's capabilities to consume products of different utility levels.

The dissimilarities are more striking. For the person experienced in domestic traditional marketing, the transition to international e-marketing process is often difficult because of the lack of trusted resources in the situation analysis and marketing implementation stages. In the situation analysis, veteran marketers call upon primary research and secondary research to investigate consumer or business purchasing behavior or other motivational factors. In international e-marketing research, these two resources are difficult to commission or locate; e-marketing research for some business categories just has not been conducted. The third dissimilarity is in preparing a complementary IMC media program supported by online communications. Many countries are not as "media rich" or "media diverse" as the U.S. Creativity in alternative program development and an adjustment period to overseas conditions generally help the marketer become accustomed to local consumer attitudes.

5. Why do consumer habits differ from country to country in Europe? If you compare the populations listed in the "Europe Online" table, you will find several countries with populations of less than six million. With common ancestries, small land areas, and small populations, should purchasing and Internet habits be similar? Be prepared for a class discussion on this topic.

One of the largest factors for national organization, ethnicity, and economic development, all leading to cultural behavior is physical geography, the natural dividing features of oceans, rivers, and other large bodies of water, of mountains and plains, deserts and rainforests, and valleys and islands. These features tend to isolate populations that eventually evolve into societies with different standards, expectations, ethics, and consumption patterns. Europe has a diverse and "dividing" topography such as the Alps, the Pyrenees, valleys, rivers and seas that encouraged isolated population development, therefore, producing different expectations for wants and needs. Another differentiating activity is the manner in which food is obtained. Some "nations" are aggressive hunters or fishers while others sustain the community through agrarian labor. Different societies also use geography differently in matters of commerce. Those nations that sailed to the different continents learned of different and exotic goods that were adopted by the travelers' societies. Different patterns of behavior and different national spirits created a diversity of national unions.

6. If you were the owner of a high quality equestrian bridle shop, which two countries would you target in Europe? Why? List four reasons and explain each one. Write your explanation as a letter seeking funds from a domestic bank; the loan proceeds would be used for expanding your Web server and database systems.

After a simple search on AltaVista, the key words such as "horse," "Europe," "equestrian," many appropriate sites were produced. Horse population, English rider estimates, competition from tack and equipment shops, and rider population by European countries were detailed as well as the names of equestrian magazines and newsletters. The student can answer the question by visiting links such as :

International Horses, http://www.horse-country.com/international.html
Equiweb, http://www.equiweb.co.uk/
Elmcroft Equestrian Centre, http://www.geocities.com/Yosemite/Trails/7251/index.html

7. You are a marketer with a company involved in the EU Directive negotiations. Write a company policy on international e-commerce with regards to the legal liability of the company. Will you operate according to the laws and regulations of the host country, or will you operate according to the laws of your home country providing full disclosure of your company's accountability?

This is one of the "it depends" questions that confound international marketers and corporate legal counsel. Several points of consideration would be the number of countries that you plan to market in. Counsel would advise fewer, and the marketer would perform a situation analysis on each to arrive at a reasonable market population. Also the marketer would judge the threat of liability according to the product. If the product requires "benign "usage such as colorful kitchen wares, the marketer might operate according to the laws and relations of each host country. If the product involves more risk such as consumption of pharmaceutical products or usage of high technology medical equipment, the marketer might recommend that the company operate under the laws of the country. These factors should be closely scrutinized on a country by country basis, and the company's responsibility to fully disclose its accountability will be important in building brand loyalty in markets overseas.

8. How would you approach the Chinese population in selling them specialized work apparel? These safety garments are for workers in hazardous jobs such as steel mills, chemical factories, and hydro-electric construction projects. If you used the Internet, why so? What markets would you target and with what message? If you did not use the Web, why not? What would be your alternative promotional program? Would you consider other forms of online communications? Which ones and why?

This marketing assignment would probably require government partnering. Construction of major infrastructure projects might still be considered state secrets, and therefore, off limits to foreign companies. If the guest company is allowed to sell these safety garments directly to Chinese construction workers, probably the most credible online marketing tool would be discussion groups aimed at construction project managers. This communication might strike up word-of-mouth recognition and approval from authority figures such as these construction project managers. Considering the low penetration of the Web in mainland China, a better promotional tactic might be a sampling demonstration held at the largest construction sites. The Web might not be a good alternative considering the economic and the lack of technology capability of the construction worker market.

Chapter 18
The Ethics of Electronic Marketing

Chapter Summary

The scope, magnitude, and power of the electronic environment are rapidly becoming incomprehensible. In addition to creating myriad opportunities for its positive use and application, unethical individuals will find ample opportunity to use it in illegal, unethical, or immoral ways. The role of ethics in e-commerce is taking an increasingly larger role in the guarding against abuse that can occur in such a dynamic environment. This chapter presents an ethical foundation to the issues of customer service, privacy, security, censorship, copyright, and proprietary property. The legalities of selling across state and international borders are raised, as well as Free Speech in the context of the Internet and World Wide Web as a public forum for communication. The question of "Who should have access to the Internet?" is raised.

Core Concepts

- To discuss the basic ethics of marketing on the Internet
- To reiterate the concept that customer satisfaction leads to long-term marketing relationships
- To establish guidelines along with common sense concepts that can encourage marketers to act responsibly and ethically in the practice of electronic marketing

Chapter Outline

I. A Commitment to Customer Service
   A. Treat customers in all communications and transactions as you would like to be treated, putting the needs of the customers first
      1. Provide secure, fast connections
      2. Continually improve content in you Web infrastructure
      3. You owe your customers safe delivery and promised satisfactions for the right goods and services they order
      4. Provide twenty-four hour online response to customers or prospects questions
      5. Do not tempt them with false advertising and then expect them to be your loyal customer
      6. Be sure that orders are being filled accurately and on time
      7. Make sure to respond to the customer in a timely manner regarding items ordered that are out of stock, discontinued, or otherwise unavailable
      8. Give accurate estimates of delivery dates
      9. Provide a response to the customers order via e-mail or postal mail so they have a record of the transaction
      10. If a mistake occurs, be sure to apologize and accommodate the customer as best you can
   B. Personal privacy
      1. Providing assurance of personal privacy is a very important aspect of the ethical and moral obligations a marketer has to the consumer and the company
      2. Do not annoy potential customers by filling their e-mail boxes with unwanted solicitations and information - "spamming"
   C. To contact a large number of people like interests, you should use a mailing list
      1. For each list you create to communicate with your customers, be sure to provide an option for joining the mailing list rather then making it mandatory
      2. There should be no sending of unsolicited bulk e-mail (spam) to people who are not expecting it or no postings of inappropriate ads to newsgroups or mailing lists
      3. It is also important to provide consumers a way to terminate their subscription to your mailing list
   D. Security: validation and censorship

1. You owe them a secure transaction as they order products or services or request information online
2. If the consumer desires, you should have an alternative method of payment
3. Provide a written policy to let the customer know that the site is collecting sensitive information and how you are dealing with the security issues

E. Types of security measures:
1. Secure Sockets Layer (SSL)
2. Secure Electronic Transactions (SET)
3. Firewalls, along with encryption and frequently changed passwords are ways to help secure your systems against hackers or persons with malicious intent
4. Other issues of security include such things as validating a persons age or identity before orders are placed or sites are viewed
5. Internet Censorship
6. Legalities of selling across state lines or across international borders

F. Copyright issues:
1. Be aware of the current copyright restrictions and follow them
   a. If you decide that you would like to link to someone's site or use some material that they have developed, it is best to contact them first
   b. If you see a page that intrigues you and want to make one just like it, copying the code falls under the same category
   c. If you need graphics for you Web site, buy them, do not steal them
2. In the academic world, the Fair Use Act provides for the use of small pieces of copyrighted material for the purpose of education

G. Computer viruses are nasty annoyances that cause many problems for both the consumer and the marketer and you must take precautions to assure you are not spreading disease to your consumers

H. Another common problem is the spreading of information's on hoaxes

I. It is unlawful to copy and use software without purchasing a license (piracy)

II. Who Should Be Using the Internet

A. The marketer should ask herself the questions such as "Should there be any regulations on usage of the Internet, such as applying to children's usage or extremist militia groups in communications or informational retrieval?"

B. The balance between the First Amendment Freedom of Speech is often at odds with matters of community morals and decency

C. The following questions are still issues regarding the Internet:
1. Who should be the gatekeeper of the Internet content?
2. Is someone's desire to download indecent images and to archive the images protected by free speech?
3. Do content filters, called blocking software in the *Journal* editorial, violate the same principles of freedom of speech by the pornography disseminators?
4. Should the government decide what content is acceptable?
5. Should the online industry self-regulate itself?
6. Is access to the Internet a "universal right"?
7. Should everyone have free access to the network of the Internet as individuals now have free access to television information's and entertainment airwaves of the broadcast networks?
8. Should advertisers be allowed to place their messages anywhere on the Internet or should there be "safe" times or "channels" free of advertising?
9. Should advertising be restricted to "promotional channels" in which commercial messages are transmitted all day long like the television shopping networks?
10. How will computer-illiterate people or those without computer compete within the information economy?

Teaching Suggestions

The degree of success in electronic commerce and marketing lies in the care and conduct of future cybermerchants. If consumer and business buyers have confidence in the online commerce process, then e-commerce should be a matchless success that will create a permanent industry and benefit economies and societies all over the globe. It is unjustified to say that e-marketing will need to find its level of ethics in the coming years because ethical behavior is already a standard whether the activities are business, medicine, advertising, accounting, or any other professional endeavor. Ethics, morality, fair competition were not stressed as I completed my undergraduate studies in the early 1970s; perhaps these topics were taken for granted in the practices of the oligopolies that piloted American business during the 1950s and 1960s. Prior industrial powers, Japan and Germany, were rebuilding their internal economies and posed little threat of competition; the U.S. did not have to engage in unfair or unethical business dealings because if the domestic or international company required available products or services, the U.S. was the vendor. We've read about the decline of quality and competitiveness in the 1970s, and how U.S. business foundered until the late 1980s.

During the '80s, U.S. businesses found themselves at perceived and real disadvantages, that American products were not the goods of choice when compared to products of Japan, Germany, and other industrialized countries. Perhaps unethical practices have accompanied American business for centuries, but the visibility, scope, and sheer magnitude of greed shocked our general public. Stock brokerages' self-dealing brought respected companies down and put its executives in prison. Savings and loan associations were swindled in massive real estate fraud. As prices skyrocketed, oil companies were accused of creating fantasy oil shortages. The public began distrusting business as well as politicians and automobile dealers.

The participants in the Internet economy must learn from the past and look towards a bright future. Web merchants, providers, and suppliers must act responsibly in the short-term and long-term to gain and preserve the customers' trust. The e-commerce industry must organize to establish self-regulation to protect its interests and the interests of buyers from unscrupulous individuals and firms. In the early part of the 20th century, the advertising industry recognized a similar threat of possible government regulations and created the American Association of Advertising Agencies. The AAAA has improved the practice of advertising, demanded ethical behavior from all of its members, and has proved to be a model of self-regulation for many business groups.

The Instructor should bring these past abuses to light to compare and contrast what e-commerce and e-marketing should and should not be. Already individual rights such as privacy and medical confidentiality are being debated as to what information is appropriate for Internet transmission. Social issues of technology training, increased automation, and access to the Internet as fundamental human rights have surfaced as consequences of information networks. The student should be alert to these ethical developments and have opinions on these complex developments.

Answers to Questions and Exercises

1. Write a one-page paper on how copyright on the Internet affects the marketing process and the current copyright laws. What products or services might have their copyright protection violated by transmission over the Internet? Write an e-mail to your company's legal department asking for verification of your understanding of the Internet and copyright infringement. Include at least two online references besides those listed in this chapter.

The student may approach this question from different angles, but should be able to adequately support their opinions and concepts with references on copyright from the Internet. Here are just a few of the references that I found in a search on copyright that offer information on issues of copyright.

http://www.utsystem.edu/ogc/intellectualproperty/cprtindx.htm#top
http://www.benedict.com/
http://law.miningco.com/msub11.htm

Expression, not facts or ideas, is protected by copyright. The definition of expression, as defined by the Copyright Act of 1976, includes literary, dramatic, and musical works; pantomimes and choreography; pictorial, graphic and sculptural works; audio-visual works; sound recordings; and architectural works. The act states that an original expression is eligible for copyright protection as soon as it is fixed in a tangible form.

Therefore, almost any original expression that is created is protected as soon as it is expressed. Examples of expression from the Internet might be: an image created in Photoshop which is protected as soon as the file is saved to disk, a Web page that is protected on saving it as an HTML file, or music or video clips that are provided via electronic means. However, not absolutely everything is eligible for copyright. Items that by their very nature are not eligible for copyright protection might be: ideas, facts, titles, names, short phrases, and blank forms to name just a few. A second work that merely happens to be very similar (or even identical) to an earlier work does not infringe on copyright as long as it is independently created.

Along with copyright we must also look at Fair use and implied licenses. Fair use is a legal license to use others' work, whether they approve or not. Fair use lets us use small portions of copyrighted materials, but not as much as we'd like to. Sometimes it is necessary to ask for permission to use even small portions of copyrighted materials and it is always safest to do so. Fair use constitutes one of the most important, and least clear cut, limits to copyright. The basic problem is that words like "fair" or "reasonable" cannot be clearly defined. In the U.S., partial or limited reproduction of another's work may be permitted under this doctrine. Fair use is not really feasible for the commercial world, but often it is useful in the educational setting.

Copyright of e-mail messages on list serves is a topic for many debates on the Internet. Few who post to e-mail lists would object if their messages were forwarded to others who might be interested. However, in doing so, or in using part of a prior message in responding to an earlier message, one should be careful not to change the original author's meaning. Likewise, there are few that would object to having their messages archived, perhaps on a Web page. Archiving clearly serves the interests of list members who may occasionally want to revisit topics addressed earlier. Indeed, most would prefer having archives to seeing old topics rehashed again and again -- the reason one often sees lists of frequently asked questions (FAQs). For this reason, it would alleviate many copyright problems list owners would broadcast, at least on initial subscription, a notice about copyright policy when a subscriber requests access to the list. For example, those who post to this list retain their copyright. However, subscribers grant a non-exclusive license to the list owner, directly or indirectly, to archive, and to other subscribers to forward, any message posted here.

2. Do a search on the Internet for digital certificates. Write four or five paragraphs on how to use digital certificates for authenticating users. Do you feel that digital certificates will be useful in aiding e-commerce?

Authentication is the process of verifying that people or things you cannot see are who or what they claim to be. It is the most essential of all the security services because it is the basis of access control, permissions and authorizations, enforcing accountability, and achieving non-repudiation. One of the key applications of cryptography for authentication is the digital certificate.

Digital certificates are virtual fingerprints, or retinal scans as it were, that authenticate the identity of a person or thing in a concrete, verifiable way. The certificate itself is simply a collection of information to which a digital signature is attached by the issuer, also known as a Certificate Authority (CA). A Certificate Authority is a third-party organization that is trusted by the community of certificate users, whose role is analogous to that of a Department of Motor Vehicles (DMV), which issues driver's licenses and is broadly acknowledged and accepted as a trustworthy means of personal identification. Certificate Authorities typically offer a combination of cryptography technology, an infrastructure of highly secure facilities, and a specification of practices and liability that establish its ability to operate as a trusted third party. Customers may contract with the Certificate Authority to handle routine certificate administration tasks, or they may elect to assume responsibility for certificate issuance and revocation themselves, thereby maintaining a higher level of control. You can get a certificate from companies like VeriSign.

Every time someone sends an electronic message, they attach their Digital ID to sign and encrypt that message. The recipient of the message first uses his or her own Digital ID to verify that the author's public key is authentic, then uses that public key to verify the message itself. In addition to all the benefits of authentication they provide for electronic commerce, Digital ID also make access control more secure and easier to administer than traditional password schemes. With Digital IDs, administrators don't have to waste time replacing forgotten passwords and reminding users how to log on. Digital IDs are also easy to get, easy to use, and inexpensive.

Oddly enough, passwords still play an important role even when using digital certificates. Since a digital certificate is stored on a computer, they can only be used to authenticate the computer, rather than the user, unless the user provides some other form of authentication to the computer. Passwords or pass phrases are generally used; smart cards and other hardware tokens will be used in the future. Any company systems making limited distribution data available over the Internet shall use digital certificates to validate the identity of both the user and the server. Company-approved Certificate Authorities may only issue certificates. Certificates at the user end will be used in conjunction with standard technologies such as Secure Sockets Layer to provide continuous authentication to eliminate the risk of session hijacking.

Here are some more resources for information on Digital Certificates:
Supporting article
http://www.Internetworld.com/print/1999/05/24/ecomm/19990524-digital.html
Concerns Don't Slow E-Commerce Privacy Assurance Eases Fears
http://cyberatlas.Internet.com/market/retailing/concern.html
Internet Privacy a Complex Issue No Easy Solution to This Problem
http://cyberatlas.Internet.com/market/retailing/privacy.html

3. Viruses are a dangerous element to computer users. Do a search and find the prominent virus protection software companies. List their Web address and what products they have available.

McAfee Virus Scan (Network Associates) and Norton Utilities (Symantic) are the most commonly used virus protection and repair software currently in use. Here is a list (not inclusive) of additional products that these companies provide.

Network Associates http://www.nai.com/	Symantec http://www.symantec.com/nav/	
	ACT! 3.0	Norton Zip Rescue
McAfee Total Virus Defense	Café	pcANYWHERE32 8.0
PGP Total Netwrok Security	dbANYWHERE	pcTelecommute
Sniffer Total Network Visibility	Enterprise Suite	Symantec JITspeed
Magic Total Service Desk	Mobile Essentials	Symantec Mobile Update
Securecast	Norton 2000	TalkWorks
ETC.	Norton 2000 Corporate Edition	VisualCafé 3.0 for Win 95/98/NT
	Norton AntiVirus 5.0	VisualCafé Database Edition
	Norton CleanSweep	VisualCafé Professional Edition
	Norton CrashGuard	VisualCafé Standard Edition
	Norton Ghost	Visual Page
	Norton Safe on the Web	WinFax PRO
	Norton Secret Stuff	Corporate WinFax PRO
	Norton SystemsWorks	
	Norton Utilities 4.0	
	Norton Your Eyes Only	

4. Make a short list of things not to do with electronic mail. Make a short list of ways to make electronic commerce more appealing to consumers who have a fear of losing their privacy. What is the difference between solicited and unsolicited e-mail? Are there situations or organizations that might be appropriate for sending unsolicited e-mail?

What not to do with e-mail
SPAM
Unsolicited e-mail
Profanity; Flaming
Libel/Slander

Options for making consumers feel more secure about privacy
Privacy Policies
Digital Certificates
Seals of approval from known organizations
SSL

Solicited e-mail is e-mail that a consumer or user has requested by signing up for information or filling out a request for information form, etc. Unsolicited e–mail is e-mail sent with no permission given.

There is very little mail that should be sent unsolicited. About the only type I can think of would be inter-company mailings, but these are not truly unsolicited as employees expect to be communicated with by their employees and co-workers. There may be other correct answers to this portion of the question that will need to be evaluated on an individual basis. This is a hard concept and many people argue over what is actually SPAM. Just follow the guideline of: treat your consumers, as you would like to be treated.

5. Access the American Marketing Associations (AMA) Web page and read about the standards for ethics they provide. From your experience and dealings with the Web, do you feel that e-marketers are conducting themselves morally and ethically on the Internet? Write an e-mail to the AMA stating your observations and your opinions.

The full text of the AMA Code of Ethics can be obtained from www.ama.org. This will provide a guideline for accessing the answers that students provide for this question, however this question asks for an opinion and will based on the ethics and morality of the student and can be very individualized.

5. Conservatives and liberals disagree on content appropriateness for the World Wide Web. Investigate on the Web what measures can be taken to stop minors from viewing sites that are not appropriate. Discuss and support with URLs the different methods available. Do you feel that they are effective? Write a two-page editorial stating your opinion for your local newspaper.

A good site to begin getting information on this subject is the CyberAngels site, http://www.cyberangels.org/. This site explains the different methods for blocking, filtering, monitoring and tracking sites on the Internet. It also discusses some of the top products on the market for accomplishing these tasks. Here are some excerpts from the site and a listing of the top products.

- Net Nanny - www.netnanny.com
- CyberPatrol - www.cyberpatrol.com
- CYBERSitter - www.cybersitter.com
- SurfWatch - www.surfwatch.com

Blocking software - software that uses a "bad site" list. It blocks access to sites on the list. Some of the software companies allow you to customize the list, by adding or removing sites yourself. Other software companies try to keep the sites on their list secret and don't permit parents to add or remove sites from the list. Blocked site lists should be updated regularly. Some software companies allow you to download updated sites daily. Others may charge for updates after a certain period, and may update their lists less frequently. No matter how frequently they are updated, however, the number of Web sites published each day far exceeds the ability of the software companies to review the sites, and categorize them for "bad site" lists. Out of approximately 3 million separate Web sites in existence (each Web site may contain 2 or more separate Web pages and the number of separate files, pages and graphics online is estimated at 330 million), only a small fraction have been reviewed by all child protection software companies. The gap widens daily, with the 160,000 new Web sites registered each month. "Bad sites" will inevitably get through.

Filtering - software that uses certain keywords. It blocks sites containing these keywords, alone or in context with other keywords. Software that uses standalone keywords may often filter out harmless sites, because of the inclusion of innocent words within those sites. "Butt" may be a preselected keyword, and software that doesn't filter in context would block access to sites containing the word "button." "Sex" as a filtered term may result in the blocking of the latest Web site for "sextuplets," or "Sussex, England". The biggest problem with using keyword filtering is that innocent sites may be blocked. In addition, some Web site operators have learned to get around the filtering by misspelling the typical keywords.

Outgoing filtering - certain information that a child may want to share with others can't be shared. Information such as her name, address, or telephone number can be programmed into the software, and every time she tries to send it to someone online, it merely shows up as "XXX."

Monitoring and tracking - some software allows parents to track where their children go online, how much time they spend on the computer, and even allows parents to control what times of day their children can use the computer. Many parents who find filtering or blocking distasteful, especially with older children and teens, find monitoring to satisfy their safety concerns.

6. Visit a least three major business sites of interest to you. Find their privacy policy statement and in two-pages, summarize each policy. Do you as a consumer feel comfortable with the protection they say they are providing you? In what areas do these privacy statements compare and in what areas are they contrasting? Which company's privacy statement do you most agree with? Why?

For this question I looked at three companies that do a lot of business on the Internet. For the most part, they were all comparable. Not being a particularly wary consumer, I would feel comfortable with all of their policies to protect my privacy. However, I might find myself choosing to unsubscribe myself to their list, keeping me from being inundated with e-mail from them and their third party connections. Here is a table that compares the privacy policies and the URL for each company.

	Microsoft www.microsoft.com	***Dell Computers*** www.dell.com	**Gateway Computers** www.gateway.com
Privacy Policy Easy to find	Yes	Yes	Yes
Explain what is collected and why	Yes	Yes	Yes
Send only solicited e-mail	Yes	Yes	Yes
Do not give outside sources list of consumers (Can request to be removed from list)	Yes	Yes	Yes
Use SSL for transactions & provide other means order besides online	Yes	Yes	Yes
Explain how cookies are used	Yes	Yes	Yes
Can correct/update personal information	Yes	Yes	Yes
By using site you consent to these policies	Yes	Yes	Yes
Other features	• Children's privacy issues addressed • Use TRUSTe	• Use BBBOnline Privacy	

Chapter 19
The Future of Electronic Marketing Resources

Chapter Summary

The future is difficult to accurately predict. Just a few years ago, business professionals would have felt pressed to answer the question "What will the future hold for e-commerce?" This, the final chapter in the text, raises this very question and attempts to project the future direction of e-commerce and e-marketing. These projections are based on existing technologies and attempt to show how these will be integrated to enhance the electronic environment in unprecedented ways. Numerous examples are used to show the implications of the convergence of existing and developing technologies.

Not only are implications to e-commerce made, but projected implications on consumers are also presented. The Internet2 project is introduced and its goals are outlined in detail, as well as are forecasts for improvements in software technology. Every technology improvement discussed is presented in the context of enhancing service to the customer. The chapter concludes with the premise that successful businesses of the future will be the one's that use digital tools to reinvent the way they work. Lastly, Bill Gates' Twelve New Rules (for business in the future) are presented and discussed.

Core Concepts

- To discuss the possibilities of electronic marketing technology in the future
- To speculate on the roles of electronic marketing technology in the future
- To envision the capacities of service delivered by electronic commerce

Chapter Outline

I. What the Future Holds
   A. In the context of marketing technology, convergence is the coming together of two or more disparate disciplines or technologies to provide systems of greater benefit
      1. The fax revolution was produced by a convergence of telecommunications technology, optical scanning technology, and printing technology
      2. NGI technology will provide technology for transmission of video components, videoconferencing, video storage, video broadcasting, video delivery of satellite or cable television programming over broadband networks, and video signal switching from Asynchronous Transfer Mode (ATM) to other types of networks such as ATM-to-Ethernet, the Internet system wired into many college dormitories throughout the nation

II. Overview of ATM in the Context of NGI
   A. The Internet using a modem and telephone line is a simple, analog conversation occurring between two digitally minded machines
   B. Telephones have traditionally used analog technology, which refers to electronic transmission accomplished by adding signals of varying frequency to carrier waves of a fixed frequency of alternating electromagnetic current
   C. This is called modulation
      1. A modem is used to convert the digital information in the computer to analog phone signals for the phone line and to convert analog phone signals to digital information for the computer
      2. Basically, the modem is the translator of the digital to the analog technology and herein lies the problem
      3. Traditionally, telecommunications technology has leveraged the highly predictable nature of voice data and delivered this data efficiently by using dedicated circuits operating at a fixed bandwidth

4. The mode of delivery is through what is known as circuit switching technology, which is the foundation of the telephone network
5. Telecommunications companies are now embracing networks capable of high-speed transmission of images-broadcast television and cable
6. The networks to support the new technology have remained in a separate domain

D. The method of transmitting this data uses what are called packet switching techniques, where small parcels of data transmitted individually across digital communications networks, typically known as Local Area Networks (LANs) or Wide Area Networks (WANs)
E. There is now an increasing recognition that technology is required that is capable of meeting both styles of operation
F. The strengths of the telecommunication approach in network management and control have become extremely attractive to the computing community, where network problems, even outages, result from the use of protocols, or standards of transmitting data, that are not ideally suited to such situations
G. A variety of new standards are being created to address the current deficiencies
H. A new network protocol know as Asynchronous Transfer Mode (ATM)
I. ATM provides for a signal network service capable of supporting video, voice, and data transmission needs in a flexible and responsive way, and incorporates the following capabilities:
   1. Much higher transmission capabilities
   2. Flexibility and versatility
   3. Universality and adaptability
   4. The ability to meet the needs of each segment of the corporate network
J. ATM implies far-reaching institutional as well as technological changes
   1. Standards development continues
   2. The order of implementation of ATM technology will be the Metropolitan Area Network (MAN) level in the institutional/educational campus context, followed by the Wide Area Network (WAN) level, then the corporate Local Area Network (LAN) level, and finally the work group and desktop level implementations
K. ATM thus represents a major component of NGI since it brings inter-networking potential of the Internet together with the management capabilities of high-capacity transmission within the traditional telecommunications industry

III. NGI in the Context of Marketing to Consumers

A. Internet has placed great strains on the ability of companies to deliver on their marketing promises
   1. Internet bottleneck problem
   2. Quality of service has thus become the problem with today's Internet

IV. Internet2 Project

A. Internet2 is a part of the NGI to rededicate a communications network linking research universities as the original Internet was purposed
B. The Internet2 project is bringing focus, energy, and resources to the development of a new family of advanced applications to meet emerging academic requirements in research, teaching, and learning
C. Internet2 universities, working with industry, government, and other research and education networking organizations, are addressing the major challenges facing the next generation of university networks by:
   1. Creating and sustaining a leading edge network capability for the national research community
   2. Directing network development efforts to enable a new generation of applications to fully exploit the capabilities of broadband networks
   3. Working to rapidly transfer new network services and applications to all levels of educational use and to the broader Internet community, both nationally and internationally
D. The goals of the Internet2 project include the following:
   1. Enable a new generation of applications
   2. Recreate a leading edge research and education network capability

3. Transfer new capabilities to the global production Internet
4. Demonstrate new application that can dramatically enhance researchers abilities to collaborate and conduct experiments
5. Demonstrate enhanced delivery of education and other services by taking advantage of "virtual proximity" created by an advanced comminations infrastructure
6. Support development and adoption of advanced applications by providing middleware and development tools
7. Facilitate development, deployment, and operation of an affordable communications infrastructure, capable of supporting differentiated Quality of Service (QOS) based on applications requirements of the research and education community
8. Promote experimentation what the next generation of communications technologies
9. Coordinate adoption of agreed working standards and common practices among participating institutions to ensure end-to-end quality of service and interoperability
10. Catalyze partnerships with governmental and private sector organizations
11. Encourage transfer of technology from Internet2 to the rest of the Internet
12. Study impact of new infrastructure, services, and applications on higher education and the Internet community in general

E. Perhaps the Internet2 will bring resources of communications technology and networking delivery technology into balance

V. The Evolution of Technology

A. If the NGI will provide much relief to the problems of bandwidth thus speeding up data transmission and reducing download time, what technology would interest the e-marketer?
   1. The hardware developers are pursing compact, mobile, hand-held devices containing wireless transmission similar to a cellular telephone in function and a Palm Pilot-like computer in size
   2. An Internet appliance that would serve consumers and businesspeople alike will probably have most of the following features:
      a. Internet-ready connections
      b. Color screen for daylight viewing
      c. Sufficient power for processing
      d. Voice recognition capabilities with pen-touch stylus
      e. Memory for storage of text and graphical documents
      f. Cellular telephone for upload and replication capabilities
      g. Ear and mouth piece, possibly a headset, to eliminate noise, static, and interference

B. IBM has made a pledge to eliminate the keyboard within five years to facilitate speech-activated technologies

C. The marketer will gain the capability of sending information to be consumer as the consumer logs on to his PC or Internet appliance via Internet push technology

VI. Th Expansion in Imaginative Software

A. E-commerce software of the future will be constructed for one of two purposes:
   1. To provide knowledge and convenience to the individual consumer
   2. To provide knowledge and competitive advantage for the company through business systems

B. To attract the consumer, creative and service-oriented Web sites will render information with several platforms:
   1. Entertainment
   2. Humor
   3. Rational information
   4. Factual comparison

C. Software applications, the primary building components of Web sites, are expected to be online virtual reality simulations including:
   1. Virtual Reality Modeling Language (VRML)
   2. Three-dimensional graphic tools

3. Web browsers that can display these "virtual spaces"

D. Cyberspace is proving to be a viable place for marketing venues such as industry conferences

E. Virtual reality technology (VRML) will become increasingly important as Internet-based content is available over cable modems and the other inevitable high-speed delivery system

F. Software systems for the business-to-business organization will stress interconnectivity, bringing people and functions together over the Internet

G. The VRML Web site will be the base for e-commerce

H. VRML programs will also assist the company in employee training and product sales demonstrations

I. Portal sites should continue to mature

VII. The Success of Internet Acquisitions and Mergers

A. The late 1990's saw a flurry of interest in Internet properties by investors and Internet competitors that caused a merger and acquisition frenzy

B. These acquisitions totaled in the multi-billion dollar range, and many investors were uncertain of the true value of Internet business

VIII. The Persistence in Serving the Consumer

A. Competition will drive marketers to search for competitive advantages

B. They will leverage the strength of the Internet medium-speed, accuracy, accessibility, personalization, and convenience to the consumer and will sever marketers in ways unimaginable

C. The marketer will become an information technologist, delving more into information retrieval and information delivery and applying the same framework as he develops creative promotional programs as well as information dissemination

D. The marketer will need to be schooled in a new "science" of Internet media habits, a topic dating only from the mid nineties

E. The marketer must give consideration to user-friendly marketing processes

1. Do things in as few ways as possible
2. Design systems for a hundred times your current load
3. Move quickly but cautiously on new technology, and don't jump on the newest and coolest just because it's new and cool (Investigate technology, but don't forsake your customer's best interest)
4. Put your best people closest to the money even those aren't typically the highest-paying positions

F. Consumer concerns will continue

1. Security remains one of the top reasons Web users report for not purchasing over the Web
   a. "not trusting that my credit card number will be secure," 39%
   b. "not being able to judge the quality of the product," 39.3%
   c. Not trusting that personal information will be kept private (26.9%)
   d. Being able to find the product faster/easier by shopping locally (22.6%)
2. Supporting the notion that the Web has become an important tool to access information
3. 84% of the users report that they consider access to the Wed indispensable, nearly the same percentage as those who feel e-mail is indispensable

G. Commerce overconfidence

1. E-marketing is not the easy way out, only alternative strategy amid the hard work of marketing
2. E-marketing's efforts must be integrated among traditional promotional and sales programs to enhance the synergy gained by attentive and sensitive marketing activities

IX. Bill Gates' Twelve New Rules

A. "The successful companies of the next decade will be the ones that use digital tools to reinvent the way they work. To make digital information flow an intrinsic part of your company, here are twelve key steps:

1. Insist that communication flow through e-mail
2. Study sales data online to share insights easily

3. Shift knowledge workers into high-level thinking
4. Use digital tools to create virtual teams
5. Convert every paper process into a digital process
6. Use digital tools to eliminate single-task jobs
7. Create a digital feedback loop]
8. Use digital systems to route customer complains immediately
   a. Focus on your most unhappy customer
   b. Use technology to gather rich information on their unhappy experiences wit your product and to find out what they want you to put into the product
   c. Use technology to drive the new to the right people in a hurry
9. Use digital communications to redefine the boundaries
10. Transform every business process into just-in-time delivery
11. Use digital delivery to eliminate the middle man
12. Use digital tools to help customers solve problems for themselves

Teaching Suggestions

Instructors must keep abreast of developments in marketing information technology, electronic communications infrastructure, trends in consumer and business-to-business marketing strategy, and online marketing strategy to stay versed in the environments of the electronic marketing course. We have considered the pace of change in general business as well as in e-marketing specifically. My sense is that marketers of all kinds of products and services will be running incessantly to remain in sync with the industry. A contemporary look at this phenomenon is reported in *Blur: The Speed of Change in the Connected Economy*, by Stan Davis and Christopher Meyer. The theories and practices of electronic marketing are unfolding before us every day. News of specific business events will be chronicled in the business press. The Instructor can maintain currency by reading the online and offline business newspapers and magazines for electronic marketing content.

Answers to Questions and Exercises

1. In putting all the supporting and conflicting information into a semblance of order, marketers will have to consider the rank importance of four factors or consequences that electronic marketing may influence or may be influenced by: 1) the evolution of technology; 2) the expansion of software; 3) the success of Internet acquisitions and mergers; and 4) the driving desire for marketers to better serve their customers. In terms of electronic commerce, which factor would you consider to be most affected by e-marketing over the next decade? Specify samples to support your contention. Write a one-page memo to your strategic planning manager alerting her of future marketing forces.

The overriding determinant influencing electronic marketing's future is the human factor, the driving desire for marketers to better serve their customers. The other factors will be the means by which e-marketing will produce customer satisfaction. The evolution of technology, the expansion of software, and Internet acquisitions and mergers are tools or mechanisms to enhance the performance of electronic marketing; each is a means to an end. The student may offer different samples to support this contention. There are many such as the expansion of online customer service, company FAQs, and e-mail surveys as to customer satisfaction with company products and services.

2. Assuming the Next Generation Internet Initiative is successful and achieves the noted goals, what benefits should the small e-merchant expect from the project? What should the large national marketer expect from the project? Make a list of benefits and explain why these benefits are important to each group. Be prepared to discuss your thoughts in class.

NGI's benefits to the small merchant should include expanding the Web audience as well as increasing the current capabilities to satisfy the need for higher bandwidth applications. The wider bandwidth could lead to more complex and entertaining Web site or online promotions. NGI should provide the capacity of bringing multimedia capabilities into homes and businesses. For the large national marketer, NGI's benefits should be derived from speedier networks which are one hundred to one thousand times faster than today's Internet speed. NGI's R&D may create innovative technology advancements applications that the private sector could not afford in terms of time or money.

3. The NGI will foster partnerships among academia, industry, and governments, (federal, state, local, and foreign) that will keep the U.S. at the cutting edge of information and communications technologies. This is a lofty objective for the project. In your opinion, what are the advantages and disadvantages of these three groups (academia, industry, and government). Which have different agendas and expectations from NGI, working together? Prepare your thoughts as a three-minute speech to be given to a MIS department at a state university.

In the text of the 1998 State of the Union address, the Next Generation Internet Initiative was presented as a program "to strengthen the America's technological leadership, and create new jobs and new opportunities." The advantages of working together could pool resources and knowledge from persons with diverse experience and extend the innovation potentials of these projects. The disadvantages would come from suspicions of fair treatment for each party and which sectors will ultimately benefit from the collaboration. Free flow of information could hamper the initiative stemming from political and professional jealousies.

Here are just a few of the potential applications.

- *Health care.* Doctors at university medical centers will use large archives of radiology to identify the patterns and features associated with particular diseases. This will also help improve the accuracy of mammographies by detecting subtle changes in three-dimensional images.
- *National security.* A top priority for the Defense Department is "dominant battlefield awareness." Which would require an ability to collect information from large numbers of high-resolution sensors, automatic processing of the data to support terrain and target recognition, and real-time distribution of these data to the warfighter.
- *Distance learning.* Universities are now experimenting with technologies such as two-way video to remote sites, VCR-like replay of past classes, modeling and simulation, collaborative environments, and online access to instructional software. Distance education will improve the abilities of universities to serve working Americans who want new skills but who cannot attend a class at a fixed time during the week.
- *Energy research.* Scientists and engineers can work through "collaboratories" that combine videoconferencing, shared virtual work spaces, networked scientific facilities, and databases that increase the efficiency and effectiveness of our national research enterprise.
- *Biomedical research.* Researchers will be able to solve problems in large-scale DNA sequencing and gene identification, opening the door to breakthroughs in curing human genetic diseases.
- *Environmental monitoring.* Researchers are constructing a "virtual world" to model the Chesapeake Bay ecosystem, which serves as a nursery area for many commercially important species.
- *Manufacturing engineering.* Virtual reality, along with modeling and simulation, can drastically reduce the time required to develop new products.

4. Do research on benefits and disadvantages of analog versus digital data transmission. This research refers to technology, Asynchronous Transfer Mode. Why is ATM expected to be the technology of choice for the NGI? Summarize the benefits and disadvantages in a one-page memo and e-mail it to your instructor.

Almost everything in the world can be described or represented in one of two forms: *analog* or *digital*. The principal feature of analog representations is that they are continuous, with "no gaps" between measuring points. In contrast, digital reservations consist of values measured as discrete intervals. Digital watches are called digital because they go from one value to the next without displaying all intermediate values. Consequently, they can display only a finite number of times of the day. Watches with hands are analog because the hands move continuously around the clock face. As the minute hand goes around, it not only touches the numbers 1 through 12, but also the infinite number of points in between.

Both are methods of data transmission, an important technology for Internet communications. Analog refers to electronic transmission of signals of *varying* frequency to a carrier wave of a *fixed* frequency, a process called modulation. A modem is used to convert the digital information in the computer to analog telephone signals for transmission along phone lines and to revert the signal to digital information for the computer. ATM is also a network technology based on transferring data in cells or packets of a *fixed* size. The cell used is relatively small compared to units used with older technologies. The *small constant* cell allows ATM to transmit video, audio and computer data and assures that no single type of data hogs the line. The disadvantage in ATM transmission is that ATM creates a fixed channel for proved between two points wherever data transfer begins. This differs from TCP/IP, in which messages are divided into packets and each packet can take a different route from source to destination. The difference makes it easier to track and bill data usage across an ATM network, but also makes it less adaptable to sudden surges in network traffic.

Telecommunications networks have traditionally used analog transmission because of the highly predictable nature of voice data using dedicated circuits operating at a fixed bandwidth. Voice communication is fairly constant in the amount of data moving across the line. However, digital communications are quite different; the traffic is based on images, sounds, text, even streaming video. Digital transmissions can move in small, irregular streams of data with no predictable traffic patterns. These irregularities can cause network problems, even outages and these problems are to be addressed by the Next Generation Internet initiative.

Using ATM technology provides for a single network service cable of supporting video, voice and data transmission needs in a flexible and responsive way; the ATM protocol is a new network protocol that combines the best features of circuit and packet switching approaches:

a) Much higher transmission capabilities than existing packet or frame-based technologies
b) Flexibility and versatility in that voice, data, video, and images can be transmitted simultaneously over a single, integrated corporate network or the Internet
c) Universality and adaptability. ATM technology has the potential to support a wide variety of communications methods from network cables to high-capacity optical fiber.
d) The ability to meet the needs of each segment of the corporate network from LANs, MANs to WANs.

5. How are ATM technology, Web portals, and e-commerce tied together? Describe buying products or services by entering a portal. What is the process from entering to exiting a portal? Write a one-page explanation of online portal purchasing.

E-commerce becomes flexible and versatile using ATM's capabilities for speed, video, sound, and data transmission. Advertising messages can be crafted more persuasively with the speed, color, sound, and motion of conventional commercials. Consumers entering the Web through entry points called portals like Amazon.com, or the existing search engines such as Excite or Yahoo! can jump from site to site enjoying the features of the Web. The original revenue model of advertising on high-traffic sites has moved toward generating revenue from sales commissions drawn on sales created from traffic attracted by Web portals. Customers are tagged as they enter a specific portal, and retailers pay portals' customers like Yahoo! incentives such as "Netcentives" (www.netcentives.com) for shopping the site. These incentives (like *ClickRewards*, *ClickRewards@Work*, and Custom Loyalty Networks) are designed to build and strengthen customer loyalty to the portal and its retail sites contained within.

6. In the text, one vision of a future Internet appliance for accessing the Web is discussed. What would be your description of a consumer-oriented Internet tool that you would like to use? List the features and explain why each might appeal to the average consumer. Develop a one-page memo.

A consumer-friendly device should contain these features: low-cost, easy installation for the IP connection to the television or computer monitor, enabled for sound such as RealAudio, and uses a remote control. It would contain a color monitor for viewing the Web and would be wireless for portability. Activities should include the ability to surf the Web, read daily newspapers, access e-mail, perform online searches and shopping, and take part in computer-based training. The size and weight would approximate that of a palm computer.

7. Describe how you see programming languages such as VRML and Java enhancing Web designs of the future. Is there a danger that Web sites may be designed more for entertainment than for commerce purposes? Make a list of five commerce objectives that you would expect your Web designers to follow in preparing company Web sites. Write it as an internal company memo.

New programming languages such as VRML and Java will significantly increase the amount of interactivity that can be provided on Web sites. The increase in interactivity coupled with more realistic 3D graphics will expand the interest of the Web site. For example, a shopper might get to browse through the virtual store by walking in a VRML world or drag and drop combinations of items until she is happy with the look of the outfit, much like old-fashioned paper dolls. This enterprise, though, is not a game; it is e-commerce. Everyone in the organization must recognize that customer satisfaction is the goal or using electronic marketing resources.

The marketing communications objectives for presenting a product on a Web site are slightly altered because of the differing communications capabilities and limitations of the Web vehicle:

- Decide before beginning if the site content will be either informational such as a public service message on safe boating for example, or a commercially-oriented site selling or telling the viewer about a product or service.
- Design the site on paper for the planning of the benefits/conveniences components that you wish to present to the viewer. As usual, present the product attractively and make a strong statement of user benefit in the headline.
- Place the major content elements for the home page to be contained on the first screen. This point addresses logical site navigation: no limited scrolling down or right after the home page loads and the "document done" message is viewed.
- The designer should use the graphical and audio strengths of the Web judiciously. If the selling message of the product deserves motion, have a rationale to present as to why. The same rule for using other graphic techniques such as dissolves, transitions, video segments, running banners, Java applets and other attention-getting tactics. Colors should be chosen carefully for legibility and contrast, and testing graphics, pages, and entire sites on various and multiple monitor sizes is strongly recommended.
- Install a statistics package to monitor performance of the site and individual pages for levels of viewership. Designs are meant to be updated with fresh material, new introductions, and features. The designer should not be hesitant to change the site design. A Web site continually evolves because there is no finish line or program completion in e-marketing.

8. In the next decade, do you envision consumers becoming more or less concerned with privacy privileged information selling, or abuses of fraudulent e-merchant transactions? Address each situation and express your thoughts on consumer reactions; write a letter to the editor of your local newspaper describing your support or concerns.

The consequences of this privacy issue depend on how consumers are treated in the future. If abuses continue with great frequency, consumers will become more concerned with protecting their online privacy of privileged information. In the late 1950s, consumers were leery of a new technology called "plastic credit cards" that might compromise their financial safety. Consumers did become accustomed to paying at the point of sale register, receiving a monthly statement, and mailing a check to clear the account. Likewise persons writing bad checks or invading the checking accounts of others were arrested and prosecuted. Making public Web fraud will help to deter consumer hesitancy as a publicity campaign on Web safety protocols of SSL or SET systems. Companies or individuals selling private information should also be punished and their acts publicized. If these acts become prevalent, consumers will become paranoid about personal privacy and will shun the online medium for purposes of communications, commerce, even entertainment because of the electronic information generated.

9. You will remember this comment, "The Net, by its very nature, is hostile to profit margins." What is the basis for making this comment? How as an e-marketer would you plan strategically to foil the Net in this context? Write a one-page strategy statement that would deal with commercial Web site selling autographed photos of celebrities of mounted posters from the classical movie era?

The comment is borne of the history and culture of the Internet as a free resource for sharing and collaboration. Many veteran users, especially those in education or research, expect the Internet and its services to be free as a "universal right." These users generally forget that the Federal government built and sustained the operation of the Internet, and because of sheer economics, the Next Generation Internet initiative operation is proposed to be a cooperative venture among the government, academia, and business. The popularity of usage and continuing research in information technology makes the superintendence a costly effort that no one organization can support.

There is no "foiling the Net" because if merchandise, services, or information is perceived to be of value to the consumer, s/he will purchase the item if the item is judged reasonably priced. Satisfaction of consumers' needs and wants, regardless of the product, will overturn the hostility of the Net to profits. The Web will thereafter function as any other communications or transactions medium, merchandise as a distribution outlet for commerce.

10. Of Bill Gates' twelve new rules, which one do you as an e-marketer agree with most, and how do you plan to integrate it in to your e-commerce practices? Which rule do you disagree with most, and why do you object? Write each explanation as a book review for reference by your marketing manager. Make your opinions one-page length. Students will probably interpret this question according to their views on technology and their opinion of Bill Gates. In my opinion, his "rules" should be viewed in the context of information technology as tools for unleashing human creativity and intellectual potential. The rule that needs the most integration within the corporation is Rule 3, "Shift

knowledge workers into high-level thinking." Too many companies have untapped intellectual resources that could produce outstanding achievements if they were given appropriate assignments within the workflow process. Jealousy and "turf protection" keep many performers in the dark and out of the spotlight. Sharing information and handing off assignments puts responsibility onto the shoulders of associates who have new insights and practices that might better the company's talents and improve customer sales.

The most unrealistic rule is Rule 11, "Use digital delivery to eliminate the middle man." In this age of partnering and cooperation, support and fair play will produce an atmosphere of more cooperation and less suspicion of corporate intents. Many consultants preach of the lean company structure that out-sources critical talents and expertise. Many of these "middle men" suppliers possess reliable talents and difficult-to-replace expertise that larger organizations have come to rely upon. Eliminating all middle men will break up dependable, profitable relationships by which managers produce customer satisfaction.

Test Bank

Chapter 1
Introduction to the Resources of Electronic Marketing

Test Bank

1. Technology marketing resources include

   A. World Wide Web.
   B. Fax-on-demand information.
   C. Avatars.
   D. CD-ROM presentations.
   E. All of the above.

   Answer: E Page: 5

2. With electronic marketing resources, marketers

   A. are forced to justify higher costs to customers.
   B. must use expensive sales promotions tactics.
   C. can bring value-added services to each customer.
   D. have an easier job of selling their products or services.
   E. none of the above.

   Answer: C Page: 6

3. Online marketing resources enhance internal company communications by

   A. letting employees say what they want, when they want anonymity.
   B. completely eliminating the need for face-to-face meetings.
   C. introducing humor through cartoons and jokes.
   D. bringing back the art of correspondence.
   E. all of the above.

   Answer: D Page: 7

4. Due to online communications, marketing research has become more difficult because

   A. it is difficult to measure attitude through a web site.
   B. opinions cannot be monitored over a long period of time.
   C. people give complicated opinions in discussion groups.
   D. all of the above.
   E. none of the above.

   Answer: E Page: 7

5. Online marketing works well for strategic planning because

   A. more people are looking to the web for information.
   B. people demand faster front-door delivery after a purchase.
   C. secure electronic transactions makes internet buying safe.
   D. all of the above.
   E. none of the above.

   Answer: D Page: 8

6. The ration of business-to-business purchases over the Internet as compared to consumer purchases is

A. 50 : 50
B. 85 : 15
C. 40 : 60
D. impossible to measure because of the vastness of the web.
E. none of the above.

Answer: B Page: 8

7. Automated audio-text response systems can

A. reply to questions.
B. provide technical data and specifications.
C. provide technical support with fax-back systems.
D. maintain contact with supplies and vendors.
E. all of the above.

Answer: E Page: 8

8. In customer loyalty programs

A. it is difficult to build internet in mature products.
B. retailers dislike them.
C. behavior patterns are difficult to monitor.
D. customer databases are difficult to build.
E. past behavior will usually predict future actions.

Answer: E Page: 9

9. Online marketing can create a global reach because

A. a small company can appear to be multinational.
B. global marketing can be achieved with a keystroke.
C. the internet is an international connections of networked computers.
D. a and c above.
E. a, b, and c above.

Answer: E Page: 10

10. Improved cost management is a benefit of online marketing resources because

A. E-mail cuts the cost of long distance phone charges.
B. video conferencing can replace travel cost.
C. too many people are chasing too few budget dollars.
D. all of the above.
E. none of the above.

Answer: D Page: 11

11. Telecommuting

A. is a work arrangement that is not favored by employers.
B. allows employees to work when and where they want at their discretion.
C. allows people to work remotely, away from the central office.
D. is on the decline among employees.

E. none of the above.

Answer: C Page: 11

12. Online retailing

A. is an experimental concept still in the test stage.
B. is not being adopted because of security problems.
C. is not an alternative to shopping in a mall.
D. uses the traditional marketing process to build sales.
E. is not growing like e-marketers have predicted.

Answer: D Page: 12

13. The value of electronic tools to corporations includes

A. speed, accessibility, accuracy, and competitive advantage.
B. fax-back systems to answer customer questions.
C. the ability to personalize messages with product or service orders.
D. all of the above.
E. none of the above.

Answer: D Page: 13

14. Electronic marketing resources include

A. personal selling.
B. direct mail.
C. telemarketing.
D. radio and TV advertising.
E. outdoor advertising.

Answer: C Page: 16

15. In retail site location, electronic resources can

A. provide data on income, population profiles, and occupations.
B. household growth and traffic counts.
C. psychographic profiles.
D. a and c above.
E. a, b, and c above.

Answer: E Page: 17

16. Network based resources include

A. the internet and WWW sites.
B. advertising agencies.
C. hardware and software manufacturers.
D. sales and marketing consultants.
E. none of the above.

Answer: A Page: 16

17. The primary factor driving change in marketing today is

    A. the rapid change in computer hardware.
    B. the rapid change in computer software.
    C. consumer's increasing demand for privacy.
    D. the increasing demand for segmentation by advertisers.
    E. the reluctance of consumers to purchase over the internet.

    Answer: D Page: 19

18. The number of daily newspapers in the U.S. is

    A. 1,500.
    B. 3,500.
    C. 8,500.
    D. 2,000.
    E. none of the above.

    Answer: A Page: 19

19. In the early 1970's, households using televisions (HUT) was in the low 90% range, today it is

    A. still in the low 90% range.
    B. about 96.5%.
    C. about 50%.
    D. about 37%.
    E. increasing, but at a decreasing rate.

    Answer: C Page: 19

20. In planning for e-marketing, speed should be a major consideration because

    A. computer microprocessor speeds have reached their maximum capability.
    B. consumers expect and demand it.
    C. consumers will return to organizations that promise and deliver speed and accuracy.
    D. b and c.
    E. a and c.

    Answer: D Page: 14

21. By employing electronic marketing tools, one can become a better marketer and serve customers more effectively.

    A. True
    B. False

    Answer: A Page: 5

22. Online marketing research is virtually impossible because of the infinite data that is available to the marketer because of the extensive level of communications now possible through the internet.

    A. True
    B. False

    Answer: B Page: 7

23. Affinity marketing is not a type of customer loyalty program.

    A. True
    B. False

    Answer: B Page: 9

24. Electronic marketing resources are useful in strategic planning but not in tactical execution of e-commerce programs.

    A. True
    B. False

    Answer: B Page: 16

25. HTML is widely used as a component in optical scanning and electronic coupon dispensing.

    A. True
    B. False

    Answer: B Page: 16

Chapter 2
Concept of Electronic Commerce and the Traditional Marketing Process

Test Bank

1. In traditional marketing, a situation analysis forms the foundation of opinions and facts, with better marketing planning and marketing implementation being the result. In electronic marketing, is this also the case?

A. Yes
B. No

Answer: A Page: 24

2. One advantage of the online environment is that it makes which of the following research tools more accessible?

A. opinion studies
B. international trade figures
C. consumer behavior statistics
D. government statistics
E. all of the above

Answer: E Page: 24

3. Various marketing processes, including those done in annual cycles, are also done in electronic marketing, but there is one unique feature that e-marketing resources add beyond traditional marketing. What is that factor?

A. that it costs more to do the same processes
B. the use of computer systems
C. a bigger sales staff
D. the need to advertise on the Internet
E. interactivity between the e-marketer and the consumer

Answer: E Page: 24

4. The number of Internet users is

A. 57 million.
B. 9.5 million.
C. 62 million.
D. 7.5 million.
E. unknown due to the wide variance of estimates.

Answer: E Page: 24

5. Based on recent demographic surveys of Internet users, it is clear that

A. women do not use the Internet.
B. women make up the majority of Internet users.
C. an increasing percentage (approaching 50%) of Internet users are women.

D. children between the ages of 12-17 are the biggest users of the Internet.
E. none of the above are true.

Answer: C Page: 26

6. According to the GVU 9th survey it is apparent that Internet users, compared to the general population, are

A. more educated.
B. have higher incomes.
C. are in education-related occupations.
D. are in professional occupations
E. all of the above.

Answer: E Page: 26

7. ____________ % of all Internet users use e-mail.

A. 85%
B. 50%
C. 10%
D. 100%
E. less than 10%

Answer: A Page: 25

8. Some consumers shop and buy on the Internet while other consumers prefer to shop and buy in regular, physical stores causing which new category of consumers to emerge?

A. People who do not shop anywhere.
B. People who shop only on the Internet.
C. People who buy only in physical stores.
D. People who shop on the Internet but buying using normal channels.
E. None of the above are new consumer categories.

Answer: A Page: 26

9. Web sites preferred by teens are

A. virtually identical to those of adults.
B. X-rated sites.
C. game sites.
D. business or educational sites.
E. movie sites.

Answer: A Page: 26

10. Electronic commerce now comprises ____________ of the total U.S. economy.

A. 40%
B. a tiny percentage
C. 30%
D. 60%
E. nearly 100%

Answer: B Page: 27

11. The typical business model for start-up retail vendors on the Internet includes all of the following *except*:

A. payment by credit card.
B. immediate delivery of the purchase.
C. relatively quick home delivery.
D. easily searchable catalogs of products.
E. B and C.

Answer: B Page: 28

12. Online business activities benefit more from a short-term rather than a long-term focus.

A. True
B. False

Answer: B Page: 28

13. Of all businesses that make frequent use of the Internet, the percentage of those businesses that are actually purchasing products and services on the Internet is

A. 10%.
B. less than 10%.
C. decreasing.
D. 30%.
E. unknown.

Answer: D Page: 29

14. The percentage of product selling firms who are making use of the Internet is

A. 16%.
B. negligible.
C. at least 30%.
D. almost 90%.
E. decreasing.

Answer: A Page: 29

15. The most frequent activity engaged in by businesses on the WWW is

A. internal communications.
B. vendor support.
C. researching competitors.
D. collaborating.
E. gathering product information.

Answer: E Page: 29

16. The one-on-one basis of communication that the WWW makes possible between marketers and consumers will ideally result in a relationship which

A. benefits the marketer more than the consumer.
B. benefits the consumer much more than the marketer.
C. is mutually beneficial for the marketer and the consumer.
D. terminates with the sale.
E. provides no added value to the product.

Answer: C Page: 30

17. Most consumers report that the main irritant in the process of buying a car is

A. the high price of the car.
B. how long the purchase takes.
C. the need to select optional equipment.
D. the salesperson.
E. the need for more insurance.

Answer: D Page: 32

18. When the marketing program objective is initiating an online awareness as an extension of a product or service's promotional program, copy and graphics should

A. take on a new thematic direction.
B. adhere to existing (traditional) advertising or sales promotions themes.
C. be as bold as possible.
D. not be as important as the URL.
E. not contain any graphics.

Answer: B Page: 32

19. Informed marketers understand that "prospect" selection is more important than "product" selection.

A. True
B. False

Answer: A Page: 39

20. A major benefit to conducting market research is that it permits more

A. support for "what the boss likes".
B. subjectivity.
C. objectivity.
D. flexibility.
E. bias.

Answer: C Page: 26

21. Online marketers, besides using the Internet for selling or buying activities, can also use it for

A. employee recruitment.
B. filing legal documents.
C. disseminating fragrance samples.
D. providing relocation information (homes, apartments, schools, etc.).
E. A and D.

Answer: A Page: 22

22. The marketer must monitor and adapt to events taking place in the economic environment, such as

A. monetary exchange rates.
B. trends in wages.
C. interest rate fluctuations.
D. public values.
E. A, B, and C.

Answer: E Page: 40

23. Demographic change is an important environmental variable. Which of the following is not a key demographic concern?

A. composite age profiles
B. income clusters
C. occupational profiles
D. lifestyle clusters
E. educational levels

Answer: D Page: 42

24. A marketer will find benefit in analyzing U.S. Census data in regards to which of the following?

A. current population totals
B. population growth/decline from prior periods
C. projected population figures
D. current number of households
E. all of the above

Answer: E Page: 42

25. All successful companies are recognized by customers as having certain well developed capabilities such as, but not limited to: dependability, creativity, product selection, etc. These capabilities are called ____________and are translated into customer benefits.

A. customer advantages
B. power attributes
C. winning features
D. consumer efficiencies
E. competencies.

Answer: E Page: 43

Chapter 3
Marketing Planning Stage for Online Activities

Test Bank

1. TV commercials, newspaper and magazine ads, the tools which carry and deliver the "image" of a marketed product or service, are known as its

A. positioners.
B. branding.
C. identity.
D. product luster.
E. media tool kit.

Answer: C Page: 50

2. Given a unique product or service and a small, focused target market, a strategy designed to set a product or service apart from competitors is known as

A. niche strategy.
B. mass marketing approach.
C. undifferentiated.
D. open-ended.
E. unfocused.

Answer: A Page: 50

3. Qualities considered to be desirable by an offline market segment, such as accurate prices and quick customer responses, should be equally valued by online market segments.

A. True
B. False

Answer: A Page: 51

4. During market segmentation, the investigation of prospect clusters according to lifestyle and self-concept is referred to as

A. demographics.
B. partitioning.
C. target positioning.
D. psychographics.
E. unpopular.

Answer: D Page: 53

5. The essence of buyer benefits for a particular product or service can be communicated by creating a memorable

A. infomercial.
B. positioning line that can be delivered in an advertisement.
C. full page newspaper ad.
D. consumer report to be mailed to potential buyers.
E. public relations event.

Answer: B Page: 55

6. CDs, videos, books, and software sell well online because

A. there is very little risk associated with buying such well-known items.
B. there are few physical retail stores that sell these items.
C. usually sellers of these items do not charge for delivery.
D. federal and state laws protect online customers of these products.
E. they are at least 50% cheaper online than in physical stores.

Answer: A Page: 57

7. The top three items purchased online from June of 1997 to June of 1998 were

A. travel, computers and music.
B. music, books, investments.
C. books, software and computers.
D. software, books and music.
E. travel, investments, consumer electronics.

Answer: C Page: 57

8. All of the following work to convince a customer to bookmark your Web address *except*

A. offering an outstanding single product (narrow focus).
B. providing convenience to the company's distribution channels.
C. having a difficult-to-navigate Web site.
D. offering more expertise (deeper knowledge).
E. incorporating a "guest book".

Answer: C Page: 58

9. Specific, hard-to-find items typically sell well on the WWW.

A. True
B. False

Answer: A Page: 60

10. Generally, tangible products

A. should not be sold on the WWW.
B. present no shipping problems.
C. have proven difficult to promote online.
D. should be contained in compact, square packaging.
E. should be no bigger than a breadbox.

Answer: D Page: 60

11. Of the total number of Web sites, what percent appear in English?

A. 95%
B. 1000%
C. 33.3%
D. 80%
E. 25%

Answer: D Page: 62

12. Announcing new enterprises as part of a promotional plan is cheaper on the WWW than with traditional media.

A. True
B. False

Answer: A Page: 63

13. Registration with search engines, advertising banners, and sponsorship of discussion groups are available to marketers on the Web and are usually free of cost.

A. True
B. False

Answer: B Page: 63

14. According to economic theory, unlimited access to information which leads to perfect market knowledge of price structures will tend to cause prices to

A. increase.
B. converge.
C. go down.
D. first A, then C.
E. first C, then A.

Answer: B Page: 64

15. When using electronic tools, logistics (distribution) functions should be

A. broken down into smaller, more manageable steps.
B. eliminated completely.
C. done exactly the same as in physical retail stores.
D. designed to take advantage of online communications capabilities.
E. A and D.

Answer: D Page: 68

16. Since online media fits best into the direct marketing category, business on the WWW may have the effect of

A. creating more mass marketing strategies.
B. eliminating most TV advertising.
C. minimizing personal communications with customers.
D. federal regulation of all direct marketing efforts.
E. largely eliminating the retailer or wholesaler.

Answer: E Page: 68

17. The objective and task method in which the marketer delineates the marketing for the period and then calculates a cost for each task is also known as

A. periodic table budgeting.
B. expenditure justification method.
C. zero based budgeting.

D. objective budgeting.
E. not a very good method for online marketing purposes.

Answer: C Page: 69

18. For an online marketing effort involving a product (after the selection of a good product name) the URL for your Web site should be

A. exactly the same as the product name.
B. in the Web site but never in the URL.
C. it doesn't matter too much what the URL is.
D. as close to your competitor's as possible.
E. distinctive and tie into the actual product name.

Answer: E Page: 50

19. A mixture of both numeric goals and well thought out communication objectives lead to a much better chance for online business success.

A. True
B. False

Answer: A Page: 52

20. Good online marketers will be particularly aware of how customers will use their products and the specific advantages and positive outcomes obtained from the used of the products by doing a

A. reaction profile.
B. strategic guess.
C. cost analysis.
D. benefits analysis.
E. feature analysis.

Answer: D Page: 55

21. Bayer Pharmaceutical, in introducing its FaxBack program to furnish specific drug information to physicians, discovered which of the following unexpected benefit from the system?

A. It sharply lowered costs to communicate with the physicians.
B. It captured useful demographic data from the physicians who used the system.
C. It had cooperation from Pfizer, its competitor.
D. A much slower business operation was necessary to distribute the information.
E. A larger staff was hired to handle the physician information requests.

Answer: B Page: 56

22. A good way to predict which product categories are successful on the World Wide Web is to think of what attributes are important to consumers. Which of the following is most important?

A. faster
B. more convenient
C. more unique
D. better
E. all of the above

Answer: E Page: 58

23. One effective method for online marketers to increase consumer credibility in a Web site or product line is to

A. ask prospective customers to "trust us like your uncle."
B. display awards and certifications that have been earned on the Web site.
C. assume that consumers will naturally trust your products and company.
D. say disparaging things about your competitor's Web site.
E. hire a lawyer to review your Web site content.

Answer: B Page: 58

24. In the physical retail store context, it is often difficult and time consuming to search for unique, one-of-a-kind goods but

A. it is equally difficult and time consuming on the WWW.
B. this is the only place to look for such goods.
C. there is no market opportunity in such goods.
D. such goods will all be replaced by mass marketed items.
E. the WWW's searchability makes it easier to find such goods.

Answer: E Page: 60

25. A potentially effective approach of communication design on WWW sites, apart from heavily textual content is

A. all visual content.
B. there is no alternative since HTML is written in text.
C. intuitive, graphics based navigation.
D. using only commonly known words in the text.
E. A and C.

Answer: A Page: 62

Chapter 4
The Actions of Marketing Implementation

Test Bank

1. The implementation of marketing programs means

   A. planning marketing programs.
   A. organizing marketing programs.
   B. executing marketing programs.
   C. analyzing the results of marketing programs.
   D. All of the above.

   Answer: C Page: 73

2. Implementation actions require

   A. creativity.
   B. cunning.
   C. critical thinking.
   D. a and b above.
   E. a and c.

   Answer: E Page: 73

3. Marketing planning

   A. continually focuses on reviewing past performances.
   B. focuses on the future, typically no longer than thirty days.
   C. has no time orientation.
   D. has a long term orientation up to several months.
   E. puts plans into action immediately.

   Answer: D Page: 74

4. The goal of consumer tracking is to

   A. identify the prospect.
   B. retain and build a relationship with the customer.
   C. build a customer profile database.
   D. all of the above.
   E. b and c above.

   Answer: E Page: 75

5. "Coupon Keys" are

   A. techniques to get the customer to buy.
   B. a promotion to give instant coupons to the customer.
   C. a way to trigger the customer to pick one brand over another.
   D. electronic keys to " open the doors" to more information for the customer.
   E. identification codes.

   Answer: E Page: 75

6. Attracting new customers is about how many times more costly than selling to and servicing existing customers?

   A. equal
   B. 3 times more costly
   C. 7 times more costly
   D. 10 times more costly
   E. 20 times more costly

   Answer: C Page: 76

7. Marketers learn about customer's concerns by

   A. reading their e-mail.
   B. identifying which competitor's products they buy.
   C. reviewing competitor advertising companies.
   D. listening to their compliments and complaints.
   E. doing focus groups with retailers of their product.

   Answer: D Page: 77

8. Global Positioning Satellite Systems (GPS) can

   A. provide instant time, temperature, and weather data.
   B. track package location twenty-four hours a day.
   C. provide instant access to rock music anywhere in the world.
   D. provide global news coverage twenty-four hours a day.
   E. none of the above.

   Answer: B Page: 78

9. SOQ is

   A. a formula used to estimate how many times a web site will be hit by customers in a twenty-four hour period.
   B. a new ISP like AOL.
   C. shorthand used in Global Positioning Satellite Systems to identify the geographic area "South of Quebec".
   D. a supplier's statement of qualifications to manage a proposed project.
   E. none of the above.

   Answer: D Page: 80

10. In gaining information about a prospective supplier, a marketing manager can

   A. call current and past customers for references.
   B. call suppliers who have done business with that company.
   C. review a Dunn and Bradstreet financial profile of that company.
   D. a and c above.
   E. a, b, and c above.

   Answer: E Page: 81

11. Comparison of alternative media choices can be accomplished numerically by using which of these techniques?

    A. AOL and WWW
    B. SOQ, CEO, and ISP
    C. RAM, ROM, and GPS
    D. CPM, GRP, and TRP
    E. None of the above

    Answer: D Page: 82

12. Success in the implementation of marketing plans is

    A. guaranteed by being in the market first.
    B. enhanced by spending the most money on advertising.
    C. based on having the best marketing talent your company can buy.
    D. really a matter of luck and beyond the marketer's control.
    E. in the follow-through.

    Answer: E Page: 85

13. Excellent marketing implementation requires

    A. understanding, observation, and patience to complete the project.
    B. timing, money, and luck.
    C. talented marketers working independently.
    D. a unique product with no competition.
    E. none of the above.

    Answer: A Page: 86

14. In marketing planning, time (or timing)

    A. can be used as a competitive tactic.
    B. is available to everyone.
    C. can be used to create competitive advantage.
    D. can be employed as a marketing weapon.
    E. all of the above.

    Answer: E Page: 86

15. In planning for a twelve month period,

    A. a rigid timetable should not be set because things change.
    B. procrastination time should be built in because of stressed managers need it.
    C. it is best to be general and not specific because plans and personnel change.
    D. the objective and task method works well.
    E. all of the above.

    Answer: D Page: 86

16. Formal plans must be

    A. accurate.
    B. realistic.
    C. inflexible.

D. all of the above.
E. a and b above.

Answer: E Page: 87

17. The objective and task method of planning

A. establishes the task and its sequence among other tasks.
B. sets the months, days, and hours each task should take.
C. steps back from the targeted introduction date given the parameters that are set.
D. b and c above.
E. a, b, and c above.

Answer: E Page: 88

18. Marketing managers should be briefed on a program's progress

A. weekly.
B. monthly.
C. quarterly.
D. semiannually.
E. upon completion.

Answer: A Page: 88

19. Trust is important in selecting outside suppliers. Which of these would be the most trustworthy?

A. A relative's ad agency of software firm.
B. An old college chum of the CEO.
C. The CEO of another company with whom your CEO plays golf.
D. Any of the above are trustworthy.
E. None of the above since they all present a potential risk.

Answer: E Page: 81

20. Linear activities follow a specified sequence of events.

A. True
B. False

Answer: A Page: 88

21. Concurrent activities should not be produced independently of linear activities.

A. True
B. False

Answer: B Page: 88

22. In an electronic environment, the marketing P's should be price, place, product, and promotion.

A. True
B. False

Answer: B Page: 88

23. In developing marketing plans, the most basic questions to answer are who, what, when, where, and why.

    A. True
    B. False

    Answer: B Page: 75

24. Electronic marketing resources cannot bring the buyer and seller closer together because both can be located anywhere around the globe.

    A. True
    B. False

    Answer: B Page: 74

25. Coupon keys on mass media vehicles require careful attention to keep the vehicles' performance, or pulling power, differentiated.

    A. True
    B. False

    Answer: A Page: 75

Chapter 5
An Introduction to the Internet

Test Bank

1. The dissassembling and reassembling of a message as it is sent from origin to destination over the internet is called

A. downloading.
B. uploading.
C. packet-switching.
D. file transferring.
E. bitmapping.

Answer: C Page: 97

2. The ability to find a specific search subject by dialing into the remote host where it resides and then transferring that file to one's own computer is made possible by a networking tool known as

A. BITNET.
B. FTP.
C. packet-switching.
D. DARPA
E. HTML

Answer: B Page: 98

3. The most widely used application on the Internet is

A. the WWW.
B. Telnet.
C. News groups.
D. E-mail.
E. commercial shopping malls.

Answer: D Page: 104

4. TCP/IP protocols

A. provide standard rules for networked computers to communicate with each other.
B. are a product of ARPANET research.
C. were developed to facilitate the purchase of electronic stamps.
D. Both A and B.
E. None of the above.

Answer: D Page: 105

5. The experimental computer network developed in 1969 which connected UCLA, Stanford Research Institute, UC Santa Barbara, and the University of Utah was known as

A. ARPANET.
B. DARPA.
C. BITNET.
D. CPYNET.

E. CSNET.

Answer: A Page: 97

6. Speed upgrades to NSFNET paved the way for

A. less communication over the network.
B. higher access charge to the network.
C. lower security risks in transmission.
D. no effect on over all network traffic.
E. more and more users connected to the network.

Answer: E Page: 105

7. The composition of a URL address

A. is random.
B. reveals no information about the author/owner of the web page.
C. follows the format *scheme://host.domain [port]/path/data.*
D. follows the format *path://host.domain[port]/scheme/data.*
E. is not necessary for personal web pages.

Answer: C Page: 105

8. Examples of computers which can act as a client computer to access server computers include

A. mainframes.
B. desktops.
C. PCs.
D. B and C only.
E. All of the above.

Answer: E Page: 105

9. Listservs can be used by marketers in all of the following ways *except*

A. keeping up with competitors.
B. as powerful marketing tools.
C. to engage in direct advertising.
D. monitoring customer opinion.
E. building good will among their target audience.

Answer: C Page: 106

10. The ability to connect to a computer anywhere on the Internet and use resources physically located at another host is made possible by a communications program called

A. Telnet.
B. FTP.
C. a HyperTerminal.
D. TCP/IP protocals.
E. a host login.

Answer: A Page: 106

11. Sending information to a remote computer via the Internet is known as

A. downloading a file.
B. uploading a file.
C. teleporting a file.
D. a line of transmission.
E. upgrading data.

Answer: B Page: 107

12. The Internet is now enabled to handle real time transport of files, making ________________ possible.

A. two-way pagers
B. cellular phones
C. e-mail
D. list serves
E. audio and video streams

Answer: E Page: 108

13. A domain name can contain any of the following *except*

A. numbers.
B. spaces.
C. letters.
D. 12 letters.
E. 26 letters.

Answer: B Page: 105

14. An online company that provides access to the Internet is called a

A. Domain.
B. Internet Service Provider (ISP).
C. Name Server.
D. Web interface.
E. Administrative Contact.

Answer: B Page: 107

15. World Wide Web growth began to increase dramatically in

A. June of 1995.
B. June of 1993.
C. March of 1998.
D. June of 1996.
E. It has increased dramatically since its inception.

Answer: D Page: 103

16. J.C.R. Licklider, the first head of the computer research program at DARPA was

A. a psychologist.
B. an authority on psychoacoustics.
C. at MIT.

D. the creator of the Galactic Network concept.
E. all of the above.

Answer: E Page: 95

17. The two programs which were combined by Ray Tomlinson to invent e-mail were

A. UNIX and INWIG.
B. TCP and IP.
C. SNDMSG and CPYNET.
D. UNIX and TCP.
E. INWIG and SNDMSG.

Answer: C Page: 98

18. Electronic mail and listserv servers are provided by the networking project

A. CPYNET.
B. BITNET.
C. INWIG.
D. TCP.
E. SNDMSG.

Answer: B Page: 98

19. By July of 1995, the number of Internet hosts had increased to nearly

A. 200,000.
B. 300,000.
C. 500,000.
D. 700,000.
E. 1,000,000.

Answer: D Page: 99

20. The 1988 Internet worm crisis led to the development of

A. CERFnet.
B. CERT.
C. UNIX.
D. The NSFNET backbone.
E. TCP/IP protocols.

Answer: B Page: 101

21. World Wide Web Worms (a search technology) were joined by all of the following searching programs *except*

A. Ants.
B. Spiders.
C. Wanderers.
D. Crawlers.
E. Snakes.

Answer: A Page: 103

22. Mosaic, created at the University of Illinois, is a type of

A. database.
B. graphical web browser.
C. host.
D. server.
E. e-mail.

Answer: B Page: 103

23. When the NSFNET backbone reverted to a research network in 1995, it was replaced by

A. NAPs.
B. AT & T WorldNet.
C. Cyberstations.
D. ARIN.
E. vBNS.

Answer: E Page: 104

24. The two major web browser competitors are

A. AT&T Worldnet and Netscape®.
B. Netscape and MCI.
C. Microsoft® and Netscape.
D. Microsoft and Netcom.
E. Microsoft and AT&T Worldnet.

Answer: C Page: 104

25. RealAudio is a type of

A. file security software
B. audio streaming technology
C. communications technology for listening to music
D. verbal e-mail
E. B and C

Answer: B Page: 104

Chapter 6
Concept of the Virtual Store for Marketing Products and Services

Test Bank

1. A 1998 Arbitron survey reported what percent of participants use the Internet for shopping?

   A. 5.3%
   B. 10.0%
   C. 18.7%
   D. 21.5%
   E. 26.0%

   Answer: E Page: 112

2. The primary functions to address in managing the traditional tangible store are

   A. finance and marketing.
   B. operations and loss control.
   C. personnel staffing, training, and development.
   D. finance, marketing, and operations.
   E. location, purchasing, and inventory management.

   Answer: D Page: 112

3. The principles of retail management in a virtual environment are carried out

   A. in the front office.
   B. on the web site.
   C. in Office 2000.
   D. in the back office.
   E. at regional offices nationally.

   Answer: D Page: 112

4. The JCPenney monster web site is directed towards

   A. shoppers.
   B. the community in general.
   C. stockholders.
   D. all of the above.
   E. none of the above.

   Answer: D Page: 113

5. Which of the following is *not* an advantage of the virtual store?

   A. sales and marketing literature can be distributed on request.
   B. capital expenditure is typically less to start a virtual store.
   C. distribution channels can be expanded.
   D. the successful virtual store will eliminate the traditional store.
   E. new products or services can be tested on the Web.

   Answer: D Page: 116-117

6. Disadvantages of the cyberstore include

   A. the idea that not all products or services are appropriate for web sales exposure.
   B. that the twenty-four hour service commitment can create problems.
   C. that managing the cyberstore may take a great deal of the webmaster's time.
   D. all of the above.
   E. none of the above.

   Answer: D Pager: 119-121

7. The attributes the web can almost flawlessly deliver include

   A. consistency and privacy.
   B. accuracy and privacy.
   C. reliability and responsiveness.
   D. accessibility, reliability, and consistency.
   E. none of the above.

   Answer: D Page: 121

8. The typical demographic of cyberstore users is

   A. single females seventeen years and under still in high school.
   B. males 25 to 45 years with an average income of more than $50,000.
   C. males 18 to 24 years, single and in college.
   D. dual income married couples, 46 to 54 years with average incomes more than $100,000.
   E. retired females 64 years and older.

   Answer: B Page: 121

9. The cybermall is

   A. a high-tech chain of computer stores found in southern California.
   B. the name of America's largest mall located new Minneapolis.
   C. a group of cyberstores bonded together to give customers greater selection in one location.
   D. the largest retail web site in the U.S.
   E. none of the above.

   Answer: C Page: 122

10. A linked storefront is

   A. similar to a national retail chain like the Gap or Banana Republic.
   B. a group of traditional retail stores online with each other to provide instant access to inventory for customers.
   C. a group of stores offering complementary products like cookware and gourmet food.
   D. a storefront address hyperlinked within a popular general internet site.
   E. none of the above.

   Answer: D Page: 122

11. The main reason people are not willing to purchase from the virtual store is

   A. the cost of products are too high
   B. the range of choice is so big people cannot make a good decision.
   C. people still prefer to inspect or try on products before they buy.

D. people are concerned with how they will get service after the sale.
E. the deficient security and reliability of online shopping.

Answer: E Page: 122

12. To cybershoppers, the most important characteristic of a cybermerchant is

A. an extensively wide range of products to choose from.
B. security for online purchases.
C. vendor reliability and reputation.
D. ease of access to product information.
E. quality information regarding purchase options.

Answer: E Page: 124

13. The web presence of an online marketer can

A. make a sale.
B. provide after-sale service.
C. build customer loyalty.
D. only inform or create interest or curiosity.
E. all of the above.

Answer: D Page: 124

14. Online marketing is considered to be an extension of

A. personal selling.
B. direct marketing.
C. point-of-sale marketing.
D. advertising.
E. global marketing.

Answer: B Page: 125

15. Couponing can take the form of

A. two-for-one offers.
B. cents or dollars off at checkout.
C. coupons for the exchange of other products from the same company.
D. a and c above.
E. a, b, and c above.

Answer: E Page: 126

16. The qualities customers value in online awareness include

A. privacy.
B. accuracy of order fulfillment.
C. free twenty-four hour return and credit for unwanted items.
D. a and b above.
E. a, b, and c above.

Answer: D Page: 126

17. Identity, in e-commerce terms, is created by

    A. the company who sponsors the web site.
    B. the appearance and performance of the web site.
    C. the other storefronts to which an individual site is banded in a cybermall.
    D. all of the above.
    E. none of the above.

    Answer: B Page: 126

18. In e-commerce, the key to product or service value is

    A. the company behind the product or service.
    B. warranties and guarantees the company offers.
    C. how technological the web site is perceived to be.
    D. deliberate differentiation of product or service.
    E. none of the above.

    Answer: D Page: 127

19. The critical factor in creating and sustaining competitive advantage on the internet is

    A. the unique selling proposition of the product or service.
    B. the customerization and personalization of the product or service.
    C. the quality and value of the product or service.
    D. the security and confidentiality in purchasing.
    E. the wide range of quality and price offerings.

    Answer: B Page: 127

20. The ability to test new products or services is one the biggest advantages of the web.

    A. True
    B. False

    Answer: A Page: 117

21. The virtual store can present products or services even if the server is not running.

    A. True
    B. False

    Answer: B Page: 121

22. Men are more frequent purchasers from virtual stores than women.

    A. True
    B. False

    Answer: A Page: 123

23. Empathy for customers' wants and desires is one of the key ingredients for the success of a virtual store.

    A. True
    B. False

Answer: A Page: 124

24. The competitive difference between an online vehicle and traditional media is the online opportunity for interactivity.

    A. True
    B. False

    Answer: A Page: 125

25. The image of a company from its web site is what the marketer wants it to be and not what the viewer interprets it to be.

    A. True
    B. False

    Answer: B Page: 126

Chapter 7
The Tools of Electronic Marketing Resources

Test Bank

1. Which of the following are necessary for electronic commerce to function?

   A. Electronic equipment and networks
   B. Electronic equipment and transaction systems
   C. Electronic equipment, networks, and transaction systems
   D. Electronic equipment, networks, transaction systems, and secured transfer systems
   E. None of the above

   Answer: C Page: 136

2. In e-commerce, who defines gratification?

   A. Suppliers
   B. Web site developers
   C. Web retailers
   D. Customers
   E. Customer service representatives

   Answer: D Page: 136

3. E-commerce resource tools include

   A. CD-ROM.
   B. optical scanners.
   C. smart cards.
   D. all of the above.
   E. none of the above.

   Answer: D Page: 137

4. The technology that has been developed to integrate marketing operations and corporate strategy is

   A. enterprise reporting.
   B. data warehousing.
   C. functional integration software.
   D. a and b above.
   E. a and c above.

   Answer: D Page: 137

5. E-mail was developed in

   A. research and development labs at Microsoft.
   B. military defense research programs.
   C. the garage of a silicone valley techie.
   D. a research program at Netscape.
   E. research and educational communities.

   Answer: E Page: 138

6. GUI stands for

   A. "give us information".
   B. "going under interview".
   C. the name of a rock band like REM.
   D. graphical user interface.
   E. none of the above.

   Answer: D Page: 142

7. The name of the graphical browser that made the Web more user-friendly to navigate was

   A. Netscape Navigator.
   B. Internet Explorer.
   C. World Wide Web.
   D. Telnet.
   E. Mosaic.

   Answer: E Page: 142

8. Which of the following are recommended to be fully functional online?

   A. WWW and Usenet
   B. E-mail, www, and FTP
   C. Telnet and Usenet
   D. Newsgroups and e-mail
   E. All of the above

   Answer: E Page: 145

9. The Web was introduced to the public in

   A. 1973.
   B. 1984.
   C. 1987.
   D. 1991.
   E. 1995.

   Answer: D Page: 145

10. In recent years, web sites have come alive with the addition of

    A. motion.
    B. motion and sound.
    C. motion, sound, and voice interaction.
    D. motion, sound, and color and graphic manipulation.
    E. motion, sound, voice interaction, and color and graphic manipulation.

    Answer: D Page: 146

11. The title of the in-house staff person responsible for maintaining a web site is

    A. Web developer.
    B. Web marketer.
    C. Web assimilator.
    D. Web coordinator.

E. Web master.

Answer: E Page: 146

12. A web site enables a user an almost guaranteed instantaneous collection of information from

A. a Q&A site.
B. a FAQ site.
C. a MIDI site.
D. a MINI site.
E. none of the above.

Answer: B Page: 148

13. CD-ROMs

A. hold about 630 megabytes.
B. cannot be written over.
C. are identical to audio compact discs.
D. all of the above.
E. a and b above.

Answer: E Page: 149

14. Front-end and back-end devices are

A. similar to Netscape and Explorer.
B. multiple software applications used together to build specific systems.
C. hardware and software applications used together to build specific systems.
D. all of the above.
E. b and c above.

Answer: B Page: 151

15. The Intranet is

A. a secured communications system within the internet.
B. a quick access system between web sites similar to a hot link.
C. a newer generation online communications significantly faster than the internet.
D. a private access communications network for employees within an organization.
E. none of the above.

Answer: D Page: 152

16. The Extranet is

A. a superior version of the internet that provides voice recognition and enhanced security.
B. a private access communications network exclusively for employees of a firm.
C. a private communications network that includes selected external suppliers and clients
D. a and c above.
E. all of the above.

Answer: C Page: 154

17. Data from optical scanners can assist marketers by

    A. tracking the results of sales promotions.
    B. verifying customer identities.
    C. counting units sold in a defined time period.
    D. checking prices.
    E. all of the above.

    Answer: E Page: 155

18. A web portal is

    A. the same as a metasite.
    B. the same as a betasite.
    C. an entry point to a wide array of services and resources.
    D. all of the above.
    E. a and c above.

    Answer: E Page: 155

19. Typical problems marketers can encounter when integrating web site activities into the marketing plan include

    A. not knowing how to use a web site as a marketing tool.
    B. broken links to web pages.
    C. taking too long to download pages.
    D. all of the above.
    E. b and c above.

    Answer: E Page: 154

20. In most cases of electronic commerce, information interactivity delivers an overarching sense of customer gratification.

    A. True
    B. False

    Answer: A Page: 154

21. The database is the traditional medium of the IS Department of average to large firms.

    A. True
    B. False

    Answer: A Page: 155

22. Because of new emerging communications technology, e-mail is quickly declining in importance as a communications tool.

    A. True
    B. False

    Answer: B Page: 156

23. While e-mail messages may seem somewhat cybermall, emotions are expressed through the use of emoticons.

    A. True
    B. False

    Answer: A Page: 138

24. In marketing circles, the web is considered a killer application because of sound, visual, and interactive capabilities.

    A. True
    B. False

    Answer: A Page: 141

25. CD-ROM stands for compact disk rite-only memory

    A. True
    B. False

    Answer: B Page: 143

Chapter 8
Segmenting and Analyzing the Target Market

Test Bank

1. Approximately how many households are in the U.S.?

   A. 83 million
   B. 97 million
   C. 109.5 million
   D. 121.7 million
   E. 130 million

   Answer: E Page: 160

2. Geographic targeting can be can be used to profile

   A. individual people.
   B. zip codes and census tracts.
   C. states and counties.
   D. b and c above.
   E. a and b above.

   Answer: D Page: 160

3. Marketers can get demographic characteristics on how many different household clusters?

   A. 25
   B. 38
   C. 43
   D. 50
   E. None, because no two households are alike.

   Answer: D Page: 160

4. An example of a longitudinal database is

   A. Procter & Gamble tracking female births and the babies the women will eventually have.
   B. Disney's release of videos by generation.
   C. Ford's tracking of individuals successive car purchases.
   D. a and c above.
   E. a, b, and c above.

   Answer: E Page: 160-161

5. Databases can provide marketers with what type of data?

   A. Demographics and housing characteristics.
   B. Lifestyle and purchasing behavior.
   C. Socioeconomic and lifestyle.
   D. All of the above.
   E. None of the above.

   Answer: D Page: 162

6. Demographers have found that people with similar social, economic, and demographic characteristics tend to

   A. respond the best to e-marketing programs.
   B. freely spend large amounts of discretionary income.
   C. be equally spread throughout the U.S.
   D. be very cautious about giving out personal information.
   E. live together in clusters.

   Answer: E Page: 162

7. Successful segmentation strategies are based on

   A. accurately defining demographic profiles only.
   B. in-depth psychological analysis of representative consumers of a segment of interest to marketers.
   C. solid marketing planning and implementation of the marketing plan.
   D. demographic and psychographic profiles of the areas of highest marketing potential.
   E. none of the above.

   Answer: D Page: 162

8. A typical demographic report consists of

   A. demographics with updates and projections.
   B. age broken down by income levels.
   C. business facts.
   D. retail facts.
   E. all of the above.

   Answer: E Page: 163

9. Psychographics cluster households by

   A. income.
   B. geographic location.
   C. lifestyles.
   D. education.
   E. mental status.

   Answer: C Page: 164

10. MicroVision describes how many segments from "upper crust" to "stars and stripes" to "late-life laborers"?

    A. 18
    B. 27
    C. 39
    D. 50
    E. 56

    Answer: D Page: 165

11. While demographics deal with aggregate numbers, psychographic data identifies

    A. the number of households in each segment.
    B. the number and percent of households and population in each segment.

C. the geographic dispersion of household profiles throughout the U.S.
D. all of the above.
E. none of the above.

Answer: B Page: 165

12. Commercial suppliers of demographic and psychographic data to marketers include

A. National Decision Systems and Simmons Market Research Bureau.
B. The U.S. Department of Commerce.
C. The Federal Trade Commission.
D. Consumer Research Bureaus at major universities.
E. Industry Trade Associations.

Answer: A Page: 165

13. iVALS is used for

A. basic market planning.
B. building e-commerce web sites.
C. improving values and lifestyles of consumers.
D. affinity-mapping software.
E. none of the above.

Answer: E Page: 168

14. There are how many iVALS segment profiles?

A. 10
B. 20
C. 30
D. 40
E. 50

Answer: A Page: 168

15. Behavioral segmentation links consumer behavior to

A. their values, attitudes, and lifestyles.
B. marketing influences in an electronic environment.
C. their income level impacting on consumption.
D. their product consumption and usage levels.
E. all of the above.

Answer: D Page: 170

16. In e-marketing, tracking and profiling software is called

A. T & P's.
B. ProTracks.
C. Trackies.
D. Cookies.
E. all of the above refer to the same thing.

Answer: D Page: 170

17. "ALEXA" is a new

A. auto import sold exclusively on the internet.
B. psychographic segmentation technique.
C. database software to integrate demographic and psychographic data.
D. model for building e-commerce web sites.
E. model of advertising viewership called clickstream analysis.

Answer: E Page: 171

18. The two important areas of judgement in marketing are

A. identifying marketing objectives and establishing marketing strategies.
B. budgeting for marketing and monitoring budget expenditures.
C. product development and product improvement.
D. the creative marketing process and market segment selection.
E. all of the above are equally important.

Answer: D Page: 172

19. The key benefit to utilizing mapping software is

A. planning.
B. organizing.
C. directing.
D. controlling.
E. all of the above.

Answer: B Page: 174

20. Three types of database mapping that are useful to e-marketers include

A. site analysis, territory identification, and product movement.
B. population density, retail trade area, and income profiles.
C. database plots, ethnic profiling, and educational level profiles.
D. household income, house value, and property tax base.
E. site analysis, territory management, and database plots.

Answer: E Page: 175

21. Geo-demographic analysis provides data on both household attributes and lifestyle patterns.

A. True
B. False

Answer: B Page: 160

22. Properly maintained databases provide marketers with accurate, up-to-date information on population, households, and businesses nationwide.

A. True
B. False

Answer: A Page: 161

23. Psychographics is a customer segmentation and target market that identifies the number and concentration of households of each segment located within a trade area.

A. True
B. False

Answer: A Page: 165

24. Clickstream analysis is a study of consumer response data detailing the content and advertising banners that consumers click on during the online navigation process.

A. True
B. False

Answer: A Page: 171

25. Computer technology is the key factor in the growth of the use of demographic and psychographic data analysis and its extensive application in strategic marketing planning.

A. True
B. False

Answer: A Page: 177

Chapter 9
Integrating the Promotional Mix

Test Bank

1. One new technology, exemplified by Alexa Internet, is to deliver product or service information to Internet consumers more effectively and involves the use of what is known as

A. customization profiles.
B. personalization profiles.
C. web use tracking.
D. habit patterns.
E. navigation customization.

Answer: C Page: 181

2. Alexa Internet provides

A. summary data regarding web site sales.
B. a tool bar which lists site statistics, including "hits" and sales data.
C. alternative sites similar to the one accessed.
D. a "trust-rating" for the site accessed.
E. B and C above.

Answer: B Page: 181

3. There is no difference between the traditional promotional mix for products and services via regular channels and the electronic promotional mix.

A. True
B. False

Answer: B Page: 181

4. Which of the elements of the promotional mix below are media-based and therefore provide a tested means of communication that can be adapted for Internet communications?

A. direct marketing and sales promotion
B. advertising
C. personal selling
D. direct marketing, advertising, sales promotion and public relations
E. none of the above

Answer: D Page: 181

5. The WWW can be used as part of a "grand" promotional plan under the following circumstances:

A. at the present time, a promotional plan based solely on the WWW cannot be relied upon.
B. only in the marketing of products versus services.
C. if a traditional promotional plan has been ineffective.
D. if the majority of the target market for the commercial offering on-line.
E. if the number of households containing a computer is less than 20%.

Answer: A Page: 182

6. One of the important considerations for the marketer when developing on-line communication strategies is

A. to think about quick delivery of information.
B. to assure accuracy in delivered information.
C. to emphasize dialogue with customers not monologue.
D. there are no substantive differences communication capacity.
E. traditional media is actually better at dialogue than Internet strategy.

Answer: C Page: 183

7. Online marketers must create online awareness for their web sites in the following stages:

A. online visibility, online believability, online longevity.
B. web site advertising, then web site propagation.
C. URL notification, registration and reservation.
D. directory registration only.
E. registration in WWW, Usenet and FTP.

Answer: A Page: 183

8. Because the WWW is an anonymous marketplace, ____________ is essential in distinguishing genuine merchants from scam artists.

A. a well designed web site
B. online credibility
C. a statement of customer service policy
D. a low price
E. a high price

Answer: B Page: 183

9. One method that online marketers use to show appreciation for the customer's business by paying special attention to them is

A. giving the lowest prices possible.
B. allowing free returns.
C. personalizing with the customer's name all e-mail correspondence associated with the purchase or inquiry.
D. providing coupons for discounts.
E. being cordial in all communications.

Answer: C Page: 184

10. Online customer retention can be measured by

A. informal comments.
B. number of customers.
C. sales.
D. reorders from satisfied customers.
E. returned orders.

Answer: D Page: 185

11. One WWW approach that uses client-server applications to unilaterally send information to customers is called

A. direct marketing.
B. push technology.

C. pull technology.
D. browser technology.
E. spamming.

Answer: B Page: 186

12. __________________ is a PC/WWW channel utilizing software that integrates news wires, newspapers, magazines, using push technology.

A. Push Web
B. Point Cast
C. Push Cast
D. Net Cast
E. Net Push

Answer: B Page: 186

13. One promotion by Travelocity.com whose objective was to induce customer loyalty involved

A. $50 discounts for airline ticket purchases.
B. free rental car.
C. 1,500 bonus frequent flier miles.
D. 10% discount on hotel reservations.
E. a contest for a trip to Hawaii.

Answer: C Page: 188

14. Companies establishing businesses on the internet have been allocating up to __________ of their operating budgets on marketing activities

A. 20%
B. 10%
C. 35%
D. 50%
E. 70%

Answer: E Page: 192

15. Which of the following puts the WWW into a unique category of marketing communications?

A. The ability to provide audio.
B. The ability to provide full text advertisements.
C. The ability to provide sight, motion, color, sound and user friendliness.
D. The highest level of reach.
E. The high cost of delivering advertising content.

Answer: C Page: 193

16. Marketers on the WWW should remember that viewers are in search of

A. the cheapest deals possible.
B. the best quality products.
C. exciting shopping experiences.
D. convenience, quality, efficiency, delivery ability, and performance.
E. buyer friendly messages.

Answer: D Page: 195

17. With today's WWW marketing, which of the following is mandatory?

A. Including a web site in all advertising materials.
B. Including an e-mail address in all advertising materials.
C. Developing and obtaining a creative and catchy domain name.
D. Consistency between web address and e-mail address.
E. All of the above.

Answer: E Page: 195

18. __________ is an advertising company that conceives and produces new media campaigns and materials based on electronic vehicles.

A. An interactive advertising agency
B. A push content company
C. A WWW media company
D. Netscape
E. Nielsen Media Research

Answer: A Page: 196

19. One of the benefits of marketing via the WWW is that it will eliminate "waste coverage" of the major mass media of TV, magazines, and newspapers.

A. True
B. False

Answer: A Page: 205

20. A major consumer benefit in shopping on the WWW is

A. the ability to search for one-of-a-kind products.
B. better product descriptions.
C. better guarantees.
D. personal sales support.
E. higher trust level with the vendor.

Answer: A Page: 205

21. For sales professionals, personal communication devices are being improved rapidly by technology advancements. An example is

A. personal digital assistance (PDA).
B. alpha-numeric pagers.
C. "smart" cellular telephones.
D. GPS implementations.
E. all of the above.

Answer: E Page: 206

22. According to a study by Gupta and Pitkow, the most important way that WWW users find out about web sites is through

A. trial and error.
B. guessing.
C. television advertising.
D. printed promotional materials.
E. word of mouth contexts with friends and others.

Answer: E Page: 208

23. In defining the online communications objectives for a web site, an important issue is

A. whether the site would be linked to databases.
B. the type of television and telephone connections the target customers use.
C. whether the electronic resource(s) will support introductory mass media product merchandising.
D. how to make the web site as static in nature as possible for easy reading.
E. A and C above.

Answer: E Page: 199

24. When Biore introduced its Pore Perfect Strips product, it gave away samples to teenage girls at shopping malls. This promotion

A. could have been distributed more easily via the WWW.
B. was a failure because too much free product was handed out.
C. was a traditional promotion aimed at inducing trial of the product.
D. cannot be realistically done via a web site.
E. C and D above.

Answer: E Page: 201

25. Public relations has traditionally utilized the print and broadcast media to disseminate favorable information about a product or its producer. With the Internet,

A. no change in PR will occur unless federal regulation allows it.
B. the basic principles of PR are rendered obsolete.
C. public relations must continue to be practiced in these traditional media for efficiency's sake.
D. conservative companies and marketers don't believe in PR on the Internet.
E. new creative possibilities and new channels for PR information have emerged.

Answer: E Page: 202

Chapter 10
Using the Internet

Test Bank

1. The informal rules of behavior for the Internet have evolved over time and are generally described by the term

A. Netiquette.
B. Acceptable Net Usage (ANU).
C. Internet rules and standards.
D. FTP.
E. there are no informal rules of behavior.

Answer: A Page: 224

2. People who use various resources on the Internet come from many nations and many social classes. They are sometimes called

A. Cybernauts.
B. Internet geeks.
C. Netizens (network citizens).
D. Internet explorers.
E. Cyber critters.

Answer: C Page: 224

3. "Flaming" is

A. a practice that is encouraged on the net.
B. a practice that is funny.
C. a difficult skill to learn.
D. sending an argumentative or belligerent response.
E. burning out your computer modem.

Answer: D Page: 225

4. Typing a mail message completely in upper case is

A. more efficient than lower case.
B. is typically considered to be SHOUTING.
C. is only for printing.
D. can only be done in UNIX.
E. disables the spell checking.

Answer: B Page: 225

5. Sending e-mails on the Internet does not allow nuances and emotions of communication to be transmitted. One can simulate emotions with the use of

A. special control codes.
B. emoticons.
C. pictures.
D. extended explanations of the emotions.
E. all upper case typing.

Answer: B Page: 225

6. Multimedia capability was added to the Internet in 1993. Prior to that time all transmissions on the Internet were essentially

A. not done with a "browser".
B. in black and white.
C. character-based.
D. frequently limited to academic and research messages.
E. all of the above.

Answer: E Page: 213

7. There are numerous types of content available on the World Wide Web. These different types of content can be used tactically by both marketers and consumers.

A. True
B. False

Answer: A Page: 213

8. Marketers can use the WWW for the following activity:

A. product delivery.
B. marketing intelligence.
C. customer service.
D. product pricing.
E. b, c, and d above.

Answer: E Page: 213

9. There are two main types of commerce on the Internet. They are

A. business-to-consumer and government.
B. international and intrastate.
C. government and Fortune 500 companies.
D. business-to-consumer and business-to-business.
E. none of the above.

Answer: D Page: 213

10. As a marketer, you should never be concerned about your competitors' Web sites.

A. True
B. False

Answer: B Page: 214

11. Web sites for business-to-consumer commerce should be designed to

A. be easy to use.
B. contain a list of product categories.
C. contain an internal search engine.
D. download quickly.
E. all of the above.

Answer: E Page: 214

12. A retailer that offers online purchasing should

A. not accept credit cards
B. provide secure transmissions such as SSL encryption
C. handle all purchases via telephone
D. advise purchasers of the type of security it is using
E. b and d above

Answer: E Page: 214

13. Web sites for business-to-business commerce will

A. have much more technical informational than business-to-consumer sites.
B. be the same as business-to-consumer sites.
C. be filled with large GIF files.
D. be much more conservative than business-to-consumer sites.
E. all of the above.

Answer: A Page: 215

14. One pricing tactic that both business-to-business and business-to-consumer marketers can use effectively is

A. limited use products.
B. discounts for online sales only.
C. special credit card promotions.
D. annual purchasing volume rates.
E. none of the above.

Answer: B Page: 217

15. Most consumers like shopping on the WWW because there is no pressure from sales people.

A. True
B. False

Answer: A Page: 217

16. One of the most important reasons for consumers to shop on the WWW is

A. convenience.
B. free software.
C. saving time.
D. personalized shopping services.
E. none of the above.

Answer: A Page: 217

17. In terms of dollars, the holiday shopping season on the Internet is

A. negligible in volume.
B. much bigger than in retail stores.
C. about the same as in retail stores.
D. much heavier than normal.
E. one to two months before Thanksgiving.

Answer: D Page: 217

18. The demographics of the Internet are still changing rapidly; but which of the following is true?

A. It is mostly women who access the WWW.
B. Persons aged 50-65 access the WWW more frequently than other age groups.
C. Expert users rarely access the WWW.
D. Men access the Internet slightly more than women.
E. People from southern states use the WWW more often than other regions.

Answer: D Page: 218

19. Navigation services for the web (search engines and web directories) are increasingly used by web surfers. Among the most popular navigation services are

A. Webcrawler.
B. Yahoo!
C. Spin!
D. Four11.
E. none of the above.

Answer: B Page: 218

20. Searching is a big part of shopping or surfing on the World Wide Web and customers

A. frequently take hours to find something.
B. have limitations regarding how long they will search.
C. try to find an item once, then give up.
D. spend no more than five minutes searching.
E. only search for items using navigation services.

Answer: B Page: 218

21. When consumers search for information on the web they generate a "hit ratio" which is

A. the total number of items delivered by the search.
B. the number of items they buy.
C. the number of searches which produce successful results.
D. how often the modem downloads the search results.
E. the batting average of Manny Sosa.

Answer: C Page: 218

22. Two of the best resources for web marketing intelligence purposes are

A. consumer opinion regarding product use and missing product features.
B. customer product returns and opinion surveys.
C. product sales information and product returns.
D. industry sales information and product sales information.
E. physical store sales information and industry sales information.

Answer: A Page: 219

23. Contributions to "Deja Communities" which are forums facilitated by the web site Deja News can be viewed

A. by date.

B. by thread.
C. by the posting author.
D. a and b.
E. all of the above.

Answer: D Page: 219

24. The meta search engine Dogpile (www.dogpile.com) searches by

A. indexing individual words.
B. charging other sites a fee for promotion in its search results list.
C. blasting a search request to numerous search engines which and then produces one huge list of hits.
D. presenting the top 10 sites other people have visited for a particular search term.
E. simplifying the search.

Answer: C Page: 221

25. Boolean search strings tell a WWW search engine

A. when to turn off.
B. how many copies of the page to print.
C. whether to also search in Usenet.
D. what terms must be in the web page or what terms must not be in the web page searched for.
E. none of the above.

Answer: D Page: 222

Chapter 11
Web Page Design

Test Bank

1. In designing a Web site, all of the following are questions to be considered *except:*

A. Who will be reading the page?
B. What type of computer will s/he be using?
C. Will someone copy the site?
D. What is the purpose of the site?
E. Which search engines does your market prefer?

Answer: C Page: 231

2. Although many good editors are available to perform the coding required to build Web pages, all of the following are good reasons to learn and use HTML yourself *except*

A. the best editor can make mistakes.
B. you can get the exact effect desired in less time.
C. inputting your own code gives you more freedom.
D. using HTML helps you understand VisualBasic authoring tools.
E. you don't need an editor to build a great Web page.

Answer: D Page: 232

3. The three basic stages of designing a Web site include

A. the analysis phase, the design phase, and the building phase.
B. the objective setting phase and the building phase because there are only two.
C. the analysis phase, the drafting phase, and the publishing phase.
D. the problem phase, the design phase, and the implementation phase.
E. the baseline phase, the software phase, and the hardware phase.

Answer: A Page: 232

4. In which of the following phases of Web design would you identify your targeted audience?

A. the post-implementation phase
B. the design phase
C. the publishing phase
D. the baseline phase
E. the analysis phase

Answer: E Page: 232

5. The tactic of keeping graphic elements "one screen" as the Web page opens with no scrolling required is known as

A. home paging.
B. vertical design.
C. designing above the fold.
D. synergistic design
E. designing by the numbers.

Answer: C Page: 234

6. Sustained interactivity with a Web site, "the holistic sensation that people feel when they act with total involvement," is known as

A. sustained interactivity.
B. flow.
C. virtual engagement.
D. viewer reach/touch.
E. maximum escape.

Answer: B Page: 235

7. The main tools that marketers use to create this interactivity on a Web site are

A. well prepared narratives.
B. animation.
C. vivid pictures.
D. hyperlinks.
E. games/prizes.

Answer: D Page: 237

8. One good way to bring consumers back to a Web site is by

A. asking consumers to remember your site.
B. paying them $5 -10 for doing so.
C. not mentioning your competitors in comparison ads.
D. thanking them for visiting the site the first time.
E. offering an e-mail service for new and current specials.

Answer: E Page: 233

9. Converting existing paper-based documents to Web-based documents is no problem since print-based designs work just as well on computer screens.

A. True
B. False

Answer: B Page: 239

10. Creating concise, memorable titles to your Web documents serves the following purpose:

A. titles act as indicators of what to expect.
B. making it easier for the browser to display the Web documents.
C. titles provide an easy visual clue to identify source files quickly when you need to make changes.
D. titles are not really as important as links.
E. a and c only.

Answer: E Page: 241

11. The Head section of an HTML document

A. supplies the document title.
B. indicates to Web browsers how to index the document.

C. defines the function of the document.
D. establishes a relationship between HTML documents and directories.
E. all of the above.
Answer: E Page: 242

12. Keywords which allow your Web documents to be located by search engine word searches are contained in the

A. meta tag
B. body
C. link attributes
D. break tag
E. scripts

Answer: A Page: 242

13. When designing documents with HTML coding the actual font properties and descriptions of how the text is being used are known as

A. style formatting.
B. autocodes.
C. physical styles and logical styles.
D. font/style selections.
E. text fonts.

Answer: C Page: 244

14. Text will sometimes be displayed differently on Microsoft® Explorer and Netscape® Navigator.

A. True
B. False

Answer: A Page: 245

15. The two types of lists in block level formatting which use the <LI> tag to mark individual items in the list are

A. outline lists and table lists
B. numbered lists and bulleted lists
C. lower and higher order lists
D. undifferentiated and differentiated lists
E. content and discovery lists

Answer: B Page: 247

16. Numbered lists require the use of the following container tags:

A. <DL> and </DL>
B. <NL> and </NL>
C. <AL> and </AL>
D. <OL> and </OL>
E. <UL> and </UL>

Answer: D Page: 249

17. Lists which provide a dictionary entry-like format are called

A. definition lists.
B. dictionary lists.
C. term lists.
D. glossary lists.
E. a and/or d.

Answer: E Page: 250

18. Which of the following HTML elements can be used within a table to display the reason for or the identity of a table?

A. Either the table row or table column tag.
B. The caption tag.
C. The title tag.
D. The table row tag.
E. The ALIGN tag.

Answer: B Page: 253

19. Which of the following tags are very useful in tables?

A. CELLPADDING, CELLSPACING and SPAMMING.
B. ALIGN, CELLSPACING, ROWSPAN and CSPAN.
C. BORDER, ALIGN, CELLSPACING, CELLSPACING and ROWSPAN.
D. VALIGN, TABLESPACE, and COLSPAN.
E. None of the above.

Answer: C Page: 253

20. Interactivity on a Web page usually comes from hyperlinks which

A. force visitors to register their information.
B. encourage visitors to look at graphics or tables.
C. enable a viewer to stay in one portion of the Web page.
D. allow visitors to immediately jump (using mouse clicks) to other pages that you designate.
E. generate fast-moving images.

Answer: D Page: 254

21. One of the most visually appealing objects to put on a Web page is a picture or graphic. The HTML tag for doing this is

A. <VIS>
B. <IMG>
C. <GRAPH>
D. <PIC>
E. <SRC>

Answer: B Page: 254

22. Image maps are

A. not useful at most connect speeds.
B. the best way to present more complicated tables.
C. interactive graphical maps without clickable images.

D. interactive graphical maps with clickable images.
E. static image files that are very high resolution.

Answer: D Page: 256

23. Image maps consist of several components including which of the following?

A. A site-map file that directs the browser to the image.
B. A graphic image gif file that a user clicks on.
C. An HTML file to link the image and map files.
D. B and C only.
E. All of the above.

Answer: D Page: 256

24. Generally speaking, based on how each works, there are two types of image maps. They are

A. empty images and container images.
B. front-end and back-end.
C. client-side and server-side.
D. graphical and photo.
E. there is only one type of image map: local-side.

Answer: C Page: 256

25. Since all browsers read the same HTML code, you can

A. count on good displaying of your pages as long as your HTML is correct.
B. browsers don't read HTML code the same, but the differences are always slight.
C. assume that differences in display will not happen.
D. save time by writing the same code for both Netscape and Microsoft browsers.
E. Browsers don't read HTML code the same requiring testing on multiple browsers to be sure that your viewers see what you intended.

Answer: E Page: 257

Chapter 12
Capturing Customer Profiles and Data Management

Test Bank

1. The main entity or component of a database is

A. the field.
B. the table.
C. the record.
D. the category.
E. the cell.

Answer: B Page: 263

2. The entity or component within a database that holds information such as a name or date is

A. the table.
B. the record.
C. the field.
D. the cell.
E. the subcategory.

Answer: C Page: 263

3. The records in a database

A. hold the fields.
B. hold the tables.
C. hold information such as a name or date.
D. both a and c.
E. both b and c.

Answer: D Page: 263

4. Database design can be very complicated. Three elements that should always be present in database design to insure consistency of analysis are

A. technology, research techniques, and data.
B. names, addresses, and ages.
C. forms, tags, and attributes.
D. characters, fonts, and scales.
E. hierarchy, dependence, and decomposition.

Answer: A Page: 263

5. All of the following contribute to the ever more complex management of marketing processes *except*

A. customized products.
B. new distribution channels.
C. multiple pricing options.
D. new communications channels.
E. mass production.

Answer: E Page: 264

6. The key to managing new online marketing processes will be

A. hiring and training competent customer service representatives.
B. technology and automation.
C. more specialized education and research.
D. predicting the future with greater accuracy.
E. minimizing the impact of change until it is better understood.

Answer: B Page: 264

7. Potentially, the best database for e-commerce is

A. an operations oriented database.
B. a market intelligence database.
C. a name and address file.
D. the US Census.
E. one assembled from ongoing customer transactions.

Answer: E Page: 265

8. Transactional databases are advantageous because they always include information about

A. whether or not the customer is already buying from the marketer's company.
B. the number of potential customers in targeted household.
C. the target market a customer occupies.
D. whether or not the customer shops online.
E. broad demographic data.

Answer: A Page: 265

9. All of the following are tried and true methods of assembling databases for marketing purposes *except*

A. profiling by demographics.
B. profiling by retrographics.
C. profiling by geographics.
D. profiling by psychographics.
E. creating a proprietary database.

Answer: B Page: 265

10. Often the most difficult aspect of the data collection planning process is

A. agreeing on the need to collect data.
B. acquiring the funds for data collection.
C. getting the various departments together to create the plan.
D. implementing the plan.
E. deciding whether the plan requires evaluation.

Answer: C Page: 266

11. A "hit" can be recorded if the following occurs:

A. A request for a file has been made.
B. A successful file transfer has occurred.

C. An unsuccessful file transfer has occurred.
D. A null transfer has occurred.
E. All of the above.

Answer: E Page: 267

12. All of the following are shortcomings to issuing cookies *except*

A. multiple users of a single PC count as multiple visits by a single user.
B. many consider them to be an invasion of privacy.
C. they cannot be turned off.
D. both Netscape Navigator and Internet Explorer allow the cookie option to be turned off.
E. both a and d.

Answer: C Page: 267

13. In a database, the data in fields appear in

A. rows
B. numerals only
C. columns
D. single units
E. both a and c

Answer: C Page: 271

14. In a database, the data in records appear in

A. rows.
B. single units.
C. columns.
D. alphabetical characters only.
E. both a and c.

Answer: E Page: 271

15. When designing a database, a starting form which opens up other forms or reports is called a

A. data entry form.
B. diving board.
C. dialogue board.
D. switch board.
E. control board.

Answer: D Page: 271

16. A control is a link between a database form and its record source. The most common type of control used to display and enter data is a

A. dialogue box.
B. switch board.
C. record.
D. parameter.
E. text box.

Answer: E Page: 271

17. Internet forms that request customer information should take no longer to complete than

A. 10 minutes.
B. 3-5 minutes.
C. 1 minute or less.
D. such forms should be mailed to customers.
E. truly interested customers will complete the form regardless of how long it takes.

Answer: B Page: 272

18. Open-ended questions are an effective means of gathering qualitative data.

A. True
B. False

Answer: A Page: 272

19. The database process which synthesizes, sorts and calculates data from multiple tables is called a

A. control.
B. quanitifier.
C. query.
D. selector.
E. analyzer.

Answer: C Page: 272

20. Information that is grouped into two types can be analyzed by

A. calculating the two groups separately and then adding them.
B. Boolean operators.
C. wizards.
D. crosstab queries.
E. none of the above.

Answer: D Page: 273

21. Links between reports and their sources are created with graphical objects called

A. queries.
B. Boolean operators.
C. SQLs.
D. logos.
E. controls.

Answer: E Page: 275

22. The first step in designing a database is to determine

A. how you want the final reports to look and sketch them out on paper.
B. the purpose of the database.
C. what subjects you need to store facts about.
D. what facts you need to store about each subject.
E. how the tables will relate to one another.

Answer: B Page: 275

23. It is important to remember to duplicate information within and between tables.

A. True
B. False

Answer: B Page: 276

24. The unique field or set of fields that identifies each individual record is called the

A. primary key.
B. record key.
C. front door key.
D. field key.
E. customer key.

Answer: A Page: 277

25. One of the attractive features of using a Database Wizard to create databases is that it can be used to modify existing tables in a database.

A. True
B. False

Answer: B Page: 278

Chapter 13
Considerations for Ongoing Customer Communications

Test Bank

1. Companies who are responsive to customer e-mails often install special software systems to

A. acknowledge receipt of customer messages.
B. eliminate telephone charges to the customer.
C. reduce the need for direct contact with a customer service representative.
D. minimize the amount of time a customer has to use to communicate with the company.
E. all of the above.

Answer: E Page: 286

2. The best indicator of a product's quality is the customer's

A. initial purchase.
B. repurchase.
C. communication to the company of his or her satisfaction.
D. communication of satisfaction to friends and family.
E. use of coupons.

Answer: B Page: 286

3. It is now possible for computers to recognize and respond with equal accuracy to both written and spoken communication.
A. True
B. False

Answer: B Page: 287

4. According to a recent study, fully two thirds of all documented customer dissatifaction results from

A. product failure.
B. poor service.
C. communication breakdown.
D. bad value.
E. misleading advertising.

Answer: C Page: 289

5. A recent examination of 125 sites for customer e-mail responsiveness indicated that the most responsive sites were

A. travel sites.
B. commercial air lines.
C. wholesalers.
D. retail shopping sites.
E. government tourism sites.

Answer: Page: 289

6. Decisions concerning customer service standards should be made by

A. customers.
B. marketers.
C. managers.
D. outside consulting firms.
E. customer service representatives.

Answer: A Page: 290

7. The most important source of customer communication a company should monitor is

A. formal customer surveys.
B. complaints.
C. compliments.
D. e-mail.
E. direct customer contact.

Answer: B Page: 291

8. When resolving conflicts with customers, establishing exactly who is responsible for the problem should be accomplished first.

A. True
B. False

Answer: B Page: 291

9. The most important ingredient of a customer service program is

A. its standards.
B. superior training of representatives.
C. its activities schedule.
D. high quality of representatives' performance capabilities.
E. good form letters.

Answer: D Page: 293

10. The program or script which tells a form what to do with the data entered on it is usually placed in a directory on the Web server called the

A. file upload field
B. hidden field
C. script file
D. base directory
E. CGI-bin

Answer: E Page: 294

11. The HTML tag that possesses the most options and attributes is

A. METHOD.
B. INPUT.
C. CGI.
D. MAXLENGTH.
E. GREENIE.

Answer: B Page: 296

12. For security reasons, CGI-bin directories are usually accessible to

A. system administrators.
B. customer service representatives.
C. all web site visitors.
D. visitors with university Internet accounts.
E. "friends and family".

Answer: A Page: 298

13. The attribute which points a form to a URL which will accept its information is the

A. POINTER attribute.
B. METHOD attribute.
C. ACTION attribute.
D. INPUT attribute.
E. ACCEPT attribute.

Answer: C Page: 295

14. Software that can scan the text of an incoming e-mail and respond intelligently without human intervention is a type of software called

A. "smart readers".
B. "scan-trons".
C. "intelli-mail".
D. "robots".
E. "e-trains".

Answer: D Page: 287

15. The METHOD attribute tells the form

A. when to turn off.
B. the nature of the customer's entry into the form.
C. nothing, it doesn't speak.
D. how to send its information back to the script.
E. the validity of the data being entered.

Answer: D Page: 296

16. Getting customer information very important in business. Unfortunately the WWW is not well suited for conducting prospect, customer, supplier and ex-customer information.

A. True
B. False

Answer: B Page: 287

17. "Ask Jeeves" is an item that can be installed on your firm's home page. It is

A. a financial calculator.
B. a software navigation tool.
C. a software search tool that provides instant responses to customer inquires.

D. the only way for a customer to find out information about your site.
E. a Microsoft kids game to entertain visitors to your site.

Answer: C Page: 287

18. A good way to present your firm's detailed company or product information to customers is put a hyperlink on

A. your home page that directs customers to SEC material about your firm.
B. your home page that directs customers to the local library.
C. customers don't want to know about these things, a hyperlink is not necessary.
D. the web site of a competitor back to your site.
E. your home page that will link to an "About Us" or "About Our Products" page.

Answer: E Page: 288

19. To get customer information using your web site or via e-mail, you can

A. perform opinion polls
B. gain feedback on new product concepts
C. do customer response polls on a variety of promotions
D. survey ex-customers
E. all of the above.

Answer: E Page: 288

20. There are newsgroups on the Internet where consumers can talk about any subject including

A. how they've been treated by a company or the company's products.
B. consumers don't really use the Internet to transmit such information.
C. the newsgroups are for regular broadcast-type news.
D. newsgroups are not on the Internet, they are on cable TV.
E. newsgroups are heavily regulated by the FCC, so consumers cannot talk about much.

Answer: A Page: 289

21. Many online retailing executives know that customer service is crucially important to e-marketing success. One suggested strategy to achieve great customer service is

A. lower service standards to make them easier to attain.
B. automating functions such as order tracking and suggestive selling.
C. to hire as many customer service representatives as possible.
D. put all efforts into selling and worry about customer service later.
E. to fire any service representative who mistreats a customer.

Answer: B Page: 290

22. Customers visiting a web site almost always have questions. Often these questions are repetitious. An efficient way of handling these questions is

A. not to let visitors to your site ask these questions.
B. to put a 900 telephone number on your site for your customers to call and ask questions.
C. to ask customers to write you letter if they have any questions.
D. by preparing a FAQ page to answer simple or common customer questions.
E. to ignore all questions except for "How do I order?"

Answer: D Page: 291

23. The use of the Internet for customer surveys has become a less costly way to get input from a company's marketing segments. As a result, the results of such surveys have little credibility.

A. True
B. False

Answer: B Page: 292

24. Forms on your web site allow for

A. surveying.
B. order taking.
C. the administration of tests.
D. interactivity.
E. all of the above.

Answer: E Page: 294

25. The ________________ type is a form that displays a selection form for a web site visitor to indicate choices to a question or an ordering option.

A. CHOOSER
B. BOX CHOICE
C. CHECKBOX
D. CHEX
E. TEX-MEX

Answer: C Page: 296

Chapter 14
Establishing and Promoting the Virtual Store

Test Bank

1. I have a business idea and I'm ready to start doing business on the Internet. Which of the following is the best way to implement my decision?

A. to develop the side myself using HTML.
B. to have a Webfront store developer create my site.
C. locate my site at a stand-alone address.
D. have my site appear at a cyber-mall.
E. each of these is a decision that must be made based on my market circumstances.

Answer: E Page: 303

2. When it comes to traditional organizational responsibilities, the difference(s) between running a "real" business and running an e-commerce business is/are in the area(s) of

A. financial affairs.
B. production concerns.
C. marketing concerns.
D. both B and C.
E. there are no differences.

Answer: E Page: 306

3. Bankers are sometimes hesitant to loan money to e-businesses to pay for

A. marketing and advertising expenditures.
B. telephone equipment.
C. production equipment.
D. office furniture.
E. operating supplies.

Answer: A Page: 307

4. All of the following are important for successful e-commerce *except*

A. adequate servers.
B. well-trained technical personnel.
C. deep pile carpeting in the office.
D. quick connections.
E. ample telephone lines.

Answer: C Page: 307

5. If your web site is locate on a hosting service's equipment

A. the costs will be 5-15 time than if you would do it yourself.
B. this is not a good idea.
C. the ISP bears the expense of equipment upgrades and repairs.
D. you will always bear equipment upgrades and repairs expenses.
E. potential customers cannot view your web site.

Answer: C Page: 309

6. If you are going to build your own web storefront using virtual-store building software or some other software tool, a good (free) place to look for current information is

A. in the yellow pages.
B. the public library periodicals section.
C. in the general business press.
D. in chat rooms.
E. Web Developer News (www.internetnews.com).

Answer: E Page: 309

7. Although hardware requirements can change over time, which of the following is *not* adequate for e-commerce operations?

A. 16 or more megs of RAM memory
B. 17" color monitor
C. 56.6 baud modem
D. 133MHz PC
E. 4 gigabyte hard disk

Answer: D Page: 310

8. Service companies can take the entire burden of producing a storefront for marketers by taking the marketing plan/objectives and doing all of the programming, equipment selection, and everything entailed in a ready-to-run operation. This is called a(n) ________ system.

A. extensive
B. turnkey
C. zip
D. virtual
E. cheap

Answer: B Page: 311

9. During the design and production process of an e-commerce Web site, it is advisable for your goals and objectives to remain open-ended and flexible.

A. True
B. False

Answer: B Page: 312

10. All of the following are benefits of signing on with a cybermall *except*

A. the ease of small business to differentiate itself from the rest.
B. expanded exposure.
C. site maintenance services.
D. the selection to be found at the cybermall's address.
E. offers shoppers many hyperlinked addresses to follow from one page.

Answer: A Page: 312

11. One very popular cyber mall is ______________, with reasonable costs, sometimes as low as a flat $75 per month.

A. OpenMall
B. Internet Universal Mall
C. Uni-Mall
D. Delaware CyberMall
E. Mall of America

Answer: D Page: 313

12. Using a new marketing concept when accessing a Web site on the ShopperConnection network, a shopper will be given a chance to link to another site only

A. if s/he still has money.
B. if s/he has a special password.
C. after making an initial purchase.
D. when promising to make a purchase at the next site.
E. with an American Express Gold Card.

Answer: C Page: 314

13. When setting up an online presence, all of the following are necessary *except*

A. proficiency at a word processing program.
B. the ability to type.
C. familiarity with HTML.
D. COBOL programming knowledge.
E. understanding of advertising procedure, graphics and copy.

Answer: D Page: 314

14. _________________ has the primary responsibility for maintaining the accuracy, organization and functionality of the e-commerce web site which are crucial to the success of the site.

A. The big cheese
B. The e-commerce manager
C. The Webmaster
D. The marketing manager
E. The regional web manager

Answer: C Page: 314

15. A(n) __________is a company that provides you with a connection to the Internet as well as related Internet-based services and choosing the right one for your e-business is crucial.

A. Regional Exchange Carrier (REC)
B. WWW Interconnect (WWWI)
C. Ethernet Service Provider (ESP)
D. Internet Service Provider (ISP)
E. satellite service system (SSS)

Answer: D Page: 315

16. One drawback to using a large ISP is

A. large ISPs usually have slow connections.
B. large ISPs usually charge more per month.
C. large ISPs fail financially more often than small ISPs.

D. large ISPs have old equipment.
E. large ISPs may not be as flexible as smaller ISPs.

Answer: E Page: 315

17. If your ISP is also providing services to design and build your site including domain name registration, you want to make sure that

A. the site is working right away.
B. they pick fashionable colors for the web pages.
C. the domain name is registered to your business, not the ISP.
D. your competitors do not ever see your site.
E. they charge by the site, not the page.

Answer: C Page: 317

18. Be very careful in choosing your ISP. Per FCC regulations, you cannot change providers.

A. True
B. False

Answer: B Page: 317

19. Traditional promotion is aimed at attracting interest to your product or service. The same is true in online promotion but

A. everything is much more expensive online.
B. there is no long history on what works and doesn't work.
C. potential customers on the Internet are a lot easier to fool.
D. potential customers on the Internet are a lot more receptive to promotional messages.
E. nothing is really similar between traditional and online promotion.

Answer: B Page: 318

20. In a comparison of advertising rates between TV, newspapers, and Internet audiences

A. TV is 10 times more expensive.
B. there is no real cost on the Internet.
C. newspaper advertising is, by far, the cheapest.
D. advertisers pay about as much ($10-40 per 1000 viewers) for each medium.
E. comparison of these costs is not very important to businesses.

Answer: D Page: 318

21. Ads that appear on web pages are meant to attract viewers who will point their mouse at these advertisements to get more information. The measurement for how often viewers do this is called ____________________.

A. reader response rate.
B. reach.
C. virtual share.
D. virtual response.
E. clickthrough rate.

Answer: E Page: 318

22. Which one of the following is *not* a good tactic to consider for establishing a dialog among your target markets?

A. extensive mail surveys
B. e-mail
C. advertising
D. conference venues
E. electronic publishing

Answer: A Page: 320

23. All of the following are attributes of a successful commercial Web site *except*

A. that the content is updated regularly.
B. that navigation is clear and consistent.
C. the frequent use of large, beautiful graphics files.
D. that the organizational/institutional support is in place.
E. that the site is integrated with print media, TV, and radio.

Answer: C Page: 322

24. The GVU 9th WWW User Survey reveals that _______ of e-commerce customers have had a bad experience with purchasing online.

A. >50%
B. almost 100%
C. 20.5%
D. 1.9%
E. 0%

Answer: D Page: 323

25. The estimated number one product category for online purchases in 1999 according to Forrester Research, Forbes, and Business Week is

A. computer hardware.
B. computer software.
C. books.
D. music.
E. leisure travel.

Answer: E Page: 324

Chapter 15
Security on the E-Commerce Site

Test Bank

1. The Internet was originally designed without a very high concern about data security and was primarily intended

A. as a channel for public information.
B. for sharing information.
C. for defense contract information only.
D. for sharing documents.
E. both b and d.

Answer: E Page: 329

2. In order to provide security and privacy in Internet transmissions, the science of crytography is used to produce _____________________.

A. firewalls
B. Internet locks
C. cryptosystems
D. WWW codes
E. Hypertext Secure Code Language (HSCL)

Answer: C Page: 329

3. The two types of cryptosystems currently in use for e-commerce transactions are

A. modern and post-modern.
B. public key and centroid.
C. encryption and decryption.
D. linear and asymptopic.
E. symmetric and asymmetric.

Answer: E Page: 329

4. Both public and private keys can be used to encrypt information.

A. True
B. False

Answer: A Page: 329

5. A public key algorithm that involves the product of large prime numbers is called

A. prime time security.
B. pretty good keys.
C. RSA.
D. WWWSecure.
E. prime technology.

Answer: C Page: 330

6. Symmetric cryptosystems are easier to implement than asymmetric cryptosystems because there is only one key involved.

A. True
B. False

Answer: A Page: 330

7. The one key used in symmetric cryptosystems must be usually be delivered by

A. private keys.
B. RSA algorithms.
C. trusted couriers.
D. key-agreement algorithms.
E. parcel post.

Answer: C Page: 331

8. ________________________is the process of verifying that people or entities are who they claim to be.

A. Spot checking
B. Validation
C. Indoctrination
D. Investigation
E. authentication

Answer: E Page: 332

9. Authentication, the most essential of all security efforts, is the basis of all of the following *except*

A. permissions and authorizations.
B. achieving non-repudiation.
C. access control.
D. financial viability.
E. enforcing accountability.

Answer: D Page: 332

10. ____________________ authenticate the identity and/or status of a person in a verifiable way.

A. Notary publics
B. Digital certificates
C. Personal certificates
D. FCC certificates
E. DMV certificate

Answer: B Page: 332

11. Digital certificates are issued by

A. individual merchants.
B. Certificate Authorities.
C. credit card companies.
D. notary publics.
E. Digital Authorities.

Answer: B Page: 332

12. A digital certificate typically provides all of the following information *except*

A. corporate tax information.
B. the name and e-mail address of the holder.
C. the name of the issuer.
D. a public key.
E. the certificate validity period.

Answer: A Page: 333

13. Secure Sockets Layer (SSL) establishes a secure session between

A. the public key and the private key.
B. the modem and the remote computer.
C. the credit card company and the customers.
D. a user's Web browser and a WWW server.
E. the hard drive and the Web browser.

Answer: D Page: 335

14. The three basic requirements of channel security are that the channel is

A. private, authenticated, and reliable.
B. encrypted, temporary, and online.
C. continuous, divergent, and remote.
D. temporary, sustained, and valid.
E. there are only two requirements: authenticated and valid.

Answer: A Page: 333

15. The first phase of a "data handshake" establishes private communications

A. after both parties use a password.
B. if the transaction is a retail purchase.
C. with a key-agreement algorithm.
D. which can be mailed to each party.
E. using a digital certificate.

Answer: C Page: 333

16. Outgoing and incoming communications at each end of a secure channel require

A. one certificate and one cipher.
B. two ciphers per connection.
C. one cipher per connection.
D. two ciphers for ingoing and one for outgoing.
E. one cipher for outgoing and two for ingoing.

Answer: B Page: 333

17. The second phase of a "data handshake" performs

A. cross-checking.
B. key distribution.

C. client authentication.
D. server authentication.
E. the "hello" greeting.

Answer: C Page: 333

18. Computer hackers can cause losses to companies through

A. loss of data confidentiality.
B. loss of data integrity.
C. loss of system availability.
D. cancellation of online service accounts.
E. a, b and c.

Answer: E Page: 334

19. Surveillance and intrusion detection software is usually required in order to obtain insurance against loss.

A. True
B. False

Answer: A Page: 334

20. A technical standard for safeguarding payment card transactions on the Internet was developed by MasterCard and Visa. This is intended to be the single protocol for such protection and is called

A. Pretty Good Privacy (PGP).
B. Really Good Privacy (RGP).
C. Secure Electronic Transaction (SET).
D. public key encryption.
E. Really Sharp Authentication (RSA).

Answer: C Page: 335

21. Because it encrypts only sensitive information, SET permits Web page designers freer use of graphics in a secure mode.

A. True
B. False

Answer: A Page: 337

22. SET provides merchants and customers all of the following benefits *except*

A. special purpose digital certificates.
B. non-repudiation for dispute resolution.
C. financial performance.
D. authentication of the merchant.
E. authentication of the customer.

Answer: C Page: 338

23. The main drawback of secure system protocols such as SSL and SET is that

A. they are very difficult to remember.

B. they are extremely expensive.
C. they are likely to be hacked by moderately sophisticated computer experts.
D. they place significant loads on computer systems during transactions.
E. most parties to a transaction are not very interested in maintaining security.

Answer: D Page: 339

24. By law, a merchant may charge a customer for a credit card order only after the merchandise has been shipped.

A. True
B. False

Answer: A Page: 329

25. Idealab has a software product it calls "eWallet" which will make _________ shopping on the Internet much easier and quicker because it will work with a single click of the mouse.

A. impulse
B. home
C. automobile
D. teen
E. grocery

Answer: A Page: 340

Chapter 16
Special Opportunities for Business-to-Business Situations

Test Bank

1. There are about __________________ million companies in the world, according to the Dun & Bradstreet worldwide database.

A. 100
B. 1
C. 5
D. 40
E. less than 1

Answer: D Page: 347

2. According to Dun and Bradstreet reports, _______ American businesses currently pursue an online presence.

A. 50,000
B. 75,000
C. 100,000
D. 333,000
E. 665,000

Answer: D Page: 347

3. E-business entails the activities of marketing and selling in business-to-business transactions.

A. True
B. False

Answer: A Page: 346

4. Initially, many companies first began to use e-business capabilities to

A. automate procurement.
B. network procurement systems.
C. both A and B.
D. set up auction sites.
E. file government required business reports.

Answer: C Page: 350

5. All of the following are among the values delivered by e-business *except*

A. reach new markets.
B. build customer loyalty.
C. reduced access to information.
D. enhance human capital.
E. create new products.

Answer: C Page: 350 - 351

6. The new insurance coverage known as Net Secure protects e-commerce sites against

A. hackers.
B. spammers.
C. loss of intellectual property.
D. viruses.
E. all of the above.

Answer: E Page: 353

7. The WWW is used by consulting firms to market management and advisory services regarding which business subjects?

A. virtual seminar for e-businesses
B. consultative selling
C. partnerships
D. "service gaps"
E. all of the above

Answer: E Page: 356 - 357

8. The standard way for exchanging business to business trading information today is

A. Open Buying on the Internet (OBI).
B. approved by the Better Business Bureau.
C. via e-mail.
D. via snail-mail.
E. is very slow.

Answer: A Page: 350

9. Disadvantages of e-business business-to-business commerce include all of the following *except*

A. lost contact with distribution channels.
B. lost contact with sales personnel.
C. alienation distributors.
D. increased legal expenses to close sales.
E. loss of physical distribution locations.

Answer: D Page: 358

10. Which of the following is a strategy adopted by different e-commerce companies to appease disgruntled sales personnel and distributors?

A. Listing products on the site without providing a way to order them directly.
B. Not publicizing their sites.
C. Using sites to direct prospects to long-established dealers.
D. Selling online only at list price.
E. All of the above.

Answer: E Page: 360

11. By 2003, Forrester Research predicts business-to-business e-commerce revenues to reach

A. $100 billion.
B. $1.3 trillion.

C. $50 billion.
D. $4.2 trillion.
E. their limit.

Answer: B Page: 362

12. The Forrester Research Revenue Forecast by Industry indicates that the top 3 industries in the year 2003 will be

A. computing & electronics, utilities, and paper & office products.
B. computing & electronics, aerospace & defense, and medical.
C. computing & electronics, shipping & warehousing, and utilities.
D. computing & electronics, heavy industries, and consumer goods.
E. computing & electronics, motor vehicles, and petro-chemicals.

Answer: E Page: 362

13. ________% of all current WWW users utilize it business purposes and are considered "active business users."

A. 0
B. 34
C. Less than 5
D. 100
E. No more than 10

Answer: B Page: 347

14. In order to get a perspective on how big business-to-business e-commerce will be is to remember that

A. business products are significantly more expensive than consumer products.
B. you must take 1995 business-to-business sales and multiply by 3.
C. U.S. consumer sales will only be about 9.5% of business-to-business sales in 2001.
D. more people work for business than work in retail stores.
E. consumer sales on the Internet will be larger than business-to-business sales.

Answer: C Page: 346

15. It is conceivable that the Internet could prove to be the most effective sales tool since the telephone because it allows

A. nice pictures of products.
B. paper forms to be transmitted to sellers.
C. a more personal way to do business.
D. sales persons to smile on photographs that can be placed on Web sites.
E. companies to reach millions of potential customers quickly and cheaply.

Answer: E Page: 358

16. Marshall Industries, an electronics distributor, is an example of

A. a firm that is being very conservative about using the WWW.
B. a company that chose not to engage in e-business due to legal constraints.
C. a traditional firm that completely restructured itself to use the WWW's capabilities.
D. a company that went into bankruptcy because it did not jump into e-business.
E. a company that encourages it's customers to use the WWW, but does not do so itself.

Answer: C Page: 349

17. The new software developed by Marshall Industries which allows one site to access another site and display information located there transparently through its own site is called

A. Transparent Marketing Logistics (TML).
B. Extensible Markup Language (XML).
C. Clear Coding Language (CCL).
D. Marshall Industries Markup Language (MIML).
E. Simple Mail Tranfer Protocol (SMTP).

Answer: B Page: 348

18. E-commerce encompasses both e-business sales and online consumer sales.

A. True
B. False

Answer: A Page: 346

19. ______% of U.S. small businesses (those with less than 100 employees) are online.

A. 90
B. 20
C. 37
D. 0
E. 5

Answer: C Page: 347

20. In the 80s and 90s, the stock market propelled publicly-held companies, including Internet start-up companies, to astronomical levels of financial strength called

A. the wealth factor.
B. the hyper trend.
C. unfair to old-line companies.
D. the money initiative.
E. the Microsoft effect.

Answer: A Page: 348

21. Advertising messages for business-to-business WWW users can be aimed at them based on

A. what type of computer they are using.
B. the speed of their modem
C. how long they have been on-line.
D. their site selections and search engine choices.
E. the company's credit rating.

Answer: D Page: 349

22. Businesses are being forced to change their practices due to the Internet's capacity for

A. speed of information.
B. accuracy of information.
C. potential for customer satisfaction.

D. generating competitive pressures.
E. all of the above.

Answer: E Page: 346

23. The capabilities of the WWW and e-business systems include the use of information systems that allow firms to

A. do business at less than 10% of prior cost levels.
B. eliminate the sales function altogether.
C. forget about the need to advertise in trade journals.
D. precisely anticipate their customers actions.
E. make less in profits but provide better quality of service.

Answer: D Page: 350

24. Since the legal framework regulating digital transactions is so clear

A. no lawyers are needed.
B. there is no risk of digital signatures ever being contested.
C. Congress will not need to pass any laws regarding e-business.
D. the online business-to-business marketer should worry about advertising more than legalities.
E. actually, many contract related questions still need resolution because the legal framework is uncertain.

Answer: E Page: 358

25. One of the surprises of e-business transaction volumes is

A. the purchasing of business books from Amazon.com.
B. surplus/discounted equipment online auctions.
C. the wheelbarrow market demand.
D. how high value industrial goods cannot be sold on the WWW.
E. there are no surprises in e-business so far.

Answer: B Page: 360

Chapter 17
Implications to the International Marketing Program

Test Bank

1. The evaluation of international marketing processes and potential is conducted in much the same way as the evaluation of marketing in the U.S.

A. True
B. False

Answer: A Page: 366

2. MIT Lab founder Nicholas Negroponte expects the next wave of e-commerce growth to take place in

A. Mexico.
B. Australia.
C. the Third World.
D. Asia.
E. California.

Answer: C Page: 369

3. Two trustworthy indicators of a country's means for general consumption are its

A. sports viewership and religious membership.
B. infrastructure and economic development.
C. size and population.
D. regulatory laws and degree of personal freedom.
E. consumption history and governmental structure.

Answer: B Page: 369

4. The one country in the Americas with a completely digital telephone system is

A. Canada
B. Belize
C. U.S.
D. Brazil
E. Uruguay

Answer: E Page: 370

5. A Web page's home country can be determined by

A. the flag in the upper right-hand corner.
B. a three-number code following the domain name.
C. clicking on the "home country" link.
D. a 2-3 letter code at the end of the domain name.
E. there is no sure way to tell.

Answer: D Page: 369

6. According to the GVU 8th User Survey, European shoppers have generally been online 2-3 years longer than American shoppers.

A. True
B. False

Answer: A Page: 373 - 374

7. By the year 2002, Dataquest predicts that the number of computers connected to the Internet in Europe will reach

A. 17 million.
B. 69 million.
C. 42 million.
D. 200 million.
E. 5 million.

Answer: B Page: 374

8. The only country in Europe not yet online is

A. Finland
B. Switzerland
C. Italy
D. Spain
E. all are online

Answer: E Page: 374 - 375

9. According to a recent Jupiter survey of user perceptions, the majority of residents with household Internet access in Britain, France, and Germany report their understanding of the Internet to be

A. good.
B. total and complete.
C. moderate.
D. limited, poor, or nonexistent.
E. the same as in the U.S.

Answer: D Page: 377

10. The *China Economic Times* reported China's 64% increase in wired computers during a recent six month period as being due to the country's relatively inexpensive online fees.

A. True
B. False

Answer: B Page: 376

11. When considering an online marketing effort with international customers, you should consider the familiarity of the target market with WWW usage and other emerging online technologies.

A. True
B. False

Answer: A Page: 374

12. The most populous European countries are approaching a 10% level of WWW access, but which country has already made it to this threshold?

A. Sweden
B. Norway
C. Finland
D. Portugal
E. a, b and c

Answer: E Page: 375

13. In the U.S., the population is generally very aware of the Internet and its offerings, but in other countries this is not true. This means that

A. you can only market to countries that are aware of the Internet.
B. you should not think of e-commerce in foreign countries.
C. you may have to sell the Internet before you sell your product to international markets.
D. consumers in other countries are not interested in online marketing efforts.
E. consumers in other countries cannot afford online marketed products.

Answer: C Page: 376

14. In China, the vast majority of Internet users are male (92.8%).

A. True
B. False

Answer: A Page: 376

15. One of the big concerns about the largest Latin American countries (Brazil, Argentina and Mexico) is

A. current uncertainty in currency stability.
B. the different languages spoken there.
C. poor education levels.
D. predictions for long term GDP non growth, possibly even decline.
E. a and d.

Answer: E Page: 377

16. "Smart phones," a type of non-computer appliance which allows access to the Internet on small screens is estimated to reach ________ users by 2002, according to Jupiter Communications.

A. <1 million
B. 500,000
C. 2 million
D. 12.9 million
E. Smart phones cannot access the Internet.

Answer: D Page: 377

17. The program that you use to access the Internet on your computer, such as Internet Explorer® or Netscape Communicator® is called a "browser." The program that will do the same thing on one of the "smart phones" is called a

A. telebrowser.
B. Internet Access Applet (IAA).

C. viewer.
D. Internet dialer.
E. microbrowser.

Answer: E Page: 377

18. It is very likely that the first few generations of small screens on Internet appliances such as "smart phones" will not be able to access the full color displays of Web pages because they will have

A. no need for it.
B. small monochrome screens.
C. no consumers who wish to see them.
D. be too heavy.
E. separate, handheld screens.

Answer: B Page: 377

19. E-marketers from the U.S. should avoid the problem of assuming that all viewers of their Web sites will be from the U.S. by

A. knowing the market's language preference and removing U.S. colloquialisms in the content.
B. using a more graphical approach to Web site content.
C. not designing Web sites for non English readers.
D. publishing all Web sites in German.
E. a and d.

Answer: E Page: 377

20. Generally speaking, all countries view the Internet's effects similarly with regard to protecting citizens, economies, and cultures.

A. True
B. False

Answer: B Page: 378

21. With regard to consumer protections across the international landscapes, online marketers have been

A. ignoring all local laws.
B. adjusting their policies on protection to fit the market countries laws.
C. avoiding marketing to non-U.S. markets.
D. unconcerned with any laws whatsoever.
E. fined by European countries for failing to translate all content.

Answer: B Page: 321

22. The European Union policy, effective 1998, that forbids companies from sending personal information out of Europe unless the destination country has certain privacy provisions is called

A. ineffective by marketers.
B. too strict by marketers.
C. the EU Directive.
D. unconstitutional by the World Court.
E. b and c.

Answer: E Page: 379

23. In response to the European Union's policy, an industry group was formed to generate industry-led solutions to the EU's concerns. This industry group is called

A. Internet Systems Business Society (ISDS).
B. profits-oriented.
C. illegal.
D. the Global Business Dialogue (GBD).
E. unethical.

Answer: D Page: 379

24. A long term trend in online and international marketing is that

A. less Internet marketing will be done in Europe.
B. severely restrictive laws will hamper marketers in all countries.
C. marketing is becoming more and more similar among nations and industries.
D. it will not be profitable to market to South American countries.
E. English will be the main language for Web content.

Answer: C Page: 380

25. The 1998 French Open official tennis site received 39% of its orders from Europe. This is an indication that

a) Europeans prefer tennis over soccer.
b) these items were not available in stores in Europe.
c) Europe has more tennis fans than the U.S.
d) the U.S. is not the only country where there is an important growing online market.
e) that North American orders (49%) are clearly more important.

Answer: D Page: 380

Chapter 18
The Ethics of Electronic Marketing

Test Bank

1. It is perfectly acceptable to e-mail customers unsolicited information ("spam") as long as you use a mailing list.

A. True
B. False

Answer: B Page: 384

2. All of the following are good ways to help build your mailing lists *except*

A. providing a check box so the customer can choose whether or not to be a part of the list.
B. asking current customers to provide you with a list of people that you can e-mail.
C. selling or trading your lists with other marketers.
D. asking current customers to forward information to others who may be interested.
E. providing consumers with a way to unsubscribe from the list.

Answer: C Page: 385

3. Intranets are private networks that can be accessed by the Internet. They require protection from viruses and hackers. This is done with a(n)

A. Internet wall.
B. firewall.
C. privacy wall.
D. notice for hackers to "Stay Away!"
E. hope that nothing bad will happen.

Answer: B Page: 387

4. Firewalls can be implemented

A. by network administrators in hardware only
B. by network administrators in software only
C. to protect private networks connected to the Internet
D. by consumers who access the sites
E. by the FCC.

Answer: C Page: 387

5. International trade embargoes do not apply to business conducted on the Internet.

A. True
B. False

Answer: B Page: 387

6. Seventy percent of the complaints on the 1998 roster of Net fraud records compiled by the National Consumers League were against

A. Web auctions.

B. sites which did not validate a customer's identity.
C. governmental sites.
D. retail sites.
E. sites which present X-rated material.

Answer: A Page: 388

7. The S.A.F.E. program developed by CyberQuest

A. validates users' identities on the Internet.
B. prevents minors from accessing violent or pornographic sites.
C. tracks hackers on the internet.
D. provides an in-house escrow system to protect buyers against fraud.
E. protects users against downloading viruses from commercial sites.

Answer: D Page: 388

8. A digital certificate

A. authenticates the identity of a consumer.
B. authenticates the identity of a commercial site.
C. is awarded annually to the commercial Web site that registers the most hits.
D. confers a great deal of prestige in the online commercial community.
E. both a and b.

Answer: E Page: 388

9. Using disclaimers is a definitive way to protect your commercial site against accusations of fraud by consumers.

A. True
B. False

Answer: B Page: 388 - 389

10. When considering copyright issues, the Fair Use Act provides for

A. a solution to the dilemma such copyright issues on the Net.
B. the free use of small portions of copyrighted material for educational purposes.
C. the protection of intellectual property rights online.
D. applies only to text, not graphics.
E. the Fair Use Act does not apply to online material.

Answer: B Page: 389

11. Computer viruses can be passed to your customers

A. when a Web page is viewed.
B. when a file is downloaded.
C. when a file is downloaded and opened.
D. when e-mail is received.
E. when a Web site is bookmarked by a viewer.

Answer: C Page: 390

12. In order to copy and use software, the consumer must

A. purchase the software.
B. agree to make only one copy.
C. purchase a license.
D. both a and c.
E. both b and c.

Answer: E Page: 392

13. In America, males accounted for ________ of Internet users in 1998.

A. 64%
B. less than 20%
C. 100%
D. over 90%
E. about 50%

Answer: A Page: 393

14. In Europe, males accounted for ________ of Internet users in 1998.

A. less than 20%
B. 64%
C. 82%
D. over 95%
E. 100%

Answer: C Page: 393

15. Caucasians accounted for _________ of Internet users in 1998.

A. at least 95%
B. 87%
C. 50%
D. 100%
E. 25%

Answer: B Page: 393

16. English is the language used most frequently on the Internet, followed by

A. German, French, and Italian.
B. German, French, and Spanish.
C. French, German, and Spanish.
D. German, French and Dutch.
E. Spanish, German, and French.

Answer: D Page: 393

17. The Electronic Frontier Foundation

A. is a non-profit organization.
B. is non-partisan.
C. protects privacy on the Internet.
D. protects against censorship on the Internet.

E. all of the above.

Answer: E Page: 393

18. One of the fundamental concepts of Komenar's ten points on privacy and customer data collection is

A. marketers should collect as much information about consumers as possible.
B. marketers should pay users for their information.
C. user information belongs to the user.
D. the FCC should regulate all consumer privacy issues.
E. marketers should be able to sell consumer information any time they wish.

Answer: C Page: 385

19. Another one of the Komenar's points, which affords consumers some control over information collected by marketers is

A. that no information about a consumer should reach a second party with explicit user permission.
B. FCC standards for use of consumer information.
C. a specific process for marketers to ask permission to sell consumer information.
D. that second parties generally do not trust information not gathered by them.
E. Komenar does not believe that consumers should control any information.

Answer: A Page: 385

20. On the issue of security and privacy,

A. customers never think about security or privacy.
B. marketers should just do whatever they feel is best.
C. these issues are not important to most people.
D. customers expect security and privacy.
E. these issues must be resolved before further expansion of the Internet.

Answer: D Page: 386

21. A very professional and effective way to let visitors to your site know how you feel about consumer issues is to

A. ask them to trust you.
B. register with the FCC.
C. let all your employees know that privacy is important.
D. answer any questions you might get about privacy issues.
E. provide a written privacy policy on your Web site.

Answer: E Page: 386

22. Provision of a site with Secure Sockets Layer (SSL)

A. is the obligation of the marketer and the merchant.
B. secures credit card transactions.
C. is the responsibility of the customer.
D. uses a form of encryption to provide privacy of information
E. both a and d.

Answer: E Page: 386

23. Besides using firewalls for intranet security, one can also

A. use satellite reconnaissance for the intranet.
B. use encryption of data going into and out of the intranet.
C. instruct employees to never use the Internet.
D. not allow anyone to send anything into the intranet.
E. only use the firewall to assure complete security.

Answer: B Page: 387

24. One of the vexing problems for online marketers of adult material is

A. not having enough opportunity to reach potential customers.
B. laws against putting any adult material online.
C. the need to validate the age of a user before orders are placed or sites are viewed.
D. no demand for online adult material.
E. that credit card companies refuse to allow purchases online for such material.

Answer: C Page: 388

25. When you have a site that you wish to link to, you must

A. pay the other site $50.
B. secure written permission from the other site.
C. contact the other site and beg them for permission.
D. always insist that the other site link back to your site.
E. you don't have to ask for permission but it is generally a good idea.

Answer: E Page: 389

Chapter 19
The Future of Electronic Marketing Resources

Test Bank

1. ______________________ is the coming together of two or more technologies to provide systems of greater benefit. In the Internet world, telecommunications, television and computing are coming together to provide many new applications for consumers and e-marketers.

A. Multipicity
B. Convergence
C. Breakthrough combination
D. Technology bonding
E. Tri-communcations

Answer: B Page: 397

2. Education, government and business are collaboratively developing a high speed version of the traditional Internet which will integrate transmission of voice, video and data over the same line. This initiative is called the

A. High Speed Internet (HIS).
B. Next Generation Internet (NGI).
C. Advanced Transfer Model (ATM).
D. Cibabit Internet Code (CIC).
E. Voice Video Data Link (LSN).

Answer: B Page: 397

3. All of the following are goals of the above-referenced initiative *except*

A. to advance research in networking technologies.
B. to develop a testbed to support network research.
C. to connect over 100 sites at speeds 100 to 1000 times faster than is currently possible.
D. total commercialization of all digital transmissions.
E. to develop advanced applications not possible on today's Internet.

Answer: D Page: 397

4. ______________________ is a collaborative effort by more than 100 U.S. research universities to develop new high speed networking technologies and broadband applications. It is closely related to NGI.

A. AcademicNet
B. NewNet
C. Internet2
D. UltraNet
E. PowerNet

Answer: C Page: 398

5. A modem works by

A. translating analog phone signals to digital information.
B. translating digital information to analog phone signals.
C. converting signals of varying frequency to single frequency waves.

D. opening up a digital connection on a phone line.
E. both A and B.

Answer: E Page: 399

6. With telecommunications technology initially designed for voice communications, the amount of data moving across the line is

A. constant.
B. dedicated to multi-access.
C. variable.
D. frequently lost.
E. unpredictable.

Answer: A Page: 399

7. ______________________ is the mode of delivery of the telecommunications infrastructure that was designed for, and works very well for, voice communications. This mode of delivery is too costly and wasteful for digital communications.

A. Packet switching
B. Asynchronous Transfer Mode
C. Hyper-switching
D. Fast forward
E. Circuit switching

Answer: E Page: 399

8. Digital communication traffic is based on

A. images.
B. text.
C. sound.
D. small, irregular streams of data.
E. all of the above.

Answer: E Page: 399

9. The current telephone networks which have handled huge volumes of voice transmissions are now

A. unable to handle digital transmissions.
B. frequently breaking down, hampering both digital and voice messages.
C. handling huge volumes of digital data transmissions.
D. in need of replacement by wireless systems.
E. the best systems for the future of the Internet.

Answer: C Page: 399

10. The protocol known as ATM provides for

A. much higher transmission capabilities.
B. an open solution and an international telecommunications standard.
C. a single network that supports both digital and analog communication.
D. flexibility; easily handling voice, video and images.
E. all of the above.

Answer: E Page: 400

11. Internet telephony is an evolving service that is starting to become popular with users because it is essentially free telephone service. But quality is not optimal. There is a tradeoff between _____________ and _____________.

A. cost and access
B. access and reliability
C. bandwith and reliability
D. high speed and low speed
E. Internet2 and NGI

Answer: C Page: 400

12. Internet 2 provides a communications network linking

A. all Internet search engines.
B. major research universities.
C. government and business sites.
D. satellite and ground systems.
E. U.S. east and west coast networks.

Answer: B Page: 401

13. Internet 2 specific objectives include all of the following *except*

A. enhanced collaborative research and experimentation.
B. better distance education.
C. encouraging partnerships between government and the private sector.
D. development of commercial university research online publishing sites.
E. the standardization of work practices among institutions.

Answer: D Page: 401

14. The capabilities of the Internet currently exceed the available technology.

A. True
B. False

Answer: A Page: 403

15. A hand-held device with wireless transmission capability which would have numerous features, including Internet access, voice recognition, memory for storage of documents is called

A. a pipe dream.
B. an Internet appliance.
C. a telephone.
D. a computer.
E. an Internet organizer.

Answer: B Page: 403

16. Major hardware and software companies are working on speech activated technologies which will make computers easier to use and will

A. have computers talk to us and become our friends.

B. make computers automatic.
C. eliminate the keyboard.
D. allow computers to teach university classes.
E. result in computers "talking" to each other.

Answer: C Page: 403

17. E-marketers will use virtual reality simulations to engage customers in their web sites sometimes through interactive participation. In some cases, this will involve the use of a virtual reality "avatar" which is

A. a special kind of computer mouse.
B. a fictional electronic horse.
C. an animated figure representing a person.
D. a type of Internet telephone.
E. a software application that allows a customer to spend money at a site.

Answer: C Page: 404

18. Virtual reality technology, because it is so fascinating to users, will become an important type of content on e-marketing Web sites. But, because of high bandwidth requirements, it will do so only

A. if users can get accustomed to the slightly disorienting nature of VR.
B. when the cost of VR drops.
C. if corporate sponsors use the technology in commercials.
D. as high bandwidth services, such as cable modems, are used by consumers.
E. if approved by the FCC.

Answer: D Page: 405

19. Portals receive sales commissions for directing traffic to their e-commerce partners whether or not a transaction occurs.

A. True
B. False

Answer: B Page: 406

20. According to the 1997 GVU 8th User Survey, the number one consumer issue with regard to Internet use is

A. navigation.
B. censorship.
C. privacy.
D. cost of Internet service.
E. federal taxes on Internet purchases.

Answer: C Page: 408

21. In the same survey, the percentage of users who considered access to the WWW indispensable was

A. less than 10%
B. 10 to 20%.
C. 20 to 30%.
D. 40 to 50%.
E. 84%.

Answer: E Page: 408

22 . In the last year, numerous big mergers have been announced of firms who were trying to develop vertical integration strategies. There are two types of firms generally involved, Internet companies and ______________________.

A. hardware companies
B. manufacturing firms
C. media companies
D. financial services companies
E. retailing companies

Answer: C Page: 406

23. Because of the huge amounts of digital innovations taking place right now, the marketer must be ____________________ in order to know about and manage information retrieval and information delivery in order to incorporate these into promotional programs.

A. a computer programmer
B. an information technologist
C. a hardware specialist
D. able to read all technical journals
E. a behavioral expert

Answer: B Page: 407

24. One of Bill Gates' "12 New Rules of Business" is to "use digital systems to route customer complaints immediately." He thinks that an e-marketer's greatest information opportunity is

A. an unhappy customer because they help you improve your service or product.
B. what managers think of customers.
C. what distributors think of customers.
D. information from "cookies."
E. when a customer is completely satisfied.

Answer: A Page: 407

25. Marketers might be tempted to think in complex technological terms but sometimes the best approach is the simplest. Which of the following is a simple approach that e-marketers should embrace in the design of their web sites?

A. To do things in as few ways as possible.
B. To design systems for 100 times your current load.
C. Not to jump on the newest technology just because it's new and cool.
D. Not to forsake your customers' best interests.
E. All of the above is good, simple advice.

Answer: E Page: 407